THE EPISTLE TO THE HEBREWS

The Epistle to the Hebrews

A COMMENTARY

The Most Reverend DMITRI
Archbishop of Dallas and the South

ST VLADIMIR'S SEMINARY PRESS
CRESTWOOD, NEW YORK 10707
2003

The benefactors who made this publication possible wish to dedicate it in thanksgiving for the ministry of His Grace Bishop Dmitri, and for their children, Michael, David, King, Olivia, Karl, and Sophia.

Library of Congress Cataloging-in-Publication Data

Royster, Dmitri, 1923-
    The Epistle to the Hebrews : a commentary / The Most Reverend Dmitri.
        p.   cm.
Includes index.
   ISBN 0-88141-247-3
  1. Bible. N.T. Hebrews—Commentaries.   I. Title.
  BS2775.53.R69 2003
  227'.8707—dc21

2003046566

Copyright © 2003
ST VLADIMIR'S SEMINARY PRESS
575 Scarsdale Rd., Crestwood, NY 10707
1-800-204-2665

ISBN 0-88141-247-3

PRINTED IN THE UNITED STATES OF AMERICA

Contents

Foreword 7

Preface 13

Chapter 1 17

Chapter 2 29

Chapter 3 45

Chapter 4 57

Chapter 5 71

Chapter 6 85

Chapter 7 101

Chapter 8 119

Chapter 9 131

Chapter 10 151

Chapter 11 173

Chapter 12 203

Chapter 13 227

Index of Scripture References
   in the Epistle to the Hebrews 247

Foreword

The Epistle to the Hebrews, a Commentary, is the fourth in a series of studies of the New Testament by Archbishop DMITRI of Dallas and the South (OCA). The first three studies addressed particular themes and aspects of the four canonical Gospels. Entitled *The Kingdom of God, The Parables,* and *The Miracles of Christ,* they offered commentary on the texts and events related to these topics. The present volume also highlights several important themes but does so in the context of a commentary, verse by verse, of an entire book of the New Testament. The results are illuminating and instructive for anyone seeking an understanding of the Epistle to the Hebrews from the perspective of the Orthodox Church.

With frequent mention of the specific placement of selected readings from the Epistle in the Church's liturgical and sacramental celebrations, the *Commentary* is particularly useful for those responsible for preaching and teaching in the Church—the clergy. Noteworthy here is the fact that readings from Hebrews are prescribed during the two most important times in the Orthodox liturgical year: the days prior to the celebration of the Nativity of Christ and the Great Fast before the Feast of Feasts, Pascha.

The controversial issue regarding authorship of the Epistle to the Hebrews does not play a major role in the *Commentary.* Archbishop DMITRI refers repeatedly to "the Apostle" (obviously St. Paul) as the author of the letter and cites several holy fathers as well as general liturgical practice to support this contention. Yet, he allows that scholars disagree about this matter and in the Preface states simply and directly that his only wish is to explore the richness of the letter's message "for the edification of our people."

His comment regarding "the edification of our people" reveals much about the methodology employed in the present volume. The author is an Orthodox bishop. During the rite of his consecration to this high office, the opened Gospel (with pages down) was placed over his head as he knelt before the altar table. Prayers commending him to a "valiant preaching of the Gospel" in a life "under the yoke of the Gospel" were said.[1]

Obviously his view of the Bible can be none other than that of the Church. In the Church the Bible is viewed *as a whole.* It is much more than an historical document: a disparate collection of books in frequent (apparent) conflict with one another, written by various and occasionally unknown authors for differing purposes at distinct historical times and places. It is *canonical* Scripture, i.e., the foundational written expression of the Church's *depositum fidei*—faith and life in Jesus Christ as the Son of God and Savior of the world. This perception of Scripture implies a certain methodology in the interpretation of Scripture, one employed by such holy fathers as St. Ambrose of Milan (cited in this regard in the Preface), who allows *Scripture to interpret Scripture.* Archbishop DMITRI utilizes this method throughout the *Commentary.* An outstanding example is found in the treatment he accords Hebrews 11:1, the famous verse defining faith as "the substance of things hoped for, the evidence of things not seen." To shed light on this one Biblical passage, he cites no fewer than eight others. Liturgical texts and the writings of the holy fathers, ranging from St. Ignatius of Antioch (†98-117 AD) to the nearly contemporary bishop and saint, Nikolai Velimirovic (†1956), also are referred to consistently and abundantly. Connections are made between the Epistle's passages and the sacraments of baptism, chrismation, confession, the Holy Eucharist and priesthood, not to mention the holy icons, the Great Fast and particular feastdays—especially those of the Theotokos. Extensive and timely references to the original Greek text are also made as certain key words and phrases are examined. In several places the Masoretic and Septuagint versions of sections from the Old Testament are compared.

[1] All citations from the liturgical rites and prayers for the consecration of a bishop may be found in Isabel Hapgood, *Service Book of the Holy Orthodox-Catholic Apostolic Church* (a translation from Church Slavonic), 4th edition (Antiochian Orthodox Archdiocese, 1965).

The Archbishop's above-mentioned interest in "the edification of our people" inspires as well a distinctly pastoral concern to permeate the volume. In Orthodox Tradition, a bishop is not only the principal teacher in the Church; he also holds the chief pastoral office. The two functions are considered inseparable, for "Where there is no vision, the people perish" (Prov 29:18 KJV). At his consecration a bishop is commissioned to be an imitator of Jesus Christ, "the true shepherd who didst lay down thy life for [the] sheep; to be a leader of the blind, a light to those who are in darkness, a reprover of the unwise, a teacher of the young, a lamp to the world."

Consistent with the magnitude of his churchly office and its clearly stated pastoral purposes, the author endeavors to persuade, to console, to enlighten and ultimately to lead the souls entrusted to his care to salvation in Jesus Christ, the Son of God—the Head and High Priest of the Church, which is his Body, the "fulness of him who fills all in all" (Eph 1:22). In this regard the Archbishop endorses the view that the overall message of the Epistle to the Hebrews is the fulfillment of the Old Covenant of ancient Israel in the New Covenant of Jesus Christ (which is superior to the Old in every way).[2]

His endorsement here is not to be misconstrued as a misguided *triumphalism*. It is rather a strong yet pastoral reminder concerning the words of Scripture that in Jesus Christ and the Church God's Truth in all its fulness (Eph 4:21) has been revealed: "The Lord has sworn, and will not repent" (from the Greek—change His purpose or design; cf. Ps 109/110:4 and Heb 6:18-20). Implied in it is the awesome responsibility those sacramentally ordained to pastoral ministry in the Church (bishops and presbyters) bear regarding the flock entrusted to their care. As St. John Chrysostom explains:

> For the Church is Christ's own Body, according to St. Paul, and the man who is entrusted with it must train it by unremitting vigilance to prevent the slightest spot or wrinkle or other blemish of that sort from marring its grace and loveliness. In short, he must make it

[2]Cf. Cronk, George, *The Message of the Bible: An Orthodox Christian Perspective* (St Vladimir's Seminary Press, Crestwood, NY, 1982), 203–204.

worthy, as far as lies within human power, of that pure and blessed Head to which it is subjected (*On the Priesthood,* IV, 2).

I

Two particular and central themes of the Epistle occupy places of dominance in the *Commentary.* The first, termed by the Archbishop as "the Apostle's major doctrinal theme," is the *priesthood of our Lord Jesus Christ.*[3] Following a plan presented by St. John Chrysostom, a threefold definition of this priesthood is set forth in Chapter 5.

1. A priest is taken from among men; such a selection helps to ensure that his actions will be motivated by love, compassion and mercy.

2. A priest is appointed by God to represent men before God.

3. A priest accomplishes this representation by offering gifts and sacrifices for sins.[4]

The Lord Jesus Christ fulfills and perfects all these categories of priesthood. Taking on completely our corrupted human nature, He is fully a man and beset with weakness. He is tempted like we are yet knows no sin, weeping three times over our sins in His compassion for us (cf. Heb 5:7; Lk 19:41; Jn 11:35). He is appointed by His Father to be "a priest forever, after the order of Melchisedec" (Heb 5:6), that mysterious king of peace and righteousness who appears to Abraham (Gen 14), making offerings of bread and wine and receiving tithes from the great patriarch. He has no genealogy and no successors. He enters not the earthly but the heavenly sanctuary once for all (Heb 7:27) and does so as our forerunner (Heb 6:20), making intercession for us (Heb 5:7). He learns obedience through His suffering (Heb 5:8) and offers Himself as the perfect offering on behalf of all and for all. And in our own "holding fast" (Heb 4:14) to the profession of faith once and for all delivered by Him to the saints, summarized in the Creed, experienced in the liturgical and sacramental mysteries of the Church and made manifest in godly living,

[3]Ibid., 43.
[4]Ibid., 43–46.

we anticipate our own entrance into the sanctuary above the heavens and "the rest of God."[5]

II

The above-cited Scriptural passage, "Holding fast to the profession of faith" (Heb 4:14), expresses well the second major theme developed in the *Commentary*.[6] Covering a full 25 pages and having as its focus Chapter 11 of the Epistle, this section of the *Commentary* first explores the *meaning* of faith as "the substance of things hoped for, the evidence of things not seen"(11:1). This difficult verse teaches us that the promises of God acquire substance through faith. Faith and hope save us, and things that are seen are neither faith nor hope; therefore they cannot save (cf. Rom 8:24). But faith is hope not only in the promises of God; it is trust in the witness of those through whom God has spoken.

The witnesses to that "fatherland of the heart's desire" (an expression from the hymnography of the *Panikhida*—Funeral Service) presented in Hebrews are those who anticipated its coming and thereby lived truly the life of faith (Abel, Enoch, Noah, Abraham, Sara, Moses, and other righteous of the Old Testament). The *Commentary* is particularly rich in the way it reveals all these examples of faith as portents of the advent, the cross, the death and the resurrection of Jesus Christ.

> And these all, having obtained a good report through faith, received not the promise: God having provided some better thing for us, that they without us should not be made perfect (Heb 11:39-40).

[5]*Commentary*, 4:14.

[6]*Commentary*, 3:1, provides a definition of the Greek word, *homologia,* which is much broader than the content of a creed or a doctrinal system. The word implies that our life is a continuous confession of faith and of thanksgiving, or worship. As the author states: "Our Church's understanding of the name it most often uses to describe itself, Orthodox, is twofold: the right way of worship and the right teaching."

In Jesus Christ, His Incarnate Word, God calls the whole human race to Himself. The Hebrews were the forerunners, those chosen to prepare the way for this universal calling. But the holy ones of the Old Testament "could not have had their hope completed ('should not be made perfect') without the participation of those who put their faith in the Incarnate Word, in Him who is the one promised, prophesied and prefigured in the Old Testament."[7]

III

A suitable concluding word to this Foreword, one which not only summarizes well the purpose and pastoral tone of the *Commentary*, but provides also a wonderful glimpse into the heart and faith of its author is found in the exposition of Hebrews 3:13 ("But exhort one another daily, while it is called To day; lest any of you be hardened through the deceitfulness of sin"):

> What the Apostle says to his brethren can be said to us and to our generation in these terms: when we see a brother or a sister beginning to weaken or lose interest, we must come to his rescue. We, for our part, must never let laziness and lack of enthusiasm for Christ and His way take hold of us. Our own example of dedication cannot but be contagious in the community. This is to be maintained daily, "while it is called To day." To day reminds us of the Lord's command to His disciples to work while it is still day—as long as one lives and as long as the world lasts (Rom 13:11; II Pet 3:10). St. Basil the Great *(Letter XLII,* To Chilo, no. 5) says that "Today means the whole time of our life," and St. Cyril of Jerusalem (*Catechetical Lecture, XV,* no. 32), explains it as "continually."

Fr. Paul Lazor
October 18, 2002
The Holy Apostle and Evangelist Luke

---

[7] *Commentary*, 202.

Preface

This beautiful epistle reveals perhaps more clearly than any other part of the New Testament the way in which Jesus Christ fulfilled the prophecies of the Old Testament. Further, it contains the most detailed and systematic exposition of the doctrine of our Lord's person and work, especially of His priesthood.

It was taken for granted by many of the great Fathers of the Church that St. Paul was the author of the Epistle to the Hebrews, but even in their times there were others who doubted it. Modern biblical scholars generally question his authorship and some reject it outright, bringing forth arguments based on style and language or on differences between the known epistles of St. Paul and that addressed to the Hebrews on a number of themes, such as justification. Neither this noun nor the verb "justify" occurs in this Epistle.

St. John Chrysostom, whose commentary in the form of homilies is the most complete analysis that has come down to us, has no doubt about it. In fact, he even defends and explains his stand:

> Why, then, not being a teacher of the Jews, does he send an Epistle to them? And where were those to whom he sent it? It seems to me in Jerusalem and Palestine. How, then, does he send them an Epistle? Just as he baptized, though he was not commanded to baptize. For, he says, "I was not sent to baptize": not, however, that he was forbidden, but he does it as a subordinate matter. And how could he fail to write to those, for whom he was willing even to become accursed? [Romans 9:3] Accordingly he said, "Know ye that our brother Timothy is set at liberty; with whom, if he come shortly, I will see you [Hebrews 13:23]." (*On Hebrews,* Homily 1, no. 2)

There is also an ancient testimony of Clement of Alexandria, cited by Eusebius in his *History of the Church*:

> The Epistle to the Hebrews he attributed to Paul, but says that it was written for Hebrews in their own language, and then accurately

13

translated by Luke and published for Greek readers. Hence, in the
Greek version of this epistle, we find the same stylistic color as in
the Acts. The usual opening—"Paul, an apostle"—was omitted,
with good reason. As Clement says: "in writing to Hebrews already
prejudiced against him and suspicious of him [Acts 21], he was far
too sensible to put them off at the start by naming himself." (Book
VI, no. 14)

Still, it is not our purpose to enter into a discussion of the authorship of the Epistle; we only wish to explore the richness of its message for the edification of our people.

We have tried to follow the principle of interpretation laid down
by St. Ambrose of Milan (*Letter XLIII*, no. 3), that Scripture is to be
explained by Scripture itself. The thought expressed in almost every
verse of the Epistle to the Hebrews has a parallel or related idea in
either the Old Testament or in other books of the New. To be sure,
there are direct quotes, principally from the Psalms, that show how
the person and work of the Savior was prophesied and then fulfilled.
It is evident throughout the Epistle that its author was deeply aware
of the unity of the two Testaments. New Testament quotations are
from the Authorized or King James Version. Quotations from the
Old Testament, particularly the Psalter, are usually according to the
Septuagint (denoted LXX), the Greek translation of the Old Testament used by the Apostles and the Church from the beginning.
Psalm numbers are written with the Septuagint number first, followed by the number given in the Masoretic text, as in Psalm 50/51.

What has been of great importance to us is the testimony of the
holy Fathers of the Church, which is to be found in the abundant
quotations in their doctrinal and pastoral writings of passages from
this Epistle. We make no claim to completeness in this respect, and
there could well be some significant ones that we have missed. Since
the Fathers were concerned often with the meaning of these passages, it has seemed appropriate to us to show how they made use
of them. Very often, especially when dealing with heretics, the passages are simply proof-texts for the Orthodox doctrine they were

defending. The bulk of these quotations may be found in the two collections, the *Anti-Nicene Fathers* (ANF) and the *Nicene and Post-Nicene Fathers* (NPNF). Also heavily quoted is the *Commentary on the Gospel of St. Luke* by St. Cyril, Patriarch of Alexandria and the *Discourses* of St. Symeon the New Theologian.

Another source, to which we have had recourse from time to time, is the liturgical texts, hymns, verses, and readings, which convey to the worshipping people of God the true meaning of familiar verses from the Epistle to the Hebrews.

In view of the fact that English translations of certain words and phrases do not always capture the full sense of the Greek expressions behind them, we have called attention to certain ones, giving the Greek words with alternative and, in our opinion, more accurate meanings. We have transliterated these Greek words according to the most common scheme, but we ask our readers to take note of the following: we have used *e* for "ε"; *ē* for "η"; *o* for "ο"; *ō* for "ω"; *b* for "β" (even though the pronunciation is now more like "v"); *y* for "υ", except in the combination "ευ", which we give as *ev*; and in words that have the "rough breathing" over the first vowel or diphthong we have used an initial h.

Chapter 1

v. 1. God, who at sundry times and in divers manners spake in time past unto the fathers by the prophets,

Since the Epistle is addressed to the Hebrews, the Apostle opens with a declaration with which they would agree without question: that God had spoken to their forebears through the prophets. These men, generation after generation, had proclaimed the will of God for His people, passed judgment in His name on this people's way of living, and foretold things to come, especially those that had to do with their deliverance and salvation. He had spoken over a long period of time and in many different ways. No one part of His revelation of Himself was complete, as is evident from the vocabulary; in fact, the expression translated "at sundry times" in the Greek original is the adverb, *polymerōs,* literally "in many parts," and behind "in divers manners" is another adverb, *polytropōs.* The revelation was, so to speak, progressive: He revealed many things to Moses, and others to Isaiah and Jeremiah among the prophets. Clement of Alexandria speaks of this progression as "leading from the beginning of knowledge to the end" (*Stromata,* chap. xvi). He would also add the *polypoikilōs* of Ephesians 3:10 ("manifold" or "many-faceted"), an adjective describing the wisdom of God, to the two adverbs of this verse (*op. cit.,* chap. iv).

This "end" was the revelation in Jesus Christ, the complete revelation. "No man hath seen God at any time; the only-begotten Son, which is in the bosom of the Father, He hath declared Him [made Him known]" (John 1:18).

St. John of Damascus testifies to the fact that it was through the Holy Spirit that God spoke to those of old times, and further, continues to speak to God's servants, pastors and teachers, even now (*Exposition of the Orthodox Faith,* Book IV, chap. xvii; see also St. Basil the Great, *On the Holy Spirit,* chap. xxvi, no. 63). There is abundant evidence of the work of the Holy Spirit in the carrying out of God's purposes throughout the Old Testament: I Kings/I Samuel 16:13; Judges 6:34; Ezekiel 11:5, etc. The latter reads, "And the Spirit of the Lord fell upon me, and said unto me, Speak; Thus saith the Lord."

v. 2. Hath in these last days spoken unto us by his Son, whom he hath appointed heir of all things, by whom also he made the worlds;

Now the same God speaks to His people in a direct way, that is, in and by His Son, for whom and by whom all things were created (Colossians 1:16). With reference to "His Son," St. Cyril of Jerusalem says that He is "Son by nature, without beginning . . . eternally begotten by an inscrutable and incomprehensible generation" (*Catechetical Lecture IX,* no. 4).

God's final revelation of truth is made once and is complete in itself. In the expression, "in these last days," we understand that since Christ's coming into the world, no greater or further revelation can be expected and that the final period of history has begun.

The Son or Word of God was the active agent in the creation. In Genesis, each act of creation is preceded by the expression, "and God said." God's very Word created, a fact which is confirmed by the Apostle John at the beginning of His Gospel: "All things . . . were made by Him [the Word], and without Him was not made anything that was made." The Psalmist says: "By the Word of the Lord were the heavens made" (Psalm 32/33:6). "And knowing also that the Word, the Wisdom, the Son Himself was the Image of the Father, he [St. Paul] says in the Epistle to the Colossians [1:16-17], '. . . for by Him were all things created, that are in heaven, and that are in earth, visible and invisible . . .'" (St. Athanasius, *Defense of the Nicene Definition,* chap. iv, no. 17).

The Word of God, as God's Son, is the natural heir to all things, but now, having taken on human nature, He is appointed heir so that all men might become heirs through Him. "The Spirit Himself beareth witness with our spirit, that we are the children of God: and if children, then heirs of God, and joint-heirs with Christ" (Romans 8:16-17). St. Gregory of Nyssa (*Against Eunomius,* Book II, no. 6) clarifies this heirdom with relation to the Father:

> For the Heir of all things, the Maker of the ages, He who shines with the Father's glory and expresses in Himself the Father's person, has all things that the Father Himself has, and is possessor of all His power, not that the right is transferred from the Father to the Son, but that it at once remains in the Father and resides in the Son.

The emphasis of the first identifying clause, "whom He hath appointed" is on the human nature of the Lord, and the second, "by whom He also made" on His divine nature (St. John Chrysostom, *On Hebrews,* Homily 1, no. 2).

v. 3. Who being the brightness of his glory, and the express image of his person, and upholding all things by the word of his power, when he had by himself purged our sins, sat down on the right hand of the Majesty on high;

The Person about whom the Epistle is written is now fully identified. St. John has called the Word "the true Light, which lighteth every man on coming into the world" (1:9). He declares in his First Epistle that "God is light" (1:5). Jesus Christ, the Son of God, who calls Himself "the light of the world" (John 8:12), is Light of Light, as we confess in the Creed. Now the Son, who is appointed heir in the flesh and who is the Creator in His divinity, is called "the brightness [*apavgasma* in Greek, "effulgence" or "reflection"] of the glory" of God. We recall that the Lord spoke of the glory that He had with the Father before the world was (John 17:5), and that St. Paul, in two places, calls Christ "the image [*eikōn*] of God" (II Corinthians 4:4 and Colossians 1:15).

The Son is the "express image [character] of His [God's] person," the expression of all that the Father is: He is of the same nature, of the same essence. Here "person" is translated from *hypostasis,* the technical term used in the Nicene Creed that refers to the three who make up the Holy Trinity (see St. Gregory of Nyssa, *ibid.*).

The Apostle has already said that it was by the Son that God made the world, that is, all things. He is more—He is the Sustainer of all things, and creation not only owes its existence to Him, but also its continuation and preservation. He "upholds" all things by nothing more than the "word of His power." The Son, who is the Word and has all power sustains by His word the entire created universe (*ibid.*).

This verse, it can be said, contains a summary of the doctrine of Christ. After establishing His divinity and His providential care for His creation, the writer now turns to His redeeming work on behalf of fallen man. The eternal Word came into the world, became man and gave His life in sacrifice for the sins of the world. This act was the culmination of His work, for, having identified Himself completely with man's condition, He underwent, without sinning Himself, the consequences of sin, that is, death. He offered the one perfect life—which was not deserving of death—for all, so that He might conquer death by rising from the dead (St. Ambrose, *On the Christian Faith,* Book III, chap. xi, nos. 78-81).

When He had completed His earthly work, He ascended into heaven, not only as God, but as Man, man perfected and deified (see the three "Sessional Hymns" at Matins for the Ascension). His sitting down "on the right hand of the Majesty on high" signifies that now as God-Man He has power over all things in heaven and earth (St. Ambrose, *ibid.*).

The theological content of these first three verses finds liturgical expression in this troparion: "With My word I have established heaven and earth, for I was with the Father; and with My word I uphold all creation, for I am Word and Wisdom and Power, the Father's Image, His fellow-worker and His equal in might" (Great and Holy Monday, Compline, Ode 2 of the Canon).

v. 4. Being made so much better than the angels, as he hath by inheritance obtained a more excellent name than they.

As St. Paul points out in another place, "Christ Jesus humbled Himself, and became obedient unto death, even the death of the cross, wherefore God also hath highly exalted Him and given Him a name which is above every name" (Philippians 2:8-9). The work of Jesus Christ as God-Man reached its climax with His glorification (by which word St. John describes His crucifixion) and His exaltation, so that human nature which He assumed became even greater than that of the angels, and as a result of His work He was given a name that is above all names, that is, Lord (Philippians 2:10-11). But the name that He has by right and by nature is that of Son, for it is in this name that we know of His relation to the Father (St. John Chrysostom, *op. cit.*, Homily 2, on v. 4).

In His eternal being, the glory of God always belonged to Him, for He spoke of the glory He had "with the Father before the world was" (John 17:5), but now this glory and exaltation pertain to Him as the great High Priest, and through Him, will belong to those who believe on Him. As Lord, He now reigns and will come again as King and Judge, having made for Himself a kingdom of priests and kings. "He loved us and washed us from our sins in His own blood, and hath made us kings and priests unto God . . ." (Revelation 1:6); "and we shall reign on earth" (Revelation 5:10). His glorification, ascension and reign were accomplished so that those who believe on Him may be glorified, ascend, and reign.

Finally, it should be noted that when verbs such as "being made" or "becoming" and "by inheritance obtained" or "inherited" are used, they must be understood with reference to the work of the Incarnate Word, and not the Godhead or Divinity, which is, of course, uncreated. (See both St. Ambrose and St. John Chrysostom, in the works cited above.)

*v. 5. For unto which of the angels said he at any time, Thou art
my Son, this day have I begotten thee? And again, I will be to
him a Father, and he shall be to me a Son?*

For further evidence of the Son's unique relationship to the
Father and His natural superiority to the angels, the Apostle turns to
the Old Testament and shows what David said about the Son, and
further how this could refer to Christ alone. The Psalmist, as the
ancestor of Christ in the flesh, prophesied often concerning Him.
The Messiah or Savior was to be born of "the seed of David"
(Romans 1:3). He is eternally the Son of God, but when He is born
into the world, the Father declares to Him, "Thou art my Son, this
day [today] have I begotten thee" (Psalm 2:7). This is the way in
which St. John Chrysostom (*ibid.*, on v. 5) interprets "today." He says
" 'today' seems to me to be spoken here with reference to the flesh."
Origen calls it an "eternal today" which is God's time, and emphasizes that the Son is eternally begotten of the Father (*Commentary
on St. John's Gospel*, no. 32; see also St. Basil the Great, *Letter 38*, "To
His Brother Gregory," no. 7).

In another Psalm (88/89:26), David records the words of the
Messiah, "He shall cry unto me, Thou art my Father, my God, and
the rock of my salvation." These words recall those spoken by God
to Solomon referring to his son, David, as a prefigure of the Christ,
the expected King, whose throne will be eternal and whose reign
will include all peoples (II Samuel/II Kings 7:14; see Psalm 2:7-8).
That these things were never said to any angel and that they did not
really refer to David, but to his descendant according to the flesh,
St. Peter makes clear in his sermon on the day of Pentecost (Acts
2:25-36).

*v. 6. And again, when he bringeth in the firstbegotten into the
world, he saith, And let all the angels of God worship him.*

The Son is the Only-begotten of the Father; on coming into the
world He becomes the "First-begotten." In the Psalm cited above

(88/89), the following verse (27) foretells this: "And I shall make Him first-born [*prōtotokon*], higher than the kings of the earth." St. Paul writes to the Romans (8:29): "For whom He did foreknow, He also did predestinate [or "fore-ordain"] to be conformed to the image of His Son, that He might be the firstborn among many brethren." St. Athanasius, in his *Second Discourse against the Arians* (chap. xxi, nos. 62-63) explains the difference between "Only-begotten" and "First-begotten": The Word is "Only-begotten, because of His generation from the Father . . . and First-begotten, because of His condescension to the creation and His making the many His brethren." Further, the risen Christ is called the "firstborn of every creature" and the "firstborn from the dead" (Colossians 1:15,18; Revelation 1:5; see also St. Leo the Great, *Homily 63,* no. 3).

The word for "world" in our present verse is *oikoumenēn* in Greek, the same word used in 2:5, where the "world to come" is clearly meant. This is not the same as the word we find in John 1:10 *(kosmos)*. The Apostle's choice here, with the addition of "again" *(palin;* the order is "When again He bringeth") could make the "bringing in" refer to the second coming, when the Son of Man will come "in His glory, and all the holy angels with Him" (Matthew 25:31). This is not, however, the meaning that some of the holy Fathers give this verse. For St. John Chrysostom it means: when He came into His inheritance, that is, the whole world (*op. cit.,* Homily 3, no. 1).

"Let all the angels of God worship Him" is quoted literally from Deuteronomy 32:43; a similar expression is found in Psalm 96/97:7. In the latter passage, it is clearly prophetic of the God-Man Jesus Christ's victory, at which the angels worship Him. He is due the same honor and worship as the Father, as He Himself tells us (John 5:22-23). He, glorified and ascended into heaven, is worshipped by "ten thousand times ten thousand, and thousands of thousands of angels" (Revelation 5:8-14).

v. 7. And of the angels he saith, Who maketh his angels spirits, and his ministers [leitourgous] *a flame of fire.*

In order to show that the Son of God is not an angel and not created, and in order to contrast the angels and the Son, the Apostle reminds his readers again of what is said of the angels in the Psalms, in this case Psalm 103/104:4. The angels are beings created as servants and ministers of God to proclaim His word and will. They are bodiless spirits that do His bidding, accomplish His purposes, and manifest His presence, even with fire, darkness and tempest, as on Mt. Sinai (Deuteronomy 4:11). St. Gregory of Nyssa makes use of this verse to counter Eunomius' teaching that the Christ is an "angel of the God over all," and he demonstrates that when the name "angel" was applied to the Son by Moses and Isaiah, it was to be understood with reference to the divine economy and to describe functions or specific missions (*Against Eunomius*, Book XI, no. 3).

v. 8. But unto the Son he saith, Thy throne, O God, is for ever and ever: a sceptre of righteousness is the sceptre of thy kingdom.

Now he recalls that in Psalm 44/45:6, the Son is called God, completing the contrast between created beings and the eternal Son of God begun in the preceding verse. Two symbols of royal power, the throne and the sceptre, as used: they refer not only to the eternal kingship of the Son, but to Him as God-Man, who, in His role or ministry as King, now reigns in the Church. The kingdom established by Christ is the kingdom of righteousness, justice and equity (see St. John Chrysostom, *ibid.,* no. 2).

v. 9. Thou hast loved righteousness, and hated iniquity; therefore God, even thy God, hath anointed thee with the oil of gladness above thy fellows.

This verse is a quotation of the next verse of Psalm 44 (v. 7). Again the Apostle turns from what belongs to the Son in His eternal being with the Father to the life and work of the Incarnate Son, the God-Man. His was a totally righteous life; He taught and practiced righteousness, and He expressed His approval of righteous people and their behavior. In the same manner, His life was a constant battle against iniquity and unrighteousness. Christ, whose name means "anointed," was anointed by God for His earthly ministry, as Prophet, Priest and King, just as the prophets, priests and kings were anointed under the Old Covenant. Since He had taken on human nature, all men are His fellows, but He is unique among them and superior to them. St. Cyril of Jerusalem (*Catechetical Lecture XI*, no. 15), after citing Baruch 3:35-37, goes on to add:

> Seest thou herein God become man, after the giving of the law by Moses? Hear also a second testimony to Christ's Deity, that which has just now been read, "Thy throne, O God, is for ever and ever." For lest, because of His presence here in the flesh, He should be thought to have been advanced after this to the Godhead, the Scripture says plainly, "Therefore God, even thy God, hath anointed thee with the oil of gladness above thy fellows." Seest thou Christ as God anointed by God the Father?

v. 10. And, Thou, Lord, in the beginning hast laid the foundation of the earth; and the heavens are the works of thine hands:

This verse is quoted from Psalm 101/102:25, and continues the principle enunciated in verse 2, that it was the Word of God who was the very agent of the creation of the earth and the heavens. This is brought out by St. Athanasius in his *First Discourse against the Arians:* "Moreover by saying that He it is who has 'laid the foundation of all things,' he [the Apostle] shows that He is other than all things originate. But if He be other and different in essence from their nature, what comparison of His essence can there be, or what likeness to them?" (chap. xiii, no. 57 [6]). He is, of course, using this verse as evidence that the Son is not a created being, as the Arians claimed (and as some still claim today).

vv. 11-12. They shall perish; but thou remainest; and they all shall wax old as doth a garment; and as a vesture shalt thou fold them up, and they shall be changed: but thou art the same, and thy years shall not fail.

Continuing the quotation from Psalm 101/102 (here v. 26), the Apostle explains that all created things are changeable by nature and shall perish, since they came into being from non-existence. They grow old and can be discarded or changed; the figures the Psalmist uses are reminiscent of those used by Isaiah (34:4 and 51:7-8). God alone (in this case, pointing specifically to the Son) is immutable and remains the same. Through the Prophet Malachi (3:6), God says: "I am the Lord, I change not." Our writer, later in this Epistle, says of the Son, "Jesus Christ [is] the same yesterday, and today, and for ever" (13:8). "Years" cannot really be applied to the being of God, but since man's life is measured in years, it is appropriate to stress that God does not grow old with the passing of man's years. St. Irenaeus (*Against Heresies,* Book IV, chap. iii, no. 1), in his refutation of the Gnostics' frivolous objection that God will change when heaven and earth pass away, since heaven is His throne and earth His footstool, brings forward this Psalm and the reference in Isaiah (51:6) as evidence of God's immutability and of their ignorance of Scripture.

v. 13. But to which of the angels said he at any time, Sit on my right hand, until I make thine enemies thy footstool?

We recall that in verse 3 the Apostle has asserted that this Son of God, "when He had by Himself purged our sins, sat down on the right hand of the Majesty on high." That is, He took the place that was His, but now with the human nature He had assumed and deified. Jesus Christ Himself had made the first verse from Psalm 109/110 apply to Himself, when He asked the Pharisees, "What think ye of Christ? whose son is he?" When they answered that he is the son of David, He then asked them how David could call him Lord (Matthew 22:42-45). God has never said to any angel, "Sit on my right hand," but only to Christ who, having completed His saving mission on earth, ascended into heaven and sat down on the right hand of the Father.

All of Christ's enemies will be destroyed. "But who are His enemies? All the wicked and those who set themselves to oppose the will of God" (*First Epistle of Clement*, chap. xxxvi). Christ "must reign, till He hath put all enemies under His feet." But "the last enemy that shall be destroyed is death" (I Corinthians 15:25-26).

v. 14. Are they not all ministering spirits, sent forth to minister for them who shall be heirs of salvation?

Finally, by means of a rhetorical question, we are told the purpose of the existence of the angels. They do God's bidding (Psalm 102/103:20), and they have been sent to serve and assist those who believe in Christ to become heirs of salvation. Christ is the Heir and has given us an inheritance, which is salvation, and thus we become co-heirs with Him. "In Christ we have obtained an inheritance" (Ephesians 1:11; see also Romans 8:17).

Christ said: "He that hath seen me hath seen the Father" (John 14:9). "Nor, on seeing an angel would a man say that he had seen the Father; for angels, as it is written, are 'ministering spirits, sent forth to minister,' and are heralds of gifts given by Him through the Word to those who receive them. . . . And he who hath seen the Son, knows that, in seeing Him, he has seen, not an angel, nor one merely greater than angels, nor in short any creature, but the Father Himself." (St. Athanasius, *Third Discourse against the Arians*, chap. xxv, no. 14).

As "spirits," the angels are not to be confused with the Holy Spirit. "The Spirit is called on as Lord of life, and the angels as allies of their fellow-slaves and faithful witnesses of the truth" (St. Basil the Great, *On the Holy Spirit*, chap. xiii, no. 29).

The first chapter of Hebrews very skillfully identifies the Person who is the subject of the whole Epistle. He is the Son of God, the express Image of the Father. He is eternal and unchangeable, and was the active agent in the creation itself. He is not an angel and was not created, for the angels were created to be ministers and servants of God's will. The same Son became one with the human race, taking on our nature, without ceasing to be what He always was. As God-Man, He purged our sins, made us heirs to salvation, and gave us eternal life.

This identity is revealed in a recurring interweaving of references to the Son in His eternal being and to His work as the God-Man: as Prophet (God spoke to us through His Son—v. 2), as Priest (He by Himself purged our sins—v. 3), and as King (He sat down on the right hand of the Majesty on high—v. 3) and that He obtained a more excellent name than the angels (v. 4), that is, Lord.

The Hebrews to whom the Epistle is addressed should have been the first to recognize this Person—Jesus Christ. They had been prepared to know Him by the prophets, among whom the principal is David, as the several quotations from the Psalms show.

Chapter 2

v. 1. Therefore we ought to give the more earnest heed to the things which we have heard, lest at any time we should let them slip.

In the first chapter, the Apostle has written about the Son of God, both in relation to His saving work (the dispensation or economy) and in relation to the creation, to His sovereignty, His equality with the Father, and to His reign over men and the powers above. All of this has been *heard* from the Lord Himself and from the eye-witnesses of the events of His life (see St. John Chrysostom, *On Hebrews*, Homily 3, no. 5).

Now he urges the Hebrew Christians and, of course, all Christians, to "give the more earnest heed" to all that has been heard, passed on or transmitted by those reliable witnesses. (The essence of the Tradition is the passing on from one generation to the next of the message that was given by Christ to men in its fullness.) Since a comparative, "more earnest," is used (see also II Corinthians 7:13,15), we should conclude that this exhortation recalls how poorly the Law was heeded by their ancestors. "Why 'more earnest?' Here he meant 'more earnest' than to the Law: but he suppressed the actual expression of it, and yet makes it plain in the course of reasoning, not in the way of counsel, nor of exhortation. For so it was better" (St. John Chrysostom, *ibid.*).

As he does in several of the numerous admonitions throughout the Epistle, the Apostle addresses his people in the first person plural, thus identifying himself as a member of the same community. He warns them of the consequences of neglecting Christ or perhaps having divided interests. The verb translated "give heed" (*prosechein* in Greek) occurs often in the New Testament with the meaning of "beware of," especially of false teachings; among other places, see Matthew 7:15; Luke 20:46; I Timothy 4:1; Titus 1:14, and in this

Epistle, 7:13. The first result of indifference to the "things" (which have been passed on to those whom he undertakes to warn) will be "letting them slip," that is, forgetting the vital importance of those "things" to their salvation. The verb "let slip" (in Greek, *pararreō*) is found in the Old Testament: in Proverbs 3:21, with the meaning of "pass one by" or "forget"; and in Isaiah 44:4, with reference to waters that pass or course by.

The Hebrews of old drifted away and fell into the error of idolatry because of inattention to the Law, and did not learn from it what it prefigured (Luke 24:27). This new generation of Hebrews, although they have become believers, have now turned indifferent, and are in danger of apostasy.

vv. 2-3. For if the word spoken by angels was steadfast, and every transgression and disobedience received a just recompense of reward, how shall we escape, if we neglect so great salvation; which at the first began to be spoken by the Lord, and was confirmed unto us by them that heard him;

The angels, being ministering spirits, have always been God's servants and messengers in His revelation of Himself and of His will to man; they are man's servants in that they are at the service of those who are to be heirs of salvation (see 1:14). God has spoken to men through the angels, not only in giving the Law (Acts 7:53; Galatians 3:19), but also in those acts and commands by which He directed the course of Israel's history. All of these things are included in "the word spoken by angels." This word was steadfast—true, faithful, confirmed. How? It was from God and therefore was confirmed again and again; the very prophecies contained in the word have now come to pass.

Further, God's justice was not violated in that all transgressions against the Law and every disobedience to it had dire consequences, just as obedience and observance of it were rewarded with blessings. How much greater, then, are the consequences of obedience and disobedience to Christ? The reminder of the consequence of not paying attention or being indifferent to the Law suggests that apostasy or heresy, of which some of the Apostle's readers may be guilty, will also have its recompense (St. Athanasius, *First Discourse Against the Arians*, chap. xiii, no. 59 [8]).

Christians' neglect of what Christ has given them will surely have greater consequences than those that came to the Hebrews of old (St. Symeon the New Theologian, *Discourse V*, "On Penitence," no. 10). Christ has given salvation, "so great salvation," not from earthly tribulations, but from spiritual destruction. Christ's salvation signifies the dissolution of death's finality and the defeat of the devil, and grants the Kingdom of Heaven and eternal life. The Old Law, as a type of the New, promised deliverance from earthly hardships and a recompense of earthly blessings in exchange for observing the Law. Yet, even in the Old Covenant, salvation that was more than earthly deliverance was promised to Israel (Isaiah 45:17).

Now this word of salvation was first preached by the Lord Himself, the Son of God made Man, and it was confirmed by the eye-witnesses of the Word. St. Athanasius, the great defender of the Son's divinity and equality with the Father, commenting on verse 3, offers it in order to refute the Arians' claim that the words "made" (1:4) and "better" or "more excellent" (7:22; 8:6) are proof of the similarity between the angels' ministry and the Lord's. These are of a different nature, since the angels were ministers of the very uncreated Son of God, who became man for the sake of mankind's salvation. The Saint says,

> Whereas the Word is not in the number of originate things, but is Son of the Father, therefore, as He Himself is better and His acts better and transcendant, so also is the punishment worse. Let them [the Arians] contemplate the grace which is through the Son, and let them acknowledge the witness which He gives even from His works, that He is other than things originated, and alone the very Son in the Father and the Father in Him. (*ibid.*)

*v. 4. God also bearing them witness, both with signs and won-
ders, and with divers miracles, and gifts of the Holy Ghost,
according to his own will?*

This verse completes the question begun in the preceding verse.
The faithfulness of the apostles' testimony is attested to by God the
Father Himself, who worked signs, wonders and an abundance of
miracles in them. Thus, those who had not actually seen and heard
the Lord could believe the apostles' preaching because of the wonders that accompanied it.

It was further confirmed by gifts of the Holy Spirit. St. Ambrose
stresses the meaning of the Greek word *merismois,* translated as
"gifts." It refers to what the Holy Spirit "distributes" in accordance
with His will, for example, the power to work wonders. The Saint
sees in this phrase proof of the Holy Spirit's personhood:

> But in truth the Holy Spirit is not a minister but a witness of the
> Son, as the Son Himself said of Him: "He shall bear witness of Me"
> [John 15:26]. The Spirit, then, is a witness of the Son. He who is a
> witness knows all things, as God the Father is a witness. For so you
> read in later passages, for our salvation was confirmed to us by God
> bearing witness by signs and wonders and by manifold powers and
> by distributions of the Holy Spirit. He who divides as he will is cer-
> tainly above all, not amongst all, for to divide is the gift of the
> worker, not an innate part of the work itself. (*On the Holy Spirit,*
> Book I, chap. iii, no. 48)

We recall that on the day of Pentecost, the apostles were filled
with the Holy Spirit and were empowered to proclaim the salvation
that was in Christ (see St. Cyril of Jerusalem, *Catechetical Lecture
XVI,* nos. 3 and 24). Their work was confirmed by the working of
miracles, as we see throughout the Book of Acts (4:31; 14:3; 15:12),
which is the history of the first generation of the Church. St. Paul
elsewhere refers to signs, wonders and miracles as proof of true
apostleship (II Corinthians 12:12).

In verses 3 and 4, mention is made of all three Persons of the
Holy Trinity, the Lord Jesus Christ, God the Father, and the Holy

Spirit, as having taken part in the proclamation of the Good News among men.

> *v. 5. For unto the angels hath he not put in subjection the world*
> *to come, whereof we speak.*

In a sense, then, the world of the Old Testament was subject to the angels, but only in that they were God's intermediaries in the giving of the Law and in general making His will known to man. The "world to come" (see 1:6) is subject to the Son: with His coming into the world, the world to come, the new age, has already been inaugurated. From the perspective of the Old Testament, the "world to come" points to the world initiated by Christ. Now, after His coming, it is understood both as the kingdom He established in this world and the kingdom of the world or age to come, in which He will deliver up His kingdom to the Father (I Corinthians 15:27-28).

In recounting the goodness of the Lord toward the house of Israel, Isaiah the Prophet speaks of the "angel of His presence," who "saved them: in His love and in His pity He redeemed them; and He bare them, and carried them all the days of old" (63:9; see also Psalm 90/91:11-12, "He shall give His angels charge over thee . . .").

It is not that the angels have been put aside as God's messengers, as New Testament events clearly show, but now the Father has spoken to His people more directly through His Son. It is of the world as the inaugurated new age, and the world of the kingdom of heaven of which the writer speaks. "See how he makes the comparison . . . there [in the Old Covenant], 'by angels,' and here [in the New], 'by the Lord'—and there, 'a word,' but here, 'salvation' " (St. John Chrysostom, *ibid.*).

> *v. 6. But one in a certain place testified, saying, What is man,*
> *that thou art mindful of him? or the son of man, that thou*
> *visitest him?*

The vagueness of the reference, "one in a certain place," is probably deliberate, since the Apostle counts on the familiarity of his readers (Hebrews, after all) with the passage from Psalm 8:4-8 that is quoted here in verses 6-8, "What is man ... thou hast put all things under His feet."

After God had created all things, the heavens and the earth, the light, the firmament, the dry land and the waters, vegetation, the lights, sun, moon and stars, the living beings, then, on the sixth day, He created man, the crown of His creation, and gave him dominion over all the earth. Man, then, was called into being from nothing, as was every other created thing, but he is first in God's mind, because of the fact that it was only in man that God put His own image. God's intervention in the created world and in man's affairs (His "visiting" him) was out of His loving concern, His Providence—He has always been concerned about man and man's relation with Him.

But now we must ask this question: Are these things simply applicable to mankind as a whole, without any reference to Christ? The Apostle's intent in quoting this Psalm has to be discerned in relation to his question in 1:5 and his assertion in 2:5. The theme of the whole passage is the work of the Son of God on behalf of the human race, whose nature He took upon Himself. St. John Chrysostom tells us that

> although these things were spoken of human nature generally, they would nevertheless apply more properly to Christ according to the flesh. For this, "Thou hast put all things in subjection under his feet," belongs to Him rather than to us. For the Son of God visited us when we were nothing: and after having assumed our nature, and united it to Himself, He became higher than all. (*op. cit.*, Homily 4, no. 2)

St. Augustine (*On the Psalms,* Psalm VIII, nos. 10-12) would deny that "son of man" is no more than a periphrasis for "man" in accordance with Hebrew poetic parallelism. For him, the word "or" in this verse establishes the difference. Man refers to Adam, who was no son of man, and Son of man, to Christ who was born of a woman (of the race of man). Adam's having lost his glory and honor, as well as his dominion over God's creation because of sin, and Christ's overcoming the devil and regaining what Adam lost, determine the quality of their relationship to God; thus the two verbs "art mindful" and "visitest." Adam, because of sin, distanced himself from God, who is still mindful of him to provide for his salvation; Christ, who in the dispensation was perfectly obedient to God's will, was thereby close to Him.

v. 7. Thou madest him a little lower than the angels; thou crownedst him with glory and honor, and didst set him over the works of thy hands:

The creation account in Genesis makes no mention of the angels, yet they are present and involved in human history from the beginning, having been created before the world was (St. Basil the Great, *Hexameron,* Homily 1, no. 5). Their existence and nearness to God, their function and role as doers of His will gave them a certain superiority over men. But there is a radical difference between the very mode of their existence and that of man. Man is created in the image of God and after His likeness, and thus has attributes like God's. Men and women are creative and are allowed to participate in the creative act of the procreation of children. They are "crowned" with glory and honor, in that they have been set as king and queen over creation. This reference to man's destiny given him at creation is reflected in the essential formula of the Rite of Matrimony: "O Lord our God, crown them with glory and honor." God's plan for man in relation to the whole created order was revealed to him at the beginning, when he was set over the works of God's hands (Genesis 1:26-30). The same words are applied to him in the fulfilling of his destiny in the kingdom of heaven (Revelation 21:26). (See St. Gregory of Nyssa, *Against Eunomius,* Book I, no. 16, where he examines the meaning of "subjection" in Scripture.)

v. 8. Thou hast put all things in subjection under his feet. For in that He put all in subjection under Him, He left nothing that is not put under Him. But now we see not yet all things put under Him.

Up to this verse, the Apostle, in repeating David's words, seems to have in mind mankind in general, although, as we have noted, they are especially applicable to the perfect Man, Jesus Christ. From this point on, he is clearly speaking of Christ, and in so doing he captures the full meaning of the Psalm. David's words, typically, are not only profoundly sensitive meditations on the relation between God and man, they are also prophetic; of this we have an example in verse 9 below. We also remember how in the first chapter references to the Son of God move back and forth from the Son of God as the eternal Word of God, and Creator, to the Son of God of the dispensation, in the incarnation. Finally, we may call to mind that the Word of God, in becoming incarnate, identified Himself totally with mankind, so that what was man's also became the property of the Son of Man, Jesus, and even to a higher degree. (Our device for noting the change of subject noted above is the use of capital letters for the third person pronouns as they begin to be applied to the Son of God in this and the following verses of this Epistle.)

The world was created by Him and for Him—the Son (Colossians 1:16). In this sense, all things are and have always been subject to Him. This subjection demonstrates the omnipotence of both Father and Son in their equality; St. Ambrose (*On the Christian Faith*, Book IV, chap. xi, nos. 139-141) refutes the Arian notion that there is a difference between the power of the Father and that of the Son, which they made claiming St. Paul's use of "of whom are all things" applied to the Father and "through whom are all things" applied to the Son (I Corinthians 8:6)

> Certain it is, then, that between Father and Son there can be no difference of Power. Nay, so far is such difference from being present, that the same Apostle has said that all things are "of" Him, by Whom are all things, as followeth: "For of Him and through Him and in Him are all things" [Romans 11:36]. (*ibid.*, no. 141)

Yet, we find in the last part of this verse a statement which at first glance seems to be a contradiction: "But now we see not yet all things put under Him." However, we know that the redemptive work of the Savior consisted of delivering man from bondage to sin and death. The victory over death has already been won by His resurrection. On the other hand, death must still be destroyed; when it is, the work of the Savior will be complete, and all things will be put under Him (I Corinthians 15:28; see also St. John Chrysostom, *ibid.*).

v. 9. But we see Jesus, who was made a little lower than the angels for the suffering of death, crowned with glory and honor; that He by the grace of God should taste death for every man.

This verse explains how Jesus, in becoming one with the human race, has become for but a short time lower than the angels. It is for the suffering of death, because the angels do not die. But in the resurrection, the whole thing is reversed: He is crowned with glory and honor. In other words, what was man's destiny, his calling, has been realized by Jesus Christ. His death was "for every man," not because He had to die, but He did so by the grace of God for man's salvation. (See St. Athanasius, *The Incarnation of the Word of God,* no. 10; St. Cyril of Alexandria, *Commentary on the Gospel of St. Luke,* Homily 37.)

v. 10. For it became Him, for whom are all things, and by whom are all things, in bringing many sons unto glory, to make the Captain of their salvation perfect through sufferings.

When the Apostle says, "It became Him" (that is, "It was fitting for Him"), he may have had in mind the possible reaction of his readers, the Hebrews, to the idea of the Saviour's suffering and death. He means that the whole way of salvation designed by God (the incarnation, the suffering and death of His only-begotten Son) was entirely consistent with His natural loving-kindness and benevolence. "What He has done is worthy of His love for mankind" (St. John Chrysostom, *ibid.*, no. 4; also St. Athanasius, *ibid.*).

While the Apostle may be speaking of the Father when he says, "for whom" and "by whom are all things," it is equally applicable to the Son, as is explained in I Corinthians 8:6: "But to us there is but one God, the Father, of whom are all things, and we in Him; and one Lord Jesus Christ, by whom are all things, and we by Him." He is the very reason for and the cause of the existence of all things. The divine initiative and the will to save all created things belongs to the very One whose will it was that they exist. The saving work and will of Jesus Christ was the will of the Father (St. Athanasius, *Encyclical to the Bishops of Egypt and Libya*, no. 15).

The very purpose of man's creation was to know God and to share in His blessedness and glory. Man had not achieved his purpose, so God, who loved His creation, proposed to bring men, "many sons," to glory, that is, to participation in the divine life (II Peter 1:4); hence the Incarnation: wherein the Son of God became man to *lead* men to salvation. Now this leader, Christ, is one with the human race, but He is also God. He is the Captain (*archēgos*, "leader," "cause" or "author"), in that He undergoes on behalf of all men what they must undergo, suffering and death. Thus, as such, His work is accomplished or completed: He was glorified, "crowned with glory and honor," by His voluntary sacrifice. In this sense, He is perfected, that is, He brought His work to perfection or completion. He is the way, and no one comes to the Father except by Him (John 14:6); by the blood of Jesus, the new and living way into the presence of God is made possible (Hebrews 10:19-20).

St. Gregory of Nyssa, as an example of Christ's "leading," explains that His baptism is a sign of His burial and resurrection, and that our following Him in our own baptism, as "the Leader/Captain of our salvation," is the means whereby we imitate these saving acts and appropriate them to ourselves.

> But the descent into the water, and the trine [triple] immersion of
> the person in it, involves another mystery. . . . It was necessary that

some means should be devised by which there might be, in the baptismal process, a kind of affinity and likeness between him who follows and Him who leads the way. . . . Seeing, then, [that] the death of the Author of our life subjected Him to burial in earth and was in accord with our common nature, the imitation which we enact of that death is expressed in the neighboring element [water]. . . . By having the water thrice poured on us and ascending again up from the water, we enact the saving burial and resurrection which took place on the third day. (*The Great Catechism,* chap. xxxv)

v. 11. For both He that sanctifieth and they who are sanctified are all of one: for which cause He is not ashamed to call them brethren,

The Lord Jesus Christ, the God-Man, is one with the Father, and He became one with the human race. He is begotten of the Father, and man was created by Him, so they are all of one or from one. He, by His work of redemption, sanctifies them, and they are sanctified by Him, who is "the Way." Thus, they will also come into the glory of God and become more and more like Him.

The God-Man is infinitely superior to men, yet in His condescension, His humiliation, men are His brethren. His not being ashamed to call them brethren emphasizes His loving-kindness because of which He made them so. The Apostle no doubt has in mind the heresy alluded to in I John 4:1-3, that is, that the Incarnate Word only appeared to have real humanity ("flesh") and to suffer and die. This destructive notion, Docetism, continued to plague the Church in the second century, as we see in St. Irenaeus' condemnation of it (*Against Heresies,* Book III, chap. xviii); it has surfaced from time to time ever since.

St. Cyril of Alexandria says, "having transferred to Himself our poverty, He is sanctified with us, although He is Himself the Sanctifier of all creation; that thou mightest not see Him refusing the measure of human nature" (*op. cit.,* Homily 12). St. Symeon the New Theologian (*Discourse IX,* no. 5) reminds us that "we who have been baptized in the Name of Father, and of the Son, and of the Holy Spirit, bear the name of Christ's brethren."

v. 12. Saying, I will declare thy name unto my brethren, in the midst of the church will I sing praises unto thee.

Christ's brotherhood with all men is already foretold in prophecy. Here the Apostle quotes Psalm 21/22:22; although it is rooted in David's experience, its meaning and its truth are shown by this Epistle to apply more properly to the Son of God. The first words of the Psalm, one may remember, were uttered by Jesus on the Cross, "My God, my God, why hast thou forsaken me?" Jesus, as the Leader, the "Captain of our salvation," of mankind, praises God with them in the midst of the congregation (*Epistle of Barnabas,* chap. vi).

v. 13. And again, I will put my trust in him. And again, Behold I and the children which God hath given me.

In the same vein, the Apostle quotes David (II Kings/II Samuel 22:3) and Isaiah (8:18) to show that Christ, who has clothed Himself with flesh, and consequently has taken on brotherhood with man, has put His trust in God, and looks upon all men as children given Him by the Father. So, it is together with these children and as one of them that He trusts in God (see John 17:1-26, the high priestly prayer of the Lord on the eve of His crucifixion). St. Gregory of Nyssa, speaking of Christ, tells us,

He drew with Him into the same grace all the nature that partakes of His body and is akin to Him. And these glad tidings He proclaims through the woman [Mary Magdalene], not to those disciples only, but also to all who up to the present day become disciples of the Word,—the tidings, namely, that man is no longer outlawed, nor cast out of the kingdom of God, but is once more a son, once more in the station assigned to him by his God, inasmuch as along with the first-fruits of humanity the lump is also hallowed [see Romans 11:16]. "For behold," He says, "I and the children whom God hath given me" [Isaiah 8:18]. (*Against Eunomius,* Book XII, no. 1) *v. 14. Forasmuch then as the children are partakers of flesh and blood, He also himself likewise took part of the same; that through death He might destroy him that had the power of death, that is, the devil;*

The children, His brethren, all "partakers of flesh and blood," have in common the created human nature. This is what "flesh and blood" means, and it is in contrast to the divine nature. Now, the Son of God, who had that divine nature, assumed the nature that belonged to the children that God had given Him. Thus, again, the reality of the Incarnation is stressed (see John 1:14).

Why did He do this? In order to die, and by so doing raise Himself from death and thereby break the power of the one, the devil, who held the power of death over men (Romans 5:8-10; 8:3). The Saviour's death and His victory over it provided His brothers, His fellow-human beings, with the possibility of escape from the devil's dominion (Colossians 2:14-15; II Timothy 1:10).

"The Word, therefore, by having united unto Himself that flesh which was subject unto death, as being God and Life drove away from it corruption, and made it also to be the source of life; for such must the body of (Him who is) the Life be" (St. Cyril of Alexandria, *op. cit.*, Homily 142).

v. 15. And deliver them who through fear of death were all their lifetime subject to bondage.

The fear of death is mankind's universal slavery or bondage, and as long as there was no assurance of a liberation or deliverance from that fear, man was easy prey to the power of Satan. Release from this bondage of fear is granted to all men by the death of Christ and His victory over it in the resurrection. For those who believe in Him, while they still have to die, there is a twofold deliverance: not only has all debt been paid for man's sins by Christ, but now they have the knowledge that death is not final and that they too will be victorious over it. "Thou seest that in casting out the tyranny of death, he also overthrew the strength of the devil. For he who has learned to study innumerable truths concerning the resurrection, how should he fear death? How should he shudder any more?" (St. John Chrysostom, *ibid.*, no. 6).

v. 16. For verily He took not on him the nature of angels; but He took on him the seed of Abraham.

Christ's appearance among men was not in the form of an angel—He did not become an angel, nor did He assume the nature of angels. The reality of the Incarnation, of God's taking flesh, is again emphasized by the declaration that He became a descendant of a real historical figure, Abraham, and did not just assume the appearance of man. Here, the expression "took on" ("took hold of" or "established an identity with," *epilambanetai* in Greek) indicates specifically that He did this in order to save the nature that He took on and those who shared or partook of that nature. It may be added that the declaration that He "took not on Him the nature of angels" means that the angels were not in need of redemption, for, "are they not all ministering spirits, sent forth to minister for them who shall be heirs of salvation?" (Hebrews 1:14). His pursuit of man was due to man's having turned away from Him (see St. John Chrysostom, *op. cit.,* Homily 5, no. 1). His plan and design for man's ultimate exaltation is also suggested by this verse. St. Cyril of Alexandria (*op. cit.,* Homily 23) uses this passage to refute the Nestorian teaching that the man Jesus was coupled to the Word of God only by a "connection" (*synapheia* in Greek) rather than by a "union" *(henotēs).*

v. 17. Wherefore in all things it behooved Him to be made like unto His brethren, that He might be a merciful and faithful high priest in things pertaining to God, to make reconciliation for the sins of the people.

How complete was His taking hold of mankind and becoming of the same nature, being made "like unto His brethren?" The

Apostle says, "in all things"—in other words, He was born, grew up, suffered and finally died. Why did He do this? In order to become "a merciful and faithful high priest." A priest who offers must partake of the nature of those for whom he offers. It was out of His love for man, His will to be merciful to us, that He became our High Priest. It is important to note that He did not make a sudden appearance as an adult, but that "He hallowed conception and birth, and as He grew up, bit by bit, blessed every age" (St. Symeon the New Theologian, *Discourse V,* no. 10). "In all things" means, of course, all things but sin (Hebrews 4:15; St. John of Damascus, *Exposition of the Orthodox Faith,* Book IV, chap. xiii; St. Symeon, *Discourse XXXII,* no. 5).

It was this kind of priest that was necessary to man in his relation to God, "in things pertaining to God," for no man was able to offer the sacrifice that would purify man from his sins (St. John Chrysostom, *ibid.*). Through sin, man had become an enemy of God (Romans 5:10).

The Greek term *hilaskesthai,* translated "to make reconciliation," is related to *hilastērion,* as in Romans 3:25, where it is translated "propitiation," and to *hilasmos,* as in I John 2:2 and 4:10, where it is also translated "propitiation." In other places in the New Testament (for example, Romans 5:10; II Corinthians 5:18), "reconcile" and "reconciliation" translate forms of *katallassō* and *katallagē,* apparently meaning "reconcile" without any notion of sacrifice. In any event, reconciliation of man with God was accomplished in Christ (II Corinthians 5:19) and sealed by His death. Thus, we see the sacrifice of Christ as the expiation for man's sins, payment of the debt all men owed because of their sins, in that He "purchased" the Church, the community of the redeemed, "with His own blood" (Acts 20:28). St. Athanasius (*op. cit.,* no. 20 [5]) lists among the reasons for Christ's "bodily appearance" among men the following:

> The death of all was accomplished in the Lord's body, and that death and corruption were wholly done away by reason of the Word that was united with it. For there was need of death, and

death must needs be suffered on behalf of all, that the debt owing from all might be paid.

v. 18. For in that He himself hath suffered being tempted, He is able to succor them that are tempted.

The chapter ends with another emphasis on the reality of the Incarnation. In the Saviour's earthly life, He not only was born, developed, grew and suffered, but He was even tempted as all men are. However, in His sinlessness, He resisted and overcame all temptation, but He knew man's temptation both as the omniscient God and from His experience as man. Hebrews 4:15 says, "He was in all points tempted like as we are, yet without sin." This qualifies Him to come to the aid of those who are tempted, that is, of all His brethren, as their merciful and faithful High Priest. "For He knows what temptation is, not less than we who have suffered, for He Himself also suffered" (St. John Chrysostom, *ibid.*).

St. Ambrose, in his *Treatise on the Gospel According to St. Luke* (Book IV, nos. 17-35), explores rather fully the nature of the temptations of mankind, and shows how the Lord, one by one, overcame those that that are at the root of all man's sins:

> These three kinds of vice are shown to be near the sources of all offenses, for the Scriptures would not have said, "All the temptations being ended" [Luke 4:13], if the substance of all transgressions were not in these three, of which the seeds are to be feared in their very beginning. Thus the end of temptations is the end of desires, because the causes of temptations are the causes of desires. Then, the causes of desires are the delight of the flesh, the appearance of glory, and the greed for power. (*ibid.*, no. 35)

Chapter 3

v. 1. Wherefore, holy brethren, partakers of the heavenly calling, consider the Apostle and High Priest of our profession, Christ Jesus;

At the beginning of this chapter, we find a kind of summation of all that has been stated before in the first two chapters. Because of the readers' acceptance of and faith in all that Christ is and all that He did, they are addressed as "holy brethren, partakers of the heavenly calling." They all share in a vocation that requires that they live in anticipation of a heavenly, not earthly, reward, that is, life in the kingdom of heaven. "Seek nothing here, if ye have been called yonder—yonder is the reward, yonder the recompense," St. John Chrysostom urges his people and us (*On Hebrews*, Homily 5, no. 5). His brothers in the faith are called holy because, by their faith and membership in the Body of Christ, they are called to be saints (Romans 1:7), and the great salvation that has been given to them makes them citizens of God's heavenly kingdom (Ephesians 2:19).

Just as in Chapter 2 (vv. 1-4), where the Hebrew Christians are urged to look to Christ, now they are exhorted to direct their whole mind to Him as the only way to salvation. Such is the meaning of the Greek verb *katanoēsate*, translated "consider." According to St. Symeon the New Theologian, it is

> a terrible misfortune that we who have been born of God and become immortal and partakers of a heavenly calling, who are "heirs of God and fellow-heirs with Christ" [Romans 8:17], and have become citizens of heaven [Philippians 3:20], have not yet come to the realization of so great blessings. (*Discourse VIII*, no. 3)

Christ is called both "the Apostle" and "High Priest" of their profession. This is the only instance of the application of the name "Apostle" to Christ, but it is obviously appropriate in view of His repeated claim to having been sent by the Father (John 4:34). It is a one-word résumé of His prophetic ministry. His high priesthood has already been mentioned briefly in Chapter 2 (v. 17), and will be explored in detail later.

The word "profession" here translates the Greek *homologia*. Its meaning for Greek-speaking Hebrews was much broader than the content of a creed or a doctrinal system. It was often used in the Old Testament for confession of sins, profession of faith, and, significantly, for giving thanks to and glorifying God (see Leviticus 22:18 and Deuteronomy 12:6,17 LXX). We must remember that the reconciliation brought about by the Incarnate Son of God consisted of restoring to man what he had lost by his sin, the God-centered life, the life that is a continuous confession of faith and of thanksgiving, or worship. Our Church's understanding of the name it most often uses to describe itself, Orthodox, is twofold: the right way of worship and the right teaching.

> *v. 2. Who was faithful to Him that appointed Him, as also Moses was faithful in all his house.*

The Son of God became the Son of Man specifically that He might become our merciful and faithful High Priest. This faithfulness is manifest in His carrying out the mission for which He had been sent. The Greek word translated "appointed" is *poiēsanti,* which is usually translated "made" or "created." In fact, the Arians had used this passage from Hebrews, along with certain others, to prove that the Son was a created being. The Fathers of the Church, however, explain that terms such as "made," "created," and "formed" are appropriately applied to the Son only in His work among men as a Man, in carrying out the divine will (St. Athanasius, *On the Opinion of Dionysius,* no. 11; *Second Discourse against the Arians,* chap. xiv, nos. 6-11; also St. Gregory of Nyssa, *Against Eunomius,* Book VI, no. 2). A quote from St. Ambrose is typical of the patristic response to the Arians:

You see what it is in respect whereof the writer calls Him created: "In so far as He took upon Him the seed of Abraham"; plainly asserting the begetting of a body. How, indeed, but in His body did He expiate the sins of the people? In what did He suffer, save in His body—even as we said above: "Christ having suffered in the flesh?" In what is He a priest, save in that which He took to Himself from the priestly nation? (*On the Christian Faith,* Book III, chap. xi, no. 86)

Now the Apostle brings in Moses, making a comparison between him and Jesus. He too was faithful in all that God had given him to do: bear witness to His will and direct the house of Israel to its proper relationship with God. Moses' house was the people of God, the chosen people, Israel. Jesus, in His human nature, could be compared to Moses, and this is no doubt done here to gain the confidence of the Hebrews, who certainly held Moses in the highest esteem. Moses' faithfulness is fully described in Exodus 35.

v. 3. For this man was counted worthy of more glory than Moses, inasmuch as he who hath builded the house hath more honour than the house.

Here the comparison ends, and Jesus' superiority is asserted. Having begun with a reference to His human nature, the Apostle will now proceed to demonstrate wherein that superiority lies. Moses was still one member of the household, although he was its father both historically and by God's design. But the Son of God was the real builder of that house or nation, so the Master-Builder is greater in honor than any member of it, even its leader. Moses' faithfulness is then seen as a figure of the faithfulness of Christ, that is, both he and his work are to understood as types of Christ and His work (I Corinthians 10:1-4; see also St. Gregory of Nyssa, *The Life of Moses,* II). Moses, in both word and deed, prophesied the Lord Jesus Christ. Remember the words of the Lord Himself: "For had ye believed Moses, ye would have believed me: for he wrote of me." (John 5:46; see also St. John Chrysostom, *On the Gospel of St. John,* Homily 33, no. 2).

*v. 4. For every house is builded by some man; but He that built
all things is God.*

All men have the capacity for building, but they can only use
those things which God has created and provided. Thus, the Apostle is still speaking of Moses, who, only in a limited sense, built the
house of Israel, for it was God who made Moses and gave him both
the means and mission to build it. Specifically, in view of the foregoing verse, it was the Son who built that house, as He would as the
Incarnate One build His Church, as St. Cyril of Jerusalem calls it,
"His second Holy Church" (*Catechetical Lecture XVIII,* no. 25). The
house of Israel does not describe the nation as a political or geo-
graphical entity, nor does it mean the temple itself, but the whole
people of God (St. John Chrysostom, *On Hebrews,* Homily 5, no. 4).

*v. 5. And Moses verily was faithful in all his house, as a servant,
for a testimony of those things which were to be spoken after;*

As for Moses' being a servant, we note that he was faithful in all
that God had given him to do, not as a slave (which in Greek would
be *doulos*), but as a free agent who serves God in loving response to
Him. The word in the Greek text for servant is *therapōn;* it seems to
have been chosen over *doulos* to define the relationship between
God and Moses. St. Irenaeus recalls the direct testimony of God to
Moses' special calling before Miriam and Aaron (Numbers 12:7-8)
as His *therapōn* (*Against Heresies,* Book III, chap. vi, no. 5). Note that
the response of Moses and many other righteous in the Old Testament makes clear that although they were servants of God, their free
will was not destroyed by Adam's sin, but remained operative.

Now, Moses' role or purpose as a servant of God was to point to
the future. His faithfulness was testimony or surety of those things
which were to be revealed afterwards, that is, when the real head of
the house would come to take possession of what was already His
own. He tells Moses that He would "raise up a Prophet . . . like unto
me . . ." and then ". . . like unto thee," who would speak His own
words, and that those who would not "hearken unto those words,

which He would speak in His name," would be accountable for their deeds (Deuteronomy 18:15,18-19). St. Gregory of Nyssa (*ibid.*) finds at least six figures of the Incarnation in the deeds of Moses.

> *v. 6. But Christ as a Son over His own house; whose house are we, if we hold fast the confidence and the rejoicing of the hope firm unto the end.*

The Son of God is the heir, as we saw in the first chapter of the Epistle, and the house of Israel was His house. Herein lies the distinction: Christ is *over* (the head of) His own house, the house *in* which Moses was a servant, as St. Athanasius makes clear:

> Moses as a servant, but Christ as Son, and the former faithful in his house, and the latter over the house, as having Himself built it, and being its Lord and Framer, and as God sanctifying it. For Moses, a man by nature, became faithful, in believing God who spoke to Him by His Word; but the Word was not as one of things originate in a body, nor as creature in creature, but as God in flesh, and Framer of all and Builder of all in that which was built by Him. (*Second Discourse against the Arians,* chap. xiv, no. 10)

We who believe in Christ and hold to the end of our lives the assurance and the joy of the hope that Christ has given us are truly the house of Israel, the new Israel. This stress on "holding unto the end" is directed to those who may be tempted to give up and relapse into the now apostate Judaism, but it is an appropriate reminder to Christians in every generation. The Lord Himself had said: "He that endureth to the end shall be saved" (Matthew 10:22; see also St. John Chrysostom, *ibid.,* no. 5).

This confidence we must have is the gift of God whereby we are able to come to Him as free men. We can glory in or boast of the fact that God has received us into His household. The word translated "confidence" is *parrēsia* in Greek, a word rich in meaning (hence the variety of renderings in English translations), has its roots in *pas* ("all") and *rhēsis* ("speech"). It is used extensively in the New Testament, four times in Hebrews, and a few times in the Old Testament, three in Proverbs. Being traditionally a characteristic of free men, *parrēsia* reflects the freedom that is given to men in Christ. "Stand fast therefore in the liberty [freedom] wherewith Christ hath made us free, and be not entangled again with the yoke of bondage" (Galatians 5:1).

> *vv. 7-11. Wherefore (as the Holy Ghost saith, To day if ye will hear His voice, harden not your hearts, as in the provocation, in the day of temptation in the wilderness: when your fathers tempted me, proved me, and saw my works forty years. Wherefore I was grieved with that generation, and said, They do always err in their heart; and they have not known my ways. So I sware in my wrath, They shall not enter into my rest.)*

Verse 7 begins with "Wherefore" or "for this reason," and thus recalls the preceding declarations that Christ is superior to the prophets, to the angels, and finally to Moses. Because Christ is greater than all of these, the Hebrew reader of the Epistle is exhorted to "take heed" or "be on his guard," lest he commit the same error as his forefathers. However, the sentence is interrupted by a long, parenthetical quotation (vv. 7-11) from Psalm 94/95, and then continues in verse 12.

The portion of the Psalm quoted is attributed by the Apostle to the Holy Spirit, and although David did not say, "the Holy Spirit saith," he testifies to the fact that when God spoke to the people of Israel it was through the Holy Spirit (St. Cyril of Jerusalem, *Catechetical Lecture XVII*, no. 33). Concerning this passage, St. Ambrose writes,

> Therefore, according to the Apostle, the Spirit was tempted. If He was tempted, He also was certainly guiding the people of the Jews into the land of promise, as it is written: "For He led them through the deep, as a horse through the wilderness, and they labored not, and like the cattle through the plain. The Spirit came down from

> the Lord and guided them" [Isaiah 63:13-14 LXX]. And He certainly ministered to them the calm rain of heavenly food, He with fertile shower made fruitful that daily harvest which earth had not brought forth, and husbandman had not sown. Now let us look at these points one by one. God had promised rest to the Jews; the Spirit calls that rest His. God the Father relates that He was tempted by the unbelieving, and the Spirit says that He was tempted by the same, for the temptation is one wherewith the one Godhead of the Trinity was tempted by the unbelieving. (*On the Holy Spirit,* Book III, chap. viii, nos. 52-53)

"His voice" is obviously "God's voice," but such is the unity of both will and operation of the Godhead that it could be understood as the voice of the Word or of the Holy Spirit. The same Holy Spirit who will testify of Christ (John 15:26) also did testify of Him to the Jews' forefathers. This unity is indicated in St. Paul's teaching to the Romans: "But ye are not in the flesh, but in the Spirit, if so be that the Spirit of God dwell in you. Now if any man have not the Spirit of Christ, he is none of His" (8:9).

The Hebrew Christian to whom the Apostle addresses his Epistle must not follow the example of their ancestors and harden their hearts when they hear the voice of God. When did the Hebrews of old harden their hearts? In the wilderness, when there was not water to drink, and they began to murmur against Moses, to accuse him of having led them out of Egypt to make them die of thirst, and finally to ask, "Is the Lord among us or not?" (Exodus 17:1-7). In other words, they forgot the wonderful, saving work of God on their behalf. They tempted Him and tested Him, even though they had seen His works, and grieved Him, because they strayed and showed that they did not know Him or His ways. Although Moses tried to make them see that although they had not yet entered the promised land, the Lord would keep His promise to them (Deuteronomy 12:9 ff.), they still rebelled against Him. His warning to them, in His anger, was they would not enter into His rest, that is, into the promised land (Numbers 14:22-23).

v. 12. Take heed, brethren, lest there be in any of you an evil heart of unbelief, in departing from the living God.

One must be on his guard against allowing the temptation of falling away to enter his heart. This expression seems to take for granted that the true believer has the capability to resist this evil. Although the Apostle calls them brethren, perhaps to soften what he has to say, his warning is rather severe. The consequences of their falling away will be far more serious than what happened to their forefathers, both in view of the nature of the "rest" of which they will be deprived, and that while in Christ they have greater knowledge, they also obtain a greater responsibility.

God's rest, of which the Sabbath was the earthly experience of the Hebrews, and of which the Promised Land was a symbol, is really His kingdom and the faithfuls' being in it eternally. "What other rest then is there, except the Kingdom of Heaven, of which the Sabbath was an image and type?" (St. John Chrysostom, *op. cit.,* Homily 6, no. 2). The Apostle will dwell at length on the subject of God's rest in Chapter 4.

Hardness of heart, brought about by complaining against God, produces unbelief. Unbelief is evil, because it consists of departing from the living God. Man's fundamental sin is living as if God did not exist. The application of the word "living" to God emphasizes the deadness of idols, whether they be carved or painted images of imaginary deities or an all-consuming preoccupation with wealth, fame or position (see *The Shepherd of Hermas,* Book I, Vision III, chap. vii). Here we have an indication that some of the Hebrews were not only tempted to go back to their old ways, but also there seem to have been some that were drawn to paganism or were caught up in material interests.

v. 13. But exhort one another daily, while it is called To day; lest any of you be hardened through the deceitfulness of sin.

The immediate remedy proposed is mutual encouragement by exhortation. The community nature of man's relation to God is stressed here—each member has responsibility for the others (see 10:25; also St. Ignatius, *Epistle to the Ephesians,* chap. xiii).

What the Apostle says to his brethren can be said to us and to our generation in these terms: when we see a brother or a sister beginning to weaken or lose interest, we must come to his rescue. We, for our part, must never let laziness and lack of enthusiasm for Christ and His way take hold of us. Our own example of dedication cannot but be contagious in the community. This is to be maintained daily, "while it is called To day." "To day" reminds us of the Lord's command to the disciples to work while it is still day—as long as one lives and as long as the world lasts (Romans 13:11; II Peter 3:10). St. Basil the Great (*Letter XLII,* "To Chilo," no. 5) says that "Today means the whole time of our life," and St. Cyril of Jerusalem (*Catechetical Lecture XV,* no. 32) explains it as "continually."

Sin, which produces unbelief, is deceitful in that it only seems to provide happiness and fulfillment in life, but instead produces illusions and poor imitations of those goods.

v. 14. For we are made partakers of Christ, if we hold the beginning of our confidence steadfast unto the end;

Christians are made partakers of Christ as members of His Body and of which He is the Head. We have been baptized into His death, buried with Him, and have risen up to walk in the newness of life (Romans 6:3-4). We are partakers of Him in that we are nourished after our new birth by partaking of Him in the Divine Eucharist of His body and blood (St. Gregory of Nyssa, *The Great Catechism,* chap. xxxvii).

We will be partakers of Him in His kingdom, His rest, if, until the end of our lives, we hold fast to Him who is the very principle of our existence. Sometimes the initial dedication of a convert weakens and he finally falls away into unbelief. The reason may very well be that he has lost sight of the One who is the object of our faith, having replaced Him by the means designed to lead us to Him. The word "confidence" here translates a different Greek word, *hypostasis,* which means "substance" or "foundation" (see v. 6, above). Another way in which the whole phrase may be translated is, "the principle [beginning] of our substance [being]." In Christ we have a totally new life or being; the Apostle's warning is that the sense of that new life is in danger of being lost. St. John Chrysostom puts it this way, " 'If we hold fast the principle of our subsistence unto the end.' What is the principle of our subsistence? The faith by which we stand, and have been brought into being and were made to exist, as one may say" (*ibid.,* no. 6). (See also our remarks on 2:14, above: The Lord Jesus Christ shared our nature and our life so that we might be made sharers of His nature and His life by grace.)

v. 15. While it is said, To day if ye will hear His voice, harden not your hearts, as in the provocation.

Again reference is made to what was said in verses 6 through 8. There is an urgency about this warning, since it has to do with a present danger and not some future possibility. St. Cyril of Jerusalem, explaining the "Our Father," and especially the petition, "give us this day . . . " draws attention to the meaning of *sēmeron* which is used both in this verse and in the Prayer: "each day in its turn is called 'today.' " It is noteworthy also that he stresses that the Holy Bread, that is, the Body of the Lord, is the only food that is substantial and essential to all every day (*Catechetical Lecture XXIII,* no. 15).

v. 16. For some, when they had heard, did provoke: howbeit not all that came out of Egypt by Moses.

According to St. John Chrysostom, "what he says is to this effect. They also heard, as we hear: but no profit came to them. Do not suppose then that by 'hearing' what is proclaimed ye will be profited; seeing that they also heard, but derived no benefit because they did not believe" (*ibid.,* no. 5).

Both parts of this verse are really questions: "Who did provoke when they had heard?" "Was it not all who came out of Egypt under

Moses' leadership?" These questions, along with those in verses 17 and 18, insist unremittingly that present-day Hebrew believers listen to this "voice from the wilderness."

v. 17. But with whom was He grieved forty years? was it not with them that had sinned, whose carcasses fell in the wilderness?

God was indeed grieved with those who sinned and consequently fell into disbelief. They did not reach the promised land, as their carcasses fell in the wilderness during those forty years. As a matter of fact, almost all of the 600,000 perished. "Your carcasses shall fall in this wilderness; and all that were numbered of you, according to your whole number, from twenty years old and upward, which have murmured against me" (Numbers 14:29; see also 14:23 and 32:13). In this connection, St. Paul reminds us:

But with many of them God was not well pleased: for they were overthrown in the wilderness. . . . Now all these things happened unto them for types; and they are written for our admonition, upon whom the ends of the world are come. Wherefore let him that thinketh he standeth take heed lest he fall. (I Corinthians 10:5, 11-12)

Psalm 105/106 contains an extended meditation on the apostasies of Israel, deviations that continued to exist in David's time:

We have sinned with our fathers, we have transgressed, we have done unrighteously. Our fathers in Egypt understood not thy wonders, and remembered not the multitude of thy mercy. . . . Moreover they set at nought the desirable land and believed not His word. . . . So He lifted up His hand against them, to cast them down in the wilderness. (vv. 6-7,24,26)

In the Great Fast particularly Christians are exhorted to take seriously the admonition implied in this reminder of the things that happened to some of their forefathers—"and let us not perish with those whose carcasses fell in the wilderness" (Second Week of the Great Fast, Aposticha for Friday Matins).

v. 18. And to whom sware He that they should not enter into his rest, but to them that believed not?

And it was to those who did not believe and were disobedient that He declares in His wrath that they could not enter into His rest. And it was not simply a question of unbelief, but specifically the unbelief of the very people whom He had saved from slavery and to whom He had shown His power and His love:

> Because all those men which have seen my glory, and my miracles, which I did in Egypt and in the wilderness, and have tempted me now these ten times, and have not hearkened to may voice. . . . Doubtless ye shall not come into the land, concerning which I sware to make you dwell therein, save Caleb the son of Jephunneh, and Joshua the son of Nun. (Numbers 14:22,30)

v. 19. So we see that they could not enter in because of unbelief.

Since the promised land was a figure of the kingdom of heaven, God's rest, it is made clear that the main reason why one will not be able to enter that kingdom is unbelief. All of these things have been said and the example of Israel's apostasy is given to the readers of this Epistle so that they (and we) might learn (Romans 15:4) that to have professed a belief in Christ and then to have fallen away will have disastrous consequences. "Now all these things happened unto them for ensamples [types]: and they are written for our admonition, upon whom the ends of the world are come. Wherefore let him that thinketh he standeth take heed lest he fall" (I Corinthians 10:11-12).

Chapter 4

v. 1. Let us therefore fear, lest, a promise being left us of enter-
ing into His rest, any of you should seem to come short of it.

The exhortation to the Hebrew believers in Christ continues.
They have been reminded of the failure of their forefathers that were
led out of Egypt to enter into the Promised Land because of their
unbelief. Just as it was to them, a promise of entering into God's rest
has been made to those who are faithful to Christ, that is, to the
believers of the Apostle's own time. Again, we must understand that
there were signs of weakening and falling away among them.

The text uses the term "left" (in Greek, *kataleipomenēs*) because
the rest of the first promise (the land) was but a figure of the ultimate rest, and therefore the promise is still in force. Christians are
"heirs according to the promise" (Galatians 3:29); and "This is the
promise that He hath promised us, eternal life" (I John 2:25; see also
St. John Chrysostom, *On Hebrews,* Homily 6, no. 5).

In the minds of those first Jewish believers in Christ, the promise
was either misunderstood or seemed unattainable. They were
undoubtedly under stress and persecution by the non-believing
majority. Perhaps they still kept something of the often-expressed
Hebrew belief that God's displeasure with His people was manifested
in their having to undergo hardships. Then also, many of them may
have felt guilty about abandoning the traditions of their fathers. The
Apostle's warning, "let us fear," is therefore appropriate, because their
loss will be infinitely greater than that of their ancestors.

v. 2. For unto us was the Gospel preached, as well as unto them;
but the word preached did not profit them, not being mixed
with faith in them that heard it.

Both the first-century Jewish followers of Christ and those of the
time of the Exodus were given the good news ("were evangelized").

But, because of their unbelief, the latter did not profit from their hearing (see our comment on 3:16, above). The point is made that most of them did not follow the example and join themselves to those leaders who did remain faithful, Joshua and Caleb. God had said: "Doubtless ye shall not come into the land, concerning which I sware to make you dwell therein, save Caleb the son of Jephunneh, and Joshua the son of Nun" (Numbers 14:30).

> Caleb then and Joshua, because they agreed not with those who did not believe, escaped the vengeance that was sent forth against them. And see how admirably he said, not, They did not agree, but, "they were not mixed"—that is, they stood apart, but not factiously ["not in a manner characterized by dissension"] when all the others had one and the same mind. (St. John Chrysostom, *ibid.*)

The English translation "not being mixed with faith in them that heard," follows the Received Text, in which the Greek for "mixed" is *sygkekramenos* (nom. masc. sing.), and thus refers to "the word preached." St. John's commentary, however, seems to reflect another verb form, *synkekramenous* (acc. masc. pl.), and thus refers to them (who by their faith were indeed profited). It seems that the last clause of the sentence would better be translated, "because they were not mixed [united] by faith with [to] them that heard [it]."

The exhortation the Apostle makes to his own generation can well be addressed to Christians of our own time. It is still true that only hearing the Gospel is not sufficient; we must assimilate that promise and live in expectation of its fulfillment by faith:

> For if they who suffered so great distress in the wilderness were not counted worthy of [the promised] land, and were not able to attain [that] land, because they murmured and because they committed fornication: how shall we be counted worthy of Heaven, if we live carelessly and indolently? We then have need of much earnestness. (St. John Chrysostom, *op. cit.*, Homily 7, no. 1)

v. 3. For we which have believed do enter into rest, as He said, As I have sworn in my wrath, if they shall enter into my rest:

although the works were finished from the foundation of the world.

The promises of God were made to His people as a nation or community, although each member, to be sure, had his personal responsibility for maintaining his faith, as was the case with Joshua and Caleb. The same thing is true now, and the rest of which the Apostle speaks is the kingdom of heaven. But a foretaste of that kingdom is already provided in the assembly of the faithful (see 10:25), and one must be a part of that assembly. So the faithful do enter (or better, "are entering") into the rest even now, because the means for doing so has been made available in Christ. Again reference is made to Psalm 94/95:11, as evidence that because of His displeasure with those who came out of Egypt, they did not enter into the land that He had promised them.

On the other hand, as St. John Chrysostom points out,

> This, indeed, is not evidence that we shall enter in, but that they did not enter in. What then? Thus far he aims to show us that as that rest [of the original promise] does not hinder the speaking of another rest [to which the Psalmist alludes], so neither does this [exclude] that of Heaven. (*op. cit.*, Homily 6, no. 6)

The last clause, "although the works were finished from the foundation of the world," recalls our Lord's declaration, on speaking of the last judgment, that those "blessed of His Father," would "inherit the kingdom prepared for you from the foundation of the world" (Matthew 25:34). St. Paul's assurance (Ephesians 1:4) that "He hath chosen us in Him before the foundation of the world, that we should be holy and without blame before Him in love," is explained by St. John Chrysostom (*On Ephesians,* Homily 1) in this way: "That you may not then, when you hear 'He hath chosen us,' imagine that faith alone is sufficient, he proceeds to add life and conduct. To this end, saith he [St. Paul], hath He chosen us, and on this condition, 'that we should be holy and without blemish.'"

God's rest was designed to be shared by those who are created in His image, human beings, and this is promised from the beginning. This is implied in His rest after creation.

There are, then, several meanings of rest in Scriptures: 1) God's rest on the seventh day after the six days of creation, 2) the Sabbath rest, as a remembrance of the first, 3) the Promised Land, as a figure of the fourth: 4) the rest of the eternal kingdom of heaven.

v. 4. For He spake in a certain place of the seventh day on this wise, And God did rest the seventh day from all his works.

The thought at the end of verse 3 is completed here. The key reference in Genesis 2:2 is cited. Again, the means for God's rest to be shared by His people on earth was the Sabbath—their not working on the seventh day of the week was an imitation of God's rest on the seventh day. Now, as will be seen, the Sabbath was a figure of the future rest in the Kingdom of Heaven for those who believe in Him.

v. 5. And in this place again, If they shall enter into my rest.

Once more, the Psalm (called "this place") is quoted to emphasize the fact that unbelief kept the Israelites from entering the Promised Land. "And I will come down to deliver them out of the hand of the Egyptians, and to bring them up out of that land unto a good land and a large, unto a land flowing with milk and honey" (Exodus 3:8). But, because of their infidelity, there was a change in God's dealing with this people. Thus, God instructed Moses to say to them: "Doubtless ye shall not come into the land, concerning which I sware to make you dwell therein, save Caleb . . . and Joshua . . . But your little ones, which ye said should be a prey, them will I bring in, and they shall know the land which ye have despised" (Numbers 14:30-31; see v. 3 also).

v. 6. Seeing therefore it remaineth that some must enter therein, and they to whom it was first preached entered not in because of unbelief:

It has been emphasized that unbelief accompanied by disobedience, even unwillingness to be persuaded, prevented most of those who came out of Egypt (those to whom this good news was first proclaimed, *hoi proteron evangelisthentes*) from entering into the rest that God had promised them. But, under Joshua some did reach the promised land, but even then the rest that was promised was not the final one, nor was it simply to remind them of God's rest after creation. The invitation to this rest was renewed in David's time, which fact makes it clear that the promise has never been withdrawn and that it remains for some to enter into that rest. This is the heavenly rest, toward which all of God's dealings with the Hebrews pointed, and into which the Savior has already entered after His work of redemption or recreation like a forerunner (see 6:20) for all those who believe in Him and follow Him.

v. 7. Again, He limiteth a certain day, saying in David, To day, after so long a time; as it is said, To day if you will hear His voice, harden not your hearts.

The Lord's saying, "To day, if ye will hear His voice, harden not your hearts," comes to us through David (Psalm 94/95:7; see Hebrews 3: 7-8,15). So the invitation and the warning were issued again; the "to day" refers to David's time, some 500 years after they were given (see Numbers 14), "after so long a time." The Lord's "limiting" a certain day indicates that He set (in Greek, *horizei*) another day in which Israel is invited into His rest, through the faithful following of His commandments, but the warning still remains, that unbelief (hardening their hearts) will prevent their entering it. St. John Chrysostom sees in this renewal of the condition for entering God's rest hope for the sinner who turns from his unbelief and renews his faith (*On First Corinthians*, Homily 38, no. 8).

v. 8. For if Jesus had given them rest, then would He not afterward have spoken of another day.

"Jesus" here is not our Lord Jesus Christ, but Joshua. The Greek form of the Hebrew name Joshua (or Jehoshua) is *Iēsous,* or Jesus. In Acts 7:45, we again find the name "Jesus" for Joshua. He, the son of Nun, is an Old Testament figure of Jesus the Christ. His name, at first "Oshea," was changed by Moses (Numbers 13:16), who, at God's command, ordained him to be his successor (Numbers 27:18-23). He was sent with other rulers of the tribes of Israel to spy out the promised land (Numbers 13:8), and, because of his obedience and faithfulness (Numbers 14:6-9), he finally led the survivors among the Israelites into the land of Canaan (Joshua 1-4). St. Justin Martyr asks the Jews in his *Dialogue with Trypho* how it is that they attached so much importance to the changes in Abraham's and Sarah's names and failed to consider the great prophetic significance of Joshua and his name change (chap. lxxv; chap. cxiii).

This verse confirms what we have said about the rest attained by a few of the people under Joshua's leadership: that it was symbolic of the other rest, the promise of which was renewed through David and attained for the faithful in Jesus Christ. If the rest that was reached under Joshua had been the final one, and if it had no meaning other than God's favoring the Israelites over all other people, the Lord would not have spoken of another rest. It still stood in David's time, and it now stands in our time, having been made available to all who would put their faith in Christ.

v. 9. There remaineth therefore a rest to the people of God.

Now the true meaning of rest is revealed, for here the Greek word *sabbatismos* replaces the *katapavsis* of the foregoing verses of this chapter. On the other hand, while the frame of reference is the same, the Apostle obviously has a purpose in this substitution. In verses 10 and 11, he will return to the usual term, but here he must have in mind the rabbinical saying that "the Sabbath is the image of the world to come." The Sabbath rest, the rest which recalls God's resting on the seventh day, does not mean the cessation of all activity, because, as the Savior said in answer to those Jews who criticized His healing on the Sabbath, "My Father worketh hitherto, and I work" (John 5:17). In other words, His care and providence never stop. The final, ideal rest for the people of God obedient to Him is not a state of inactivity, but an end to the struggles of earthly life and doing God's service only.

v. 10. For He that is entered into His rest, He also hath ceased from His own works, as God did from his.

According to St. John Chrysostom, "As God ceased from His works, he says, so he that hath entered into His rest [hath ceased]. For since his [the Apostle's] discourse to them was concerning rest, and they were desirous to hear when this would be, he concluded the argument with this" (*op. cit.,* Homily 6, no. 7). So, again, what the believer looks forward to with confidence and assurance is this conclusion of the journey beset by hardships.

> Seest thou then the fruits of "Jerusalem that is above?" [Galatians 4:26] And what is indeed more stupendous than all is this, that our warfare is not decided, but all these things are given us before the attainment of the promise! For they indeed toiled even after they had entered the land of promise;—rather, they toiled not, for had they chosen to obey God, they might have taken all the cities, without either arms or array. Jericho, we know, they overturned, more after the fashion of dancers than of warriors. We however have no warfare after we have entered into the land of promise, that is, into Heaven, but only so long as we are in the wilderness, that is, in the present life. (St. John Chrysostom, *On Ephesians,* Homily 23, "Moral")

Another way of understanding this passage, not at all inconsistent with the above, is this: The "Captain of our salvation," who is bringing many "sons unto glory" (Hebrews 2:10), "ran the race that was set before Him" (12:2), and "is set down at the right hand of the throne of God," finished the work that He was sent to do (John

17:4), that is, having accomplished His work, entered into glory or the rest of the Kingdom. He is thus our forerunner (6:20), and those who follow Him, "look unto Him" (12:2), are encouraged, strengthened and assured of entering into that rest if they endure to the end.

v. 11. Let us labor therefore to enter into that rest, lest any man fall after the same example of unbelief.

Now, there comes the appeal to labor (or "be earnest about"), having all our mind, hope and expectation so directed, to enter into that rest.

> Faith is indeed great and brings salvation, and without it, it is not possible ever to be saved. It suffices not however of itself to accomplish this, but there is need of a right conversation ["manner of living"] . . . how shall we be counted worthy of Heaven, if we live carelessly and indolently? We then have need of much earnestness. (St. John Chrysostom, *On Hebrews*, Homily 7, no. 1; see v. 2 also)

We remember that some among the first generation of Hebrew Christians were torn between putting all their faith in Christ and the temptation to return to the sacrifices of Judaism, which had been done away with. This failure of faith is comparable to the faithlessness of the people of Moses' time. They, however, died a physical death, and were unable to reach the promised land; now the fall's consequences are spiritual death, and those who fail will not reach the rest of which the promised land was a figure.

v. 12. For the word of God is quick, and powerful, and sharper than any two-edged sword, piercing even to the dividing asunder of soul and spirit, and of the joints and marrow, and is a discerner of the thoughts and intents of the heart.

This verse together with the one that follows are said to be a brief hymn or a part of a hymn to the Logos (Word) of God. Some modern interpreters seem to avoid identifying this logos with the Logos or Son of God, preferring to see it as a reference to the whole body of revealed truth, and there are some of the Fathers who understand it as both (see, for example, St. Symeon the New Theologian, *Discourse III*, nos. 6 and 8). St. John Chrysostom identifies this "word" with the Son of God: "In these words he [the Apostle] shows that He, the Word of God, wrought the former things also, and lives, and has not be quenched" (*ibid.*, no. 2). In any event, the "Word of God" and His word are intimately united, because when God speaks to man in the New Covenant as He did in the Old, it is by means of His Son, His Word (see St. John of Damascus, *Exposition of the Orthodox Faith*, Book IV, chap. xiii).

The Word is alive, living (quick) and active, energizing (powerful), and more incisive and penetrating (sharper) than any two-edged sword. Just as a sword might "pierce to the dividing asunder of joints and marrow," in other words, in the physical body, so also the Word of God pierces the soul and spirit. It may be noted that the wording "piercing even to" translates the Greek *diiknoumenos achri,* the first word meaning "pierce" or "pass through," and the second, "up to" or "as far as." "Soul" and "spirit" are in the same form (genitive case), so the action is on both, and does not indicate separating one from the other. The same is said of "joints" and "marrow," both in the genitive case, and, further, they are not joined in the first place, so it would be meaningless to speak of dividing one from the other.

The use of the figure "two-edged sword" was perhaps suggested by the shape of the tongue, and of course, its relation to the spoken word. The tongue is likened to a sword, or even an arrow in other places in sacred Scripture (Psalm 56/57:4; 63/64:3; Jeremiah 9:8), in which the tongue is a weapon of deceit of the enemy, but in Ephesians 6:17, the "sword of the Spirit" is "the word of God." In St. John's Revelation, in his vision of the Son of man, the Word of God, he sees that "out of his mouth went a sharp two edged sword" (1:16). "And what is the Sword? The cutting of the Word, which separates the worse from the better, and makes a division between the faithful and the unbeliever ..." (St. Gregory Nazianzus, *Oration XXXIX,* "On the Holy Lights," no. xv).

The point is that the Word of God penetrates the deepest recesses of a person's being and knows what is in the heart. He is the judge, discerner and revealer of the thoughts and intents, the secrets of the heart (see Daniel 2:47 and Romans 2:16). Thus, the Apostle wants his readers to know that the kind of disbelief and disobedience that he has spoken of as obstacles to entering into God's rest are open and known to God the Word.

> *v. 13. Neither is there any creature that is not manifest in His sight: but all things are naked and opened unto the eyes of Him with whom we have to do.*

This verse completes the thought of the preceding, and it makes it clear that the "Word" referred to is the Son of God. All creatures were made by Him and they are ever in His sight. The idea of nakedness is often applied in the Scriptures to man to stress the fact that he has no cover or place to hide from his Creator God. St. Basil urges all believers to behave and act always in accordance with "the full assurance of the presence of God" (*Letter XXII,* "On the Perfection of the Life of Solitaries," no. 2). St. Athanasius makes use of this verse to show that Christ, the Word of God, is the Judge of all men (*Second Discourse against the Arians,* chap. xxi, no. 72; see also his *Paschal Letter XI,* no. 4). We find also in the Ninth Ode of the Canon of Compline on Monday of Holy Week, "The books shall be opened and the thrones shall be set up; all men shall stand naked and their deeds shall be examined. Neither witness nor accuser will be there, for everything is manifest in God's sight."

The idiom translated "with whom we have to do," would be more literally rendered "to whom we must give account" (in Greek, *pros hon hēmin ho logos*). Thus, the word *logos* which means the word in the sense of the Son's teachings or of Scriptures, and the "Word of God" that is, the Son of God, is shown to have a third meaning, the account or answer, or defense, the revelation of a man's whole spiritual state and the record of his deeds. Man's word, in this sense, is the summary of who he is.

v. 14. Seeing then that we have a great high priest, that is passed into the heavens, Jesus the Son of God, let us hold fast our profession.

The figure suggested by the term "opened" in verse 13, a translation of the Greek *tetrachēlismena,* which describes what happens to a victim in a sacrifice (gripped by the neck so as to lay bare the animal offered, or to take away the skin of the dead animal), may have been used by the Apostle to re-introduce the theme of Christ's priestly ministry (2:17 and 3:1). In other terms, a word that is properly related to sacrifice is applied to mankind in general. Since God sent "His own Son in the likeness of sinful flesh and by a sacrifice for sin He condemned sin in the flesh" (Romans 8:3), and "He hath made Him to be sin for us, who knew no sin" (II Corinthians 5:21), the Lord's sharing our nature laid bare the sins of mankind. The priest that we have is not only the one who offers but He is also the one who is offered, at once priest and victim.

The great High Priest, after His resurrection, ascended into the heavens. However, the Greek verb *dielēlythota* is more accurately understood as "passed through," rather than "passed into." The choice of terms may represent a reluctance on the part of the Apostle to "locate" physically heaven and the throne of God. All in all, the point is made no doubt to offer consolation and hope to the Hebrew Christians: that Jesus the Son of God, still having the human nature that He assumed and the divine nature that He always had, remains their great High Priest in that He continues to care for and offer intercession for His disciples (see 7:24-25).

The writer had made much of the superiority of Jesus over Moses (3:1-6), and now he proclaims His superiority over Aaron and the priests of the Old Covenant. The latter only completed the sacrifice by entering into the Holy of Holies and sprinkling the sacrificial blood on the Mercy Seat. Now our great High Priest has entered into the ultimate Holy of Holies, beyond, as it were, the heavens, to the throne of God to present Himself to the Father (see

St. John Chrysostom, *ibid.,* no. 4; also St. Ambrose, *On the Christian Faith,* Book IV, chap. ii, no. 18).

The profession or confession (*homologia,* in Greek) refers to the whole of the faith delivered by Jesus Christ to the saints, which is summarized for us in the Creed. By holding fast this confession, which we made at our baptism, which we, in the assembly of the faithful at worship, repeat, we anticipate our own entrance into the heavenly sanctuary, into which our great High Priest leads us. It is to be stressed, however, that the ability to confess the faith and hold fast to it is the result of obedience and godly living (St. Athanasius, *Paschal Letter XI,* no. 10). This entering into the rest of God is the reward for our fidelity to the Christ of our profession. Once again we are exhorted not to fall into doubt and disbelief, as did some of our forefathers.

> *v. 15. For we have not an high priest which cannot be touched with the feeling of our infirmities; but was in all points tempted like as we are, yet without sin.*

The priests of the Old Testament came from the people and were like all other men, and the atonement they made was not only for the sins of others, but also for their own sins (see 5:3). Now, this great High Priest that we have is also one of us: He assumed our whole condition, suffered, knew from experience our infirmities or weaknesses, and was even tempted, since His manhood was complete. He suffered with us (such is the meaning of being "touched with the feeling of our infirmities"—the Greek verb is *sympathēsai*). Yet, as was pointed out in the previous verse, this Jesus is the Son of God, and He is without sin. So the priesthood is perfected in that the final High Priest offers only for His fellow human beings, for He has no sin of His own for which to atone. In Him, no temptation ever resulted in sin:

> And so our Lord Jesus Christ, though declared by the Apostle's word to have been tempted in all points like as we are, is yet said to

have been "without sin," i.e., without the infection of this appetite, as He knew nothing of incitements of carnal lust, with which we are sure to be troubled even against our will and without our knowledge. (St. John Cassian, *Conference of Abbot Serapion,* chap. v)

According to St. Symeon the New Theologian,

God, who is served by myriads of powers without number, who "sustains all things by the word of His power" [Hebrews 1:3], whose majesty is beyond anyone's endurance, has not disdained to become the father, the friend, the brother of those rejected ones [the weak and the poor]. He willed to become incarnate so that He might become "like unto us in all things, yet without sin" and make us to share in His glory and His kingdom. What stupendous riches of His great goodness! What an ineffable condescension on the part of our Master and our God! (*Discourse II,* no. 5)

v. 16. Let us therefore come boldly unto the throne of grace, that we may obtain mercy, and find grace to help in time of need.

The chapter ends with the encouragement to "come boldly unto the throne of grace." Here, the Apostle uses the same wording as in 3:6, *meta parrēsias,* "with boldness or confidence." The High Priest is approachable because of His having identified Himself with us and because of His "sympathy" or "suffering" with us. We can come to the throne, where He sits on the right hand of the Father, but it is no throne of judgment—it is a throne of grace (St. John Chrysostom, *ibid.,* no. 6), God's free gift to man, His transforming power communicated to men. We can come boldly, because it is His will for us to do so, and it is there where we obtain the mercy that we sinful creatures need and seek. This gift is given to us now ("help in the time of need" is literally "help in due season" or "timely help") by the One who was like us but overcame every temptation, but we must receive that help while there is still time. The Son of God, who is also the Son of Man, will come again and will sit upon His throne and will then be the Judge (see Matthew 25; also St. John Chrysostom, *ibid.*).

It is a fearful thing to fall into the hands of the living God: for He is Judge of the thoughts and meditations of the heart. Let no man draw near in order to make trial of His surpassing faithfulness; but let us come to Christ in meekness and in fear, that we may receive mercy and find grace to help us in our time of need. (Aposticha for the Vespers of Palm Sunday Evening)

St. Cyril of Jerusalem (*Catechetical Lecture VI*, no. 21) has an additional interpretation of this "timely help," which is germane to the intention of the Apostle in this exhortation. This Saint's concern is that, in the time of temptation to apostasize or to distort the teachings of Christ, we "store in our memory" the consequences of the falling away of our ancestors and the heresies of certain notable dissenters of the past.

Chapter 5

v. 1. For every high priest taken from among men is ordained for men in things pertaining to God, that he may offer both gifts and sacrifices for sins:

The Apostle now begins to develop his major doctrinal theme—the priesthood of our Lord Jesus Christ. In Chapter 4 (v. 14) he has already said that we Christians have a High Priest and that that High Priest is Jesus the Son of God and the Son of Man. Further (v. 15), he shows that He was able to sympathize with (suffer with) us, because He became one of us. But the point is made that He "was tempted in all points like as we are," yet without sin.

In this Chapter, he first defines what a priest is: 1) he is taken from among men; 2) he is appointed by God to represent men before God; and 3) he accomplishes this representation by offering gifts and sacrifices for sins (St. John Chrysostom, *On Hebrews,* Homily 8, no. 1). The writer is not concerned here with those additional roles, some of which were of a secular nature, that the priesthood in Israel had assumed in the course of history. Rather, he refers to the priest in terms of his true Old Testament functions—the offering of gifts in worship as a sign of gratitude and homage, and of sacrifices for sin in general, and for particular sins on the Day of Atonement (Exodus 10:10).

v. 2. Who can have compassion on the ignorant, and on them that are out of the way; for he himself also is compassed with infirmity.

The priest, being a man and, therefore, a sinner, is able to have compassion on his fellow sinners. The word in Greek here for "have compassion" (*metriopathein*) is not the same word as the one translated "touched with the feeling of" (*sympathēsai*) in 4:15. This word indicates, by its prefix *metrio-* ("with measure" or "moderation"), that the priest must be moderate and tender in his judgment of the sins of others, but, on the other hand, not be over-indulgent either. The ignorant and those that are out of the way (those who have gone astray) are those who may not have sinned deliberately. Their ignorance may consist of their not knowing what God's righteousness requires, and they simply may not realize that they have sinned. In this life, where one is surrounded by sin, it is easy to be led astray, if he is not constantly on his guard. Whatever the case may be, these sins too must be atoned for (Leviticus 4:13). The priest can understand and deal gently with those of both conditions. The main reason why he can have this kind of compassion is that he himself is of the same sinful nature and is beset by the same moral weaknesses. He can fall victim to the same.

St. Gregory of Nazianzus (*Oration XXXIX*, "On the Holy Lights," no. xviii) makes a moving confession concerning his own priesthood and the kind of compassion the Savior requires of the priest:

> I, however, for I confess myself to be a man,—that is to say, an animal shifty and of a changeable nature,—both eagerly receive this Baptism, and worship Him who has given it me, and impart it to others; for by showing mercy make provision for mercy. For I know that I too am "compassed with infirmity," and that with what measure I mete it shall be measured to me again [Matthew 7:2].

Perhaps no direct reference to the high priests during the Roman era is really intended in this verse. But while the Apostle is more concerned with what generally are the functions and character of the priesthood: "he [the Apostle] appears . . . to hint at the priests of the Jews, as being no longer priests, [but] intruders and corrupters of the law of the priesthood . . ." (St. John Chrysostom, *ibid.*, no. 2).

v. 3. And by reason hereof he ought, as for the people, so also for himself, to offer for sins.

"By reason hereof," that is, because of this infirmity, the priest ought, or is obligated by law, to offer sacrifice for his own sins, and those of his household first, since he shares in that human frailty, and only then can he offer for the people (see Leviticus 4:3-21; 9:7; 16:6,11).

With this statement we begin to understand the Apostle's first point in his exposition of the Lord's priesthood: the difference between it and that of the Old Covenant, and its superiority. Our Lord Jesus Christ, who is the great High Priest that we have, has in His manhood all the requirements for this high office, but He was unlike all the priests before Him in that He had no personal sin or even a sinful nature for which to atone.

v. 4. And no man taketh this honor unto himself, but he that is called of God, as was Aaron.

In addition to the first qualification, that he be taken from among the people, the priest is called, appointed by God, to take this responsibility. No one who is himself sinful could dare to offer on behalf of others if he did not have this divine vocation and appointment.

Aaron's appointment is described in Exodus 28, and since his sons were called to the priesthood at the same time, it is clear that the office was to be hereditary. However, the method of selecting the high priests in Israel had changed radically after the Exile. They had come to be elected, appointed by secular powers, and some had even acquired the office by disgraceful means. It was no longer for life nor hereditary.

The classic case of an attempted usurpation of the priestly office, which met with disaster, that of Korah and his company, is described in Numbers 16. Moses rebuked this son (of Izhar, the son of Kohath, the son) of Levi, when he rebelled against Moses and Aaron, not being satisfied with the ministry God had given them. "And He hath brought thee near to Him, and all thy brethren the sons of Levi with thee, and seek ye the priesthood also?" (16:10; see also Jude 11).

On the divine appointment of Aaron, St. Ambrose (*Letter LXIII*, no. 48) says,

And so He Himself also chose Aaron as priest, that not the will of man but the grace of God should have the chief part in the election of the priest; not the voluntary offering of himself, nor the taking of it upon himself, but the vocation from heaven, that he should offer gifts for sins who could be touched for those who sinned, for He Himself, it is said, bears our weakness. No one ought to take this honor upon himself but they that are called of God, as was Aaron, and so Christ did not demand but received the priesthood.

St. Cyril of Alexandria reminds us that "of every one of the holy apostles we find, that he did not promote himself to the apostleship, but rather received the honor from Christ" (*Commentary on the Gospel of St. Luke*, Homily 57).

v. 5. So also Christ glorified not Himself to be made an high priest; but he that said unto Him, Thou art my Son, to day have I begotten thee.

Just as no man was appointed by other men to be a priest, and no one could attain to this office by personal efforts or ambition—even the great High Priest Jesus Christ was given it by the Father. There are numerous occasions recorded in the New Testament when the Lord attests to His having been sent by the Father and to the work He had been sent to do.

Since Eunomius had seized upon the word "made" as evidence of the Son's being a created being, St. Gregory of Nyssa points out the absurdity of the former's argument by bringing forth other passages that contain a word meaning "made," such as "He hath made Him to be sin for us" (I Corinthians 5:21). These things refer to the Lord's "dispensation of the last times," and not to His "pre-temporal existence" (*Against Eunomius*, Book VI, no. 2).

It is no accident that the Apostle has chosen, instead of simply, "But the Father . . . ," to say, "He that said unto Him, Thou art my Son, to day have I begotten thee," quoting Psalm 2:7. This eternal (such is the meaning of "to day") sonship is indeed the necessary condition for His appointment as High Priest ("the Lamb slain from the foundation of the world," Revelation 13:8). The perfect and final High Priest is the One who is forever at the Father's right hand. Now, in the incarnation of the Son, it is He as God-Man who receives this eternal appointment. His glorification begins as He enters the final, decisive part of His priestly work, His sacrifice. This is why the "great priestly prayer" begins with "Father, the hour is come; glorify thy Son . . . with the glory which I had with thee before the world was" (John 17:1,5).

> *v. 6. As he saith also in another place, Thou art a priest for ever after the order of Melchisedec.*

Now the Apostle quotes from Psalm 109/110:4. This verse from David could be nothing but a prophetic reference to Christ, because it could not be addressed to anyone else. All the priests of the Hebrew people were of the order of Aaron, his descendants under the Law. Melchisedec was unique, as he was prior to the Law, and there was no other priest of his order until Christ. Outside of the brief reference that we have in Genesis (14:18-20), we are dependent on the present Epistle for our information about him (see especially chapter 7; also St. John Chrysostom, *ibid.*).

St. Ambrose (*ibid.*, no. 49) gives the general patristic understanding of his role:

Lastly, when the succession derived through family descent from Aaron, contained rather heirs of the family than sharers in his righteousness, there came, after the likeness of that Melchisedec, of whom we read in the Old Testament, the true Melchisedec, the true King of peace, the true King of righteousness, for this is the interpretation of the Name, "without father, without mother, without genealogy, having neither beginning of days nor end of life" [Hebrews 7:3], which also refers to the Son of God, Who in His divine generation had no mother, was in His birth of the Virgin Mary without a father; begotten before the ages of the Father alone, born in this age of the Virgin alone, and certainly could have no beginning of days seeing He "was in the beginning" [John 1:1].

v. 7. Who in the days of His flesh, when He had offered up prayers and supplications with strong crying and tears unto him that was able to save him from death, and was heard in that He feared;

The Apostle continues his exposition of Christ's priesthood, one important aspect of which is intercession. His whole life was priestly; having become man in every sense, He not only could sympathize with all of man's weaknesses, anxieties and sufferings, but He accepted them as His own, or, in the words of St. Gregory of Nazianzus, "He makes His own our folly and our transgressions" (*Fourth Theological Oration*, no. v). He experienced all things pertaining to them, including the fear of death. The prayers that He offered throughout His earthly life were both on behalf of those who believed on Him (John 17:9), but also on His own behalf as a man. "But for whom did He pray? For those who believed on Him" (St. John Chrysostom, *ibid.*, no. 3).

The introductory "in the days of His flesh" makes it clear that all that follows belongs to His incarnation, that is, in and from within the human nature He had so perfectly assumed. The Apostle's words, "when He had offered up prayers and supplications with strong crying and tears unto Him that was able to save Him from death," refer specifically to His prayers on the eve of His betrayal. That as a man He would pray not to be put to death is entirely plausible; He did pray, "O my Father, if it be possible, let this cup pass from me: nevertheless not as I will, but as thou wilt" (Matthew 26:39; also Matthew 26:42). On the other hand, He had foretold His death, speaking of it many times to His disciples. Even in the prayer, "Father, save me from this hour," He adds, "but for this cause came I unto this hour" (John 12:27). And later: "And I, if I be lifted up from the earth, will draw all men unto me. This he said, signifying what death he should die" (John 12:32-33).

St. Gregory concludes that, in His divine nature, His will coincides with the Father's will *(ibid.)*. St. Ambrose asks, "Again, what was the will of the Father, but that Jesus should come into the world and cleanse us from our sins? . . . Indeed, seeing that He hath said, 'All things that the Father hath are mine' [John 16:15], nothing of a certainty being excepted, the Son hath the same will that the Father hath" (*On the Christian Faith*, Book II, chap. vi, no. 51). Thus it was as a man that He could wish to avoid death, but as God, it was His will to undergo death in order to destroy it.

Since the prayer was offered "to Him that was able to save Him from death," it may be concluded that it was a prayer for resurrection, insofar as His resurrection, as well as His death, was on behalf of all mankind. He had testified to the fact the He had the power, if He laid down His life for man, to take it again (John 10:17-18). He was heard, that is, this prayer was granted, "in that He feared" (more literally, "on account of His reverence," "respect" or "godly piety," *apo tēs evlabeias*, in Greek—His acceptance and compliance with the Father's will). He was granted resurrection so that He might grant the same to man for whom He prayed. As St. Peter reminds the Jews, on the day of Pentecost, quoting Psalm 15/16:8-11, "He [David] seeing this before spake concerning the resurrection of Christ, that his soul was not left in Hell [Hades], neither his flesh did see corruption" (Acts 2:31).

The "strong crying and tears," although not noted in the Gospel accounts, is appropriate, in view of the shameful state of mankind that had caused death in the first place. Death is a tragedy, because man was created for life, and when Jesus met it in a personal way in the death of a friend, He wept (John 11:35). Moreover, he wept over His city Jerusalem for its disobedience and unbelief (Luke 19:41).

v. 8. Though He were [a] Son, yet learned He obedience by the things which He suffered.

There is no need for the indefinite article "a" in the English translation of this verse; in fact, its use could convey the wrong meaning, since all people could be called "sons of God." The word "Son" in its predicative placement can suggest the definite article, that is, "the Son." In any event, the meaning is clear: He was the Son of God by

nature, and, thus, it is a testimony to Christ's divinity and his equality with the Father. It was in the incarnation, "in the days of His
flesh," that He experienced the things which He suffered, and
through them, as Man, He is said to have learned obedience. St. Gregory Nazianzen (*ibid.,* no. vi) explains with regard to these passages
(vv. 7-8): all of these things

> He wonderfully wrought out, like a drama whose plot was devised
> on our behalf. For in His character of the Word He was neither obe-
> dient nor disobedient. For such expressions belong to servants, and
> inferiors, and the one applies to the better sort of them, while the
> other belongs to those who deserve punishment. But, in the char-
> acter of "the Form of a Servant" [Philippians 2:7], He condescends
> to His fellow servants, nay, to His servants, and takes upon Him a
> strange form, bearing all me and mine in Himself, that in Himself
> He may exhaust the bad, as fire does wax, or as the sun does the
> mists of the earth; and that I may partake of His nature by the
> blending. Thus He honors obedience by His action, and proves it
> experimentally by His Passion.

This kind of growth is not unlike His increase "in wisdom and
stature, and in favor with God and man" (Luke 2:52). Again, St. Gregory explains: as God, ". . . these qualities in Him were [not] capable
of growth: for how could that which was perfect from the first
become more perfect, but that they were gradually disclosed and
displayed?" (*Panegyric on St. Basil,* no. 38).

v. 9. And being made perfect, He became the author of eternal salvation unto all them that obey him;

The earthly work of the Lord, as God-Man, reached its climax
and fulfillment in His death on the cross. He was made perfect,
although as Son of God He was already perfect, in that, having completed the work He was sent to do, He brought to perfection or completion that human nature He had assumed. This process involved
learning obedience and conforming to the divine will. The word
translated "made perfect," *teleiōtheis* in Greek, as used here, recalls

the "qualifying" of the priest in the Old Testament. It even means "consecration" (see Leviticus 8:33 LXX). Thus, He had brought to perfection those on behalf of whom He completed His prophetic and priestly work, that is, those who obey Him. Because of His perfect obedience, His perfect conformity with God's will, and, as the end of both, His sacrifice, He has brought men to the point at which they may come into the presence of God. He is, then, the cause of their eternal salvation. In the obedience of Christ to the Father, man is given the example of the necessity of their obedience to Him. This obedience on the part of men must also be learned by suffering. (See St. John Chrysostom, *ibid.*, no. 3.)

v. 10. Called of God an high priest after the order of Melchisedec.

The section ends with a repetition of the words of Psalm 109/110, with some differences. In verse 6, the Apostle quotes the Psalm in order to show that Christ's special priesthood was prophesied; in this verse, his intention seems to be to emphasize that the Father indeed named the Son high priest and that He has recognized Him in that office. The verb translated "called of" (or "by") God is *prosagorevtheis hypo tou theou*, which contains both ideas, the confirmation of one in an office or calling, and a salutation to Christ, as the holder of it. It may also be noted that here He is called "High Priest," whereas in the Psalm it was simply "Priest." This alteration sets the stage for the continuation of the Apostle's exposition of the doctrine of Christ's priesthood, which will continue in Chapter 6 (v. 20). Meanwhile he will address the spiritual state of the Hebrew Christians.

That Christ's priesthood after the order of Melchisedec was prophesied and therefore according to the divine plan, St. Ambrose (*op. cit.*, Book III, chap. xi, no. 89) reminds us that

> this Melchisedec, then, have we received as a priest of God made upon the model of Christ, but the one we regard as the type, the

other as the original. Now a type is a shadow of the truth, and we have accepted the royalty of the one in the name of a single city, but that of the other as shown in the reconciliation of the whole world; for it is written: "God was in Christ, reconciling the world to Himself" [II Corinthians 5:19]; that is to say, [in Christ was] eternal Godhead: or, if the Father is in the Son, even as the Son is in the Father, then Their unity in both nature and operation is plainly not denied.

v. 11. Of whom we have many things to say, and hard to be uttered, seeing ye are dull of hearing.

The explanation of the doctrine of Christ's priesthood is now interrupted, but the readers or hearers of the Epistle are promised that there is much more to be said. On the other hand, the Apostle warns them that they may not really be ready for this exposition, for they are inattentive and the teacher will find it difficult to teach such an audience. Added to this fact, the subject itself is "hard to be uttered" ("hard to interpret/explain," from Greek *dysermēnevtos*). Of course, his discourse *(ho logos)* will demonstrate that the Aaronic priesthood has been replaced by the Melchisedecan priesthood of Christ. The new loyalty demanded of them may be difficult in view of the pressure being brought to bear on them by the Jews.

The point is made also that something has happened to these Hebrew Christians: they "have become" (Greek *gegonate*) "dull" or "sluggish" *(nōthroi)* in their concern for and comprehension of the saving truth which they have received. They seem to take things for granted or they have no interest in understanding of the truth, and they are possibly tempted to return to their old ways, including the sacrifices of the temple, which point has already been made (see vv. 2:3; 3:12; 4:11).

"I think that perhaps here also except [for] a few, there are many such [as they are], so that this may be said concerning yourselves also . . ." (St. John Chrysostom, *ibid.,* no. 4). If the fourth-century Saint could say this of his generation, what could be said of ours?

v. 12. For when for the time ye ought to be teachers, ye have need that one teach you again which be the first principles of the oracles of God; and are become such as have need of milk, and not of strong meat.

The Hebrews to whom this letter is addressed have been Christians long enough ("for" or "in view of the time") to be able to teach others, but it seems that they understand far less of the rudiments ("the elements of the beginning"—in Greek *ta stoicheia tēs archēs*) of the doctrine *(logiōn)* of God than they should, and have need of being taught them again. Perhaps it was because they did not fully grasp the real significance of God's revelation to man in Christ. It may also have been because pressure from those who rejected Christ had weakened their faith in the great High Priest. It is almost certain that there were some among them who were trying to find some way to remain faithful to the old ways and to be Christians at the same time. This, of course, could be done only by undermining the doctrine of Christ as the final High Priest and the end of the old priesthood.

So, rather than progress in the their knowledge of God made known to man by Christ, they are like those who must now begin all over, like new converts. They have become "such as have need of milk," that is, only the basic principles, instead of the solid food of those who have advanced in their knowledge and in the spiritual life under the guidance of the Holy Spirit.

St. John Chrysostom accuses some of those of his time of the same sluggishness: "I am afraid that this might fitly be said to you also, that 'when for the time ye ought to be teachers,' you do not maintain the rank of learners, but ever hearing the same things, and on the same subjects, you are in the same condition as if you heard no one" (*op. cit.*, Homily 9, no. 1).

St. Augustine makes an interesting and, to be sure, a valid point on this verse:

But let us be far from supposing that there is any contrariety between this milk and the [solid] food of spiritual things that has

to be received by the sound understanding, and which was wanting
to the Colossians [2:5] and the Thessalonians [I, 3:10], and had still
to be supplied. . . . Christ crucified is both milk to sucklings and
meat to the more advanced. And the similitude of a foundation is
on this account more suitable, because, for the completion of the
structure, the building is added without the foundation being withdrawn. (*On the Gospel of St. John*, Tractate XCVIII, chap. xvi, no. 6)

*v. 13. For every one that useth milk is unskillful in the word of
righteousness: for he is a babe.*

The Apostle presses the symbol of milk (as also in I Corinthians
3:1-3) as appropriate food for beginners and for those who have not
advanced in their comprehension of the full implications of Christ's
teachings about Himself and about how they are to live. Their being
"unskilled in the word of righteousness," is their being "unskilled in
the philosophy that is above, . . . unable to embrace a perfect and
exact [strict or orderly] life" (St. John Chrysostom, *op. cit.,* Homily
8, no. 6). It means that they are not nurtured like the righteous man
"in faith and knowledge, and the observance of divine precepts," and
so do not have their souls in health (St. Athanasius, *Paschal Letter
VII*, no. 8). They had not yet become of full age in the life in Christ,
something of which they were capable if they had trained themselves (St. John Chrysostom, *ibid.*).

The whole idea can certainly be applied to a large number of
present-day Christians, whose attachment to Christ and His Church
is merely formal, an element of their "cultural heritage," and does
not contain a deep commitment to the principles of living implied
by accepting Christ and His way. Many people can say that they are
Orthodox only because their parents were; they misunderstand the
uniqueness of the Orthodox Christian life and its demands, and they
are both unable and unwilling to witness—not to mention, to
teach—to others the truth about God and man revealed by Jesus
Christ. Pastors must often give only milk to their people, because
they are either unable or unwilling to crave the solid food of full

Christian commitment. They are content to remain at the infant level in the Faith.

According to St. Basil the Great,

> Surely it is altogether childish, and like a babe who must needs be fed on milk, to be ignorant of the great mystery of our salvation; inasmuch as, in accordance with the gradual progress of our education, while being brought to perfection in our training for godliness, we were first taught elementary and easier lessons, suited to our intelligence, while the Dispenser of our lots was ever leading us up, by gradually accustoming us, like eyes brought up in the dark, to the great light of truth. (*On the Spirit*, chap. xiv, no. 33)

v. 14. But strong meat belongeth to them that are of full age, even those who by reason of use have their senses exercised to discern both good and evil.

The unique features of Christian doctrine and the way of life that goes with it are the solid food of the mature believer (those "of full age," in Greek *teleiōn*). The "use" (in Greek *hexin*, which contains a notion of permanence) referred to is the experience in the Christian life, which includes love of God and of one's neighbor, doing unto others as we would have them do to us, overcoming selfishness; in short, living simply in accordance with God's will. Such experience enables one to discern good and evil. Apparently, the recipients of this Epistle, not exercised in the Christian way, did not know how to distinguish good from evil. Like many people today, they perhaps saw no incompatibility between society's good and Christ's good.

St. Symeon the New Theologian tells us,

> We must therefore carefully discern the thoughts that come on us and set against them the testimonies from the divinely inspired Scriptures and from the teaching of the spiritual teachers, the holy Fathers, so that if we find them to agree with these witnesses and correspond to them we may with all our might hold fast these thoughts and boldly act on them. . . . Search them [the holy Scriptures] and hold fast to what they say with great exactitude and faith,

in order that you may know God's will clearly from the the divine
Scriptures and be able infallibly to distinguish good from evil and
not obey every spirit nor be carried away with harmful thoughts.
(*Discourse III*, no. 8)

How appropriately the content of this verse can be applied to the
attitude of so many Orthodox Christians in our own time. Their
rejection of the active experience of the Church—the holy mysteries, prayer, fasting, divine worship, giving alms, and so on—ill equip
them to distinguish between the life in Christ and the life recom-
mended by society. Often the moral standards of society take prece-
dence over the principles and precepts of the Lord, such as those He
enunciated in the Sermon on the Mount. They truly do not know
how to distinguish between good and evil. This call to the Hebrew
Christians grown lax in their inattention to the fullness of Christian
commitment goes out to a very large part of the people of our own
churches in our time.

Chapter 6

v. 1. Therefore leaving the principles of the doctrine of Christ, let us go on unto perfection; not laying again the foundation of repentance from dead works, and of faith toward God,

This verse has been variously interpreted. According to one understanding, these principles (or "beginnings") of the doctrine ("the word") of Christ refer to the Old Testament symbolic or typical preparation for the Gospel. Such an interpretation is somewhat plausible if the verse is translated more literally: "having left behind the doctrine [or "account"] of the principles [or "beginnings"] of Christ." In other words, all that the Old Testament was, the history of the Hebrews, their worship, and the prophecies, spoke of Christ. What the Apostle seems to have in mind is the "beginnings of the doctrine about the Messiah, Christ," that are clearly revealed in the Old Testament. So, confident that his readers have understood that Christ was promised and His coming expected, and now that the prophecies have been fulfilled, all of those types and prefigures of Him have to be left behind and attention turned toward the reality who is Christ Himself. The foundation has already been laid: "turning away from" (Greek *metanoias*) works that cannot give life ("dead works") and reliance upon faith in God. If they do not go beyond this "milk," the first principles, they will always be at the stage of "laying the foundation," and will be unable to receive the "solid food" of the doctrine of Christ's perfect priesthood, the main subject of the Epistle.

Some of the holy Fathers, however, give more emphasis to the idea that the Apostle is pointing to the elementary instruction the Hebrews received as they were preparing for admission to the communion of the Church. Having heard the principles and having laid the foundation, they must penetrate the mystery of the redemption and, finally, of utmost importance, live the life that is in harmony with these principles (St. John Chrysostom, *On Hebrews,* Homily 9, nos. 1-3; also St. Augustine, *On the Gospel of St. John,* Tractate XCVIII, chap. xvi, no. 5).

Both of the above-cited Fathers thought that it was appropriate to address the Apostle's concerns to the Christians of their own times. St. John, for examples, chides his hearers with this remark: "For oftentimes when the teacher wishes to go on further, and to touch on higher and more mystical themes, the want of attention in those who are to be taught prevents it" (*ibid.*).

Later on, St. Symeon the New Theologian (*Discourse X,* no. 2) applies this verse to the spiritual development of his monks at the Monastery of St. Mamas: "But if the basis of faith and works is not laid without fail it is impossible for any man ever to enjoy the presence of the adorable and divine Spirit and to receive His gift."

v. 2. Of the doctrine of baptisms, and of laying on of hands, and of resurrection of the dead, and of eternal judgment.

He goes on to mention the teaching (*didaches* in Greek) of "baptisms and of laying on of hands." To be sure, initiates into the Christian faith were taught about baptism and chrismation, but by the use of the plural of baptism, the Apostle may allude to the baptism of John as well as that of Christ, since some "disciples" had received only that of the Forerunner. We note, however, that the word for baptisms here is *baptismōn,* and must come from *baptismos,* precisely because it is in the plural, since the word for Christian baptism as well as John's is *baptisma,* singular (see also 9:10 and Mark 7:4). If, indeed, the Apostle has in mind in both verses 1 and 2 the Old Testament preparation for the Gospel, when he speaks of "the word of the beginnings of Christ," these "baptisms" must denote the various ablutions or water rites practiced by the Jews (St. Ambrose, *Concerning Repentance,* Book II, chap. ii, no. 11). The "laying on of hands" is used elsewhere in the New Testament to mean the conferring of the Holy Spirit after baptism ("chrismation"), as in the incident in Acts 19:1-6, and to the ordination of deacons and presbyters (Acts 6:6; 1 Timothy 4:14).

Further, in the Old Covenant, the priest laid his hand on the sacrificial victim's head, as a sign of its acceptance (Leviticus 1:4).

In any event, the four things in this list obviously formed a part of Christian catechetical instruction: baptism, chrismation, the resurrection from the dead, and eternal judgment, in their specifically Christian meaning, although the last two would have been altogether new to some Jews (Matthew 22:23).

St. Augustine, with reference to this verse, insists that the Apostle is not minimizing the importance of these foundational matters: "When he includes doctrine also in his description of the milk, it is that which has been delivered to us in the Creed and the Lord's Prayer" (*ibid.*).

v. 3. And this will we do, if God permit.

He reaffirms his plan (see 5:10-11) to carry them along to the full understanding of Christ's perfect priesthood. We have to recall his earlier reproach for their not having advanced in their knowledge and their spiritual life, and, above all, for their being tempted to return to that which they had abandoned, the sacrifices of the Old Law (St. Ambrose, *ibid.*).

v. 4. For it is impossible for those who were once enlightened, and have tasted of the heavenly gift, and were made partakers of the Holy Ghost,

Now the Apostle's warning to them becomes quite strong, for he is about to declare something impossible for them as people who have been enlightened (in Greek, *phōtisthentas*), in their having been baptized into Christ. From St. Justin Martyr on, the term "enlightenment" or "illumination" has been regularly used as a name for baptism (*Apology I*, chap. 61). He goes on to apply the same to those who have "tasted of the heavenly gift," that is, those who have experienced the forgiveness of sins (see St. John Chrysostom, *ibid.*, no. 5), and have tasted of the Bread of heaven, Christ Himself, in the

Eucharist (John 6:33-58). Those who have received the holy mysteries with faith have become partakers of the Holy Spirit, for He is thereby given to them. There is a close relationship, of course, between the "tasting" and the being "partakers," as we understand from St. Cyril of Jerusalem's explanation:

> After this the priest says, "Holy things to holy men." Holy are the gifts presented, having received the visitation of the Holy Ghost; holy are ye also, having been deemed worthy of the Holy Ghost; the holy things therefore correspond to the holy persons. Then ye say, "One is holy, One is the Lord, Jesus Christ." For One is truly holy, by nature holy; we too are holy, but not by nature, only by participation, and discipline, and prayer. (*Catechetical Lecture XXIII*, no. 19)

v. 5. And have tasted the good word of God, and the powers of the world to come,

Before stating what the impossibility is, the Apostle mentions two other gifts that have been granted to those who have become followers of Christ in His Church. Both of these are experiences of the faithful in the Church's worship, especially in the Eucharistic assembly, in which they become partakers of the kingdom of God. "Tasting the good word of God" refers to the hearing of the word, specifically the Gospel; the "powers of the world to come," to the miraculous life of those who are Christ's disciples. These "powers" are miracles: the same word *dynameis* is used to describe the miracles of Christ in the first three Gospels. They are really "signs," as St. John calls them in his Gospel, of man's restoration and reintegration by the power of the Holy Spirit.

> To live as Angels and to have no need of earthly things, to know that this is the means of our introduction to the enjoyment of the worlds to come; this way we learn through the Spirit, and enter into those sacred recesses . . . life eternal, angelic conversation [way of life]. Of these we have already received the earnest through our Faith from the Spirit. (St. John Chrysostom, *op. cit.*, Homily 9, no. 7)

v. 6. If they shall fall away, to renew them again unto repentance; seeing they crucify to themselves the Son of God afresh, and put Him to an open shame.

What is then impossible for them? Simply that, having had all this experience in Christ, if they fall away, they may not begin all over again. They cannot be baptized a second time, because they were baptized into Christ's death and they died to the old man, and this can be done but once (Romans 6:3,6; Ephesians 4:5). This verse

> must be considered as having reference to baptism, wherein we crucify the Son of God in ourselves, that the world may be by Him crucified for us, who triumph, as it were, when we take to ourselves the likeness of His death, who put to open shame upon His cross principalities and powers, and triumphed over them, that in the likeness of His death we, too, might triumph over the principalities whose yoke we throw off. But Christ was crucified once, and died to sin once, and so there is but one, not several baptisms" (St. Ambrose, *ibid.*, no. 10).

Now, we are convinced that this impossibility does not mean that one who falls away may not repent, and it certainly does not mean that the Lord would not receive him if he truly repents. St. John Chrysostom asks (*ibid.,* no. 8),

> What then (you say)? Is there no repentance? There is repentance, but there is no second baptism: but repentance there is, and it has great force, and is able to set [one] free from the burden of his sins, if he will, even him that hath been baptized much in sins, and to establish in safety him who is in danger, even though he should have come unto the very depth of wickedness. . . . It is possible, if we will, that Christ should be formed in us again: for hear Paul saying, "My little children, of whom I travail in birth again, until Christ be formed in you" [Galatians 4:19]. Only let us lay hold on repentance [see also St. Ambrose, *ibid.,* no. 12].

v. 7. For the earth which drinketh in the rain that cometh oft upon it, and bringeth forth herbs meet for them by whom it is dressed, receiveth blessing from God:

The Apostle continues his warning to the Hebrew Christians that they be on their guard against going back on their profession and baptismal promises, and thereby assent to the crucifixion of Christ at the hands of those who rejected Him as the Messiah. The admonition ends with a little parable reminiscent of the Lord's "Parable of the Sower" (Luke 8:5-15; Isaiah 5:1-7).

The word of God falls like rain upon the earth and the ground drinks it in, receives it, takes nourishment from it and produces good fruit. Those who till the soil (the ones "by whom it is dressed"), by their care, participate in the blessing God that God bestows on the land.

> For like rain, the Saviour sendeth down upon the hearts of those who hear, the word of spiritual consolation; even the sacred doctrine of salvation. If then a man be possessed of understanding, he will bring forth the fruits of an abundant intellectual harvest; but if he be careless and negligent, he of course has no claim to the praises of virtue, and instead of grapes will bring forth thorns. And what his end will be, we learn from the words of Isaiah [5:7]. (St. Cyril of Alexandria, *Commentary on the Gospel of St. Luke*, Homily 42)

v. 8. But that which beareth thorns and briers is rejected, and is nigh unto cursing; whose end is to be burned.

There is some soil, however, as in the Parable of the Sower, that receives the same rain of God's word, but because of neglect and competing interests, bears only thorns and briers. The ground is productive or unproductive because of what men do to it, but the human who is rational and sensitive could make his own mind and heart receptive to the word. Those who fail to do so are close to being rejected, cursed and finally burned. But the Apostle does not leave his readers without hope, because they may be only "nigh" to being rejected. As long as one is still nigh to that rejection with its terrible consequences, he may still root out all those thorns and briers from his spirit and remove himself from that closeness. "Oh! how great a consolation there is in this word [nigh]! . . . So that, if we cut out and burn the thorns, we shall be able to enjoy those good things innumerable and to become approved, and to partake of [the] blessing" (St. John Chrysostom, *op. cit.,* Homily 10, no. 3).

v. 9. But, beloved, we are persuaded better things of you, and things that accompany salvation, though we thus speak.

Even though he has spoken to them so strongly, he shows real affection for those to whom he addresses his letter, not just by calling them "beloved," but by expressing his confidence (saying "we are persuaded" from *pepeismetha*, passive of *peithō*) in them and hinting that he can do this in view of their past zeal. The things they have done before must have been good works, in that they accompany ("pertain to" from *echomena*) salvation. The same thought is found in Galatians 5:10, but with reference to his hope that they may do these things in the future. He is rather specific about these "things" in the next verse. That good works and salvation go hand in hand, St. Paul assures us in his counsel to Timothy to "charge them that are rich . . . that they be rich in good works, ready to distribute, willing to communicate; laying up in store for themselves a good foundation against the time to come ("for the future" from *eis to mellon*), that they may lay hold on eternal life" (I Timothy 6:17-19). "Since he was not able to say so much from things present, he confirms his consolation from things past" (St. John Chrysostom, *ibid.,* no. 4).

v. 10. For God is not unrighteous to forget your work and labor of love, which ye have shewed toward His name, in that ye have ministered to the saints, and do minister.

Apparently the very ones he is addressing have taken care and still do take care of the believers ("the saints") of the community. These are the things that they have done and continue to do that

God will not forget, because he is not unrighteous ("unjust" or even "unfaithful"). The Apostle notes that it is out of their love for God, "toward His name," because in ministering (*diakonēsantes* and *diakonountes*) to them, they are in fact serving Him. The early Church at Jerusalem was characterized by the way in which the faithful cared for the widows, orphans and needy. Twice in his *Commentary on the Gospel of St. Luke* (Homilies 77 and 104) does St. Cyril of Alexandria cite this verse to demonstrate that the labor of the saints or holy people of God on behalf of others does not go unrewarded, for in this they give proof of their forbearance in the face of conflicts and hardships.

> *v. 11. And we desire that every one of you do shew the same diligence to the full assurance of hope unto the end;*

The Apostle's fatherly concern for them is further expressed in his desire that every one of them maintain the same earnestness which was motivated by the hope given them through their faith in Christ. He uses "we" perhaps in the name of the whole Church or of all the Apostles; it is unlikely that it is simply the editorial plural.

> For this is the admirable part of Paul's wisdom, that he does not expressly show that they "had" given in, that they "had" become negligent. For when he says, "We desire that every one of you"—it is as if one should say, I wish thee to be always in earnest; and such as thou wert before, such to be now also, and for the time to come. For this made his reproof more gentle and easy to be received. (St. John Chrysostom, *ibid.,* no. 5)

The hope they are in danger of losing is the subject of St. Paul's exhortations in many of his epistles. For example, hope is that which, produced by experience born of tribulations, "maketh not ashamed because the love of God is shed abroad in our hearts by the Holy Ghost, which is given unto us" (Romans 5:3-5). The end or goal of that hope is eternal life, of which we are made heirs by the promise of justification (Titus 3:7).

The Apostle is concerned that they may have grown tired and discouraged by the tribulations they have had to undergo, and in this he rather gently encourages them to endure to the end, which endurance the Saviour Himself had set as a condition for being saved, precisely in face of the hatred inflicted upon them (Matthew 10:20-21).

v. 12. That ye be not slothful, but followers of them who through faith and patience inherit the promises.

The word that is translated here by "slothful" is the same as that translated by "dull" (of hearing) in 5:11 *(nōthroi)*, and the verb, as was pointed out before, means "become slothful." The idea is the same: the word of Christian teaching may have begun to fall on deaf ears. He is trying to persuade them not to let that happen, that is, not to let their dullness of hearing end up in despair.

In order to strengthen his plea, and to encourage them, he proposes that they be followers of those who had overcome the temptation to become impatient, to yield to pressures and finally to lose faith. In Chapter 11, he will present a long list of just men who did overcome every obstacle by faith.

> For which reason the Apostle Paul wishes that we should be imitators of them, who, as he says, "by faith and patience" possess the promises made to Abraham, who by patience was found worthy to receive and to possess the grace of the blessing promised to him. David the prophet [Psalm 98/99:1] warns us that we should be imitators of holy Aaron, and has set him amongst the Saints of God to be imitated by us. (St. Ambrose, *Letter LXIII*, no. 50)

But, even if it should be difficult to imitate those heroes of a distant past, who indeed remain the archtypes of faith, the Apostle seems to hint at the presence (by using the present tense) among them of faithful followers of Christ, who could be more visible models for them to follow.

*v. 13. For when God made promise to Abraham, because he
could swear by no greater, he sware by himself,*

Now, if the reason for their impatience, for this seems to be what
they were suffering from, was what appeared to be a delay in the fulfillment of Christ's promise to return, he reminds them that God's
promises are always fulfilled, but that sometimes there is a long
interval between the making of the promise and its fulfillment.
Abraham is given as the greatest example of one to whom God made
promise, because he faithfully held to God's original promise (Genesis 12:1-4) until it was eventually fulfilled. The beginning of the fulfillment of the promise is confirmed by reiteration of the original
and by another, that his wife Sarai (which God changes to Sarah)
would bear him a son (Genesis 17:4,16): Isaac was born twenty-five
years after the first promise, and his grandsons Esau and Jacob sixty
years later. St. Irenaeus reflects on the fulfillment of the promise to
Abraham to be the father of many nations (Genesis 17:5), in that
"the promise of God, which He gave to Abraham, remains steadfast
. . . they which are of faith are the children of Abraham" (*Against
Heresies*, Book V, chap. xxxii, no. 2).

God's swearing an oath is recorded several times in holy Scripture; one example that is particularly important for this chapter with
regard to Christ's priesthood is Psalm 109/110: "The Lord sware,
and will not repent, Thou art a priest for ever, after the order of
Melchisedec." As we shall continue to see, God's promises are irrevocable, and He will not fail to keep them.

Commenting on Genesis 22:16-17, St. Ambrose, refuting the
Arian heresy that the Son is inferior to the Father, declares that it
was the Son who spoke to Abraham: "Most fitting was the answer
which the Son of God made to these Jews, proving Himself the Son
and equal of God. 'Whatsoever things,' He said, 'the Father hath
done, the Son doeth also in like wise' " [John 5:19]. The Saint continues, "Moreover, the Son of God saith, 'Abraham saw my day, and
rejoiced' [John 8:56]. It is He, therefore, who sware by Himself,
[and] whom Abraham saw" (*On the Christian Faith*, Book II, chap.

viii, nos. 69, 72; see also St. John Chrysostom, *op. cit.,* Homily 9, no. 1).

v. 14. Saying, Surely blessing I will bless thee, and multiplying I will multiply thee.

This verse quotes the actual promise of God to Abraham. The doubling of the words " 'bless" and "multiply" is a hebraism for emphasis, characteristic of swearing an oath.

Not only is this a reference to Abraham's own offspring, although he thought that his advanced age and his wife's made children unlikely, but even here there is an implication of something much greater. Abraham would indeed have a son, and in spite of his consideration that he was too old, his total trust and faith in God was such that he was moved to ask, "Is any thing too hard for the Lord?" (Genesis 18:14). Still, the most important thing is that this son was to be the beginning of the "great nation" (Genesis 12:2), referring first to the Old Israel and then to the New, that is, the Church of all those, from all nations, that would believe in Jesus Christ.

v. 15. And so, after he had patiently endured, he obtained the promise.

Abraham's long suffering, his patient endurance was rewarded in his descendants, and thus he obtained the promise—but not all of it, for this fulfillment was but the beginning of the ultimate realization of his fatherhood of "many nations." (The verb "endure" is *makrothymēo* in Greek; it is said of God, who patiently bears persistent petitions of His people, and of love, which makes the one who has it long-suffering; see, for example, Luke 18:7 and I Corinthians 13:4.) Although he did not live to see what God had promised him, that is, that "his seed would be as the stars of heaven and as the sand which is upon the sea shore" (Genesis 22:17), we have the Lord's assurance that Abraham did see His day and rejoiced (John 8:56). The Church of many nations or peoples consists of the children of Abraham.

St. John Chrysostom points out that the mention of Abraham was for the encouragement of the Hebrew Christians who might have grown fainthearted, but he calls attention to the fact that later in the Epistle (11:39) the Apostle will indicate that most of the men and women who patiently endured did not receive the fulfillment of the promise in their lifetime. For their strengthening, he will show that his contemporaries had been witnesses and recipients of that fulfillment. Those who patiently endured throughout the Old Testament will indeed now be "made perfect," that is, they will receive their reward because of the redemption that is in Christ (*op. cit.*, Homily 11, no. 1).

v. 16. For men verily swear by the greater: and an oath for confirmation is to them an end of all strife.

God's promise to Abraham, when He first called him to leave the land of his fathers and to go to a place that He would show him, was confirmed after the ultimate test of his obedience and faithfulness. In spite of the fact that Isaac was the son through whom the promise was partially fulfilled and in whom lay all hope of descendance, Abraham would have sacrificed him, if he knew that it was God's will.

In confirming the promise, God said, "By myself have I sworn," and the Apostle tells us (v. 13), "Since God could swear by no greater, He sware by Himself." Men, of course, usually swear by someone, God, or by something, the heavens, greater than themselves, and this they do to prove that they do not intend to break their oath. Here, this is related as a fact of human life and is not an expression of approval of the practice, especially since the Lord Himself condemns it in the Sermon on the Mount (Matthew 5:33-37; see also St. Gregory of Nyssa, *On "Not Three Gods,"* 12th paragraph).

Even a human oath is designed to put an end to every dispute and controversy: it is a confirmation (see Galatians 3:15). God's unwillingness to go back on His promise is here illustrated by an analogy with human practice, but His swearing is a condescension to the difficulty the race of man has in believing, since God ought to be believed because He is God. Christ's teaching on the matter of swearing, referred to above, lays the foundation for the kind of integrity and truthfulness that should characterize His followers, that is, that their habitual truthfulness should cause them to be believed without the necessity for an oath.

v. 17. Wherein God, willing more abundantly to shew unto the heirs of promise the immutability of his counsel, confirmed it by an oath:

God knows that the human being is weak and capable of doubting even His own Word. In a sense, then, respecting man's trust in oaths of confirmation, He had deigned to emphasize the irrevocable nature of His counsel (or "will") by means of an oath. The two words "willing" and "counsel" translate the Greek *boulomenos* and *boulē*. "The counsel of the Lord endureth for ever . . ." (Psalm 32/33:11, in which "counsel" is *boulē*). The broader meaning of His promise to Israel, and through that nation to all men, that is, the promise of a Redeemer of the whole world, is what is really alluded to here. And those who have been faithful and are faithful to Him, both in the Old Covenant and in the New, are heirs to the promise. It is to them especially that the Lord wants to make this perfectly clear ("more abundantly to show"). Thus the Apostle is stressing to the Hebrew Christian the original intent of God's promise to Abraham, that is, "in thy seed shall all the nations of the earth be blessed" (Genesis 22:18). He is telling them that only in following Christ and remaining faithful can they be true Israelites and sons of Abraham, "heirs of the promise" (See Romans 4:12; also St. Cyril of Jerusalem, *Catechetical Lecture X*, nos. 14-16).

v. 18. That by two immutable things, in which it was impossible for God to lie, we might have a strong consolation, who have fled for refuge to lay hold upon the hope set before us:

The two immutable things (*pragma* in Greek, "facts" or "acts") are God's promise and His confirmation of that promise by an oath.

"The Lord hath sworn, and will not repent" (Psalm 109/110:4—the second verb in Greek, *metamelēthēsetai*, means "change His purpose or design"). These things are obviously not subject to change, for God cannot lie (or "be false"); such would be contrary to His nature. "Nothing is impossible with God, except to lie" (*First Epistle of Clement,* chap. xxvii). With these facts the Hebrews should have been well acquainted. "God is not a man, that He should lie; neither the son of man, that he should repent: hath He said, and shall He not do it? or hath He spoken, and shall He not make it good?" (Numbers 23:19; see also St. Athanasius, *Paschal Letter XIX,* no. 3).

The Hebrew Christians are reminded of these things, which must be the greatest possible consolation ("encouragement," in Greek *paraklēsin*). They have fled for refuge to Christ, as all must do when they realize the futility of all worldly hopes and when they become aware of the consequences of their sinfulness. The only hope that is set before them is Jesus Christ, the great High Priest, the Messiah. This verse also recalls their heavenly calling, which they seem to be on the verge of forgetting (see 3:1).

v. 19. Which hope we have as an anchor of the soul, both sure and steadfast, and which entereth into that within the veil:

The hope of which the Apostle speaks is that of the resurrection and life eternal, "which God, that cannot lie, promised before the world began" (Titus 1:2). One gains this by faith in Christ, if he endures to the end.

The anchor had already been used among the Greeks as a symbol of human hope. After all, it is the instrument that is used to keep a ship from being moved or even tossed about by winds and waves. So it is that the ship of one's life or his soul is kept on course through the tempests of this life. St. Paul warns the Ephesians not to be "tossed to and fro, and carried about with every wind of doctrine ..." (4:14). Strange and novel teachings about Christ can shake the feeling of security the believer has, but there are also many other setbacks and mishaps that may undermine one's faith.

There is a striking paradox in the use of anchor here, for Christian hope moors one to heaven, while an anchor is normally cast overboard so as to lay hold of the earth with its hook. The hope which is in Christ, our Anchor, is sure (or "unshakable") and steadfast (or "firm"), for it points to life in God's kingdom.

The mention of the veil recalls the veil of the temple, which separated the Holy of Holies from the outer part of the temple, where only the high priest was allowed to enter. Christ, like the high priest of Israel, has entered once and for all into the Holy of Holies, that which is "within the veil," that is, the heavenly sanctuary.

v. 20. Whither the forerunner is for us entered, even Jesus, made an high priest for ever after the order of Melchisedec.

Again, Jesus Christ, our Anchor and our Hope, has entered into the Holy of Holies, and He is a forerunner for us, because He has taken our human nature, which He assumed, with Him into the heavenly places, and those who become His by faith will follow Him into those places. St. Paul, in his Epistle to the Ephesians (1:20 and 2:6), tells us that not only has Christ, the God-Man, been raised to the heavenly places, but that we also will be raised to those heavenly places to sit together with Him.

The idea of there being a forerunner is the new element of God's new covenant with His people. (See St. Symeon the New Theologian, *Discourse XII*, no. 7; St. Athanasius, *First Discourse against the Arians*, chap. xi, no. 4, and *Paschal Letter XLV;* and St. Gregory of Nysssa, *Funeral Oration on Meletius;* also the Matins Canon to the Cross and Resurrection for Sundays, Tone 1, Ode 4.) The use of the definite article with "forerunner," missing in Greek, changes the meaning of the verse: since in the Old Testament tabernacle, the people could never follow the high priest into the Holy of Holies, the Apostle intends to call attention to the difference between the Old and the New High Priest, introducing the concept of "a forerunner." The tabernacle and the Aaronic priesthood are types, symbols or prefigures of the reality that has been given to men in Christ.

Jesus Christ is called a "high priest forever" and "after the order of Melchisedec." His priesthood is not after the order of Levi and does not end after a period of time, as did those priesthoods. With these last words, the Apostle now returns to the subject he interrupts in Chapter 5 (v. 10). A detailed explanation of the doctrine of Christ's priesthood follows in Chapter 7, where it is necessary to show those Hebrews tempted to return to the old ways, how foolish it would be to return to the prefigures when the reality has already come.

Chapter 7

We have seen that it was the Apostle's purpose in writing this Epistle to demonstrate to the Hebrews the superiority of the New Covenant over the Old, and thereby to encourage them, those who had become followers of Christ, to remain faithful to Him. He reminds them at the beginning that God "at sundry times and in divers manners spake in time past unto the Fathers by the prophets," and that "in these last days He hath spoken unto us by His Son" (1:1-2). He then gives a rather long explanation of who the Son is and what His work consisted of (chapters 1-3) and exhorts them, in view of what he has said, to remain steadfast and obedient to Him. Now after an extended exhortation, he returns to his subject, and approaches the question of the difference between the old and new priesthoods.

> *v. 1. For this Melchisedec, king of Salem, priest of the most high God, who met Abraham returning from the slaughter of the kings, and blessed him;*

Quoting Psalm 109/110:4, the Apostle concluded the sixth chapter by calling Jesus a "high priest for ever after the order of Melchisedec." At this point, he first talks about Melchisedec himself.

Except in the above-mentioned Psalm and in this Epistle, the only place in Scripture where we find the name "Melchisedec" is in the very brief story of his encounter with Abraham in Genesis (14:18-20). On the other hand, the Apostle seems to assume that the Hebrews would be familiar with a tradition that held that the Messiah was to be a royal priest of the type of Melchisedec. Psalm 109/110, after all, is a very important prophecy concerning the promised Savior, and its several verses are often quoted: "The Lord said to my Lord, Sit thou on my right hand, until I make thine enemies thy footstool. The Lord shall send out a rod of power for thee out of Zion: rule thou in the midst of thine enemies. With thee is dominion in the day of thy power, in the splendors of thy saints; I have begotten thee from the womb before the morning star. The Lord sware, and will not repent, Thou art a priest for ever, after the order of Melchisedec" (vv. 1-4 LXX).

The Genesis account is as follows: "And Melchisedec king of Salem brought forth loaves and wine, and he was the priest of the most high God. And he blessed Abram, and said, Blessed be Abram of the most high God who made heaven and earth, and blessed the most high God who delivered thine enemies into thy power. And Abram gave him the tithe of all" (14:18-20).

This "priest of the most high God" met Abraham (Abram) as he returned from his victory over the Canaanite kings and blessed him. Now, the important thing that the Apostle calls to our attention is that Abraham recognized him as the priest and accepted his blessing, and what is more, he gave him tithes of all (his booty).

God is frequently called "Most High" in the Old Testament (*ho hypsistos:* Deuteronomy 32:8; II Kings/II Samuel 22:14 LXX), especially in the Psalms, and the exact same expression "Most High God" is found in Psalm 56/57:2. It is apparently of no significance to the Apostle that this same name was given to deities of other religions.

v. 2. To whom also Abraham gave a tenth part of all; first being by interpretation King of righteousness, and after that King of Salem, which is, King of peace;

That Abraham gave tithes of all he had taken in the battles implies that even then, before the Law established the tithe, such was the divinely-instituted thank-offering.

To the Apostle, both the name of the priest and his city are significant: Melchisedec means "king of righteousness" (or "my king is righteous"), and he was king of Salem (Jerusalem), which means "peace." Thus, this royal priest is a type of Christ the Savior, the divine-human Priest-King, who has brought both righteousness and peace to the world (Matthew 3:15; John 14:27; John 16:8-10; Colossians 1:20). St. John Chrysostom show this to us:

"First" (he [the Apostle] says) "being by interpretation King of righteousness": for Sedec means "righteousness"; and Melchi, "King": Melchisedec, "King of righteousness." Seest thou his exactness even in the names? But who is "King of righteousness," save our Lord Jesus Christ? "King of righteousness. And after that also King of Salem," from his city, "that is, King of Peace," which again is [characteristic] of Christ. For He has made us righteous, and has "made peace" for "things in Heaven and things on earth" [Colossians 1:20]. What man is "King of Righteousness and of Peace?" None, save only our Lord Jesus Christ. (*On Hebrews,* Homily 12, no. 2)

Another detail mentioned in the Genesis story, not referred to in this chapter of the Epistle, is the fact that Melchisedec "brought forth bread and wine" (14:18). Although some modern commentators think that there may be no particular significance in this act other than the priest-king's offering of food and drink to the victors, the fact that it is mentioned in connection with his being the priest, quite properly leads one to the conclusion that even this is a figure of the Eucharist that Christ, prefigured by this priest-king, would institute. The priest, fulfilling his office, would offer sacrifice, and in Melchisedec's case, the offering to the most High God was bread and wine, which he then gave to Abraham and his people. Thus, Abraham, in giving the priest tithes, participated in that sacrifice: "by whose office Abraham offered sacrifice" (St. Ambrose, *On the Christian Faith,* Book III, chap. xi, no. 87).

v. 3. Without father, without mother, without descent, having neither beginning of days, nor end of life; but made like unto the Son of God; abideth a priest continually.

In the original story, Melchisedec simply appears; there is no history of his descent or lineage. These unknown particulars must have been part of the Hebrew tradition concerning him, since they are not mentioned in Genesis. St. John Chrysostom (*ibid.,* no. 3) emphasizes that he indeed had no recorded parents and no recorded beginning or end like other men, but that he did have them, and the silence concerning them is deliberate. But, his priesthood was a direct gift from God, and so he was a type of Christ, who in reality and by nature has no descent, no beginning and no end (St. Ambrose, *ibid.*, nos. 88-89). "He is the Son without lineage; and having appeared, in His good pleasure, He shall save His people" (Aposticha for Vespers for the Annunciation of the All-holy Theotokos, quoted in part).

Melchisedec's priesthood is called "continual" (*eis to diēnekes,* which expression is used to refer to Christ's priesthood in 10:12,14), but still as a type, while Christ's priesthood is forever in reality. Theodoret of Cyprus says,

> The holy Moses when writing the ancient genealogy tells us how Adam being so many years old begat Seth [Genesis 4:25], and when he had lived so many years he ended his life [Genesis 5:5]. So too he writes of Seth, of Enoch, and of the rest, but of Melchisedec he mentions neither beginning of existence nor end of life. Thus as far as the story goes he has neither beginning of days nor end of life, but in truth and reality the only-begotten Son of God [is the one who] never began to exist and shall never have an end. . . . Then, so far as what belongs to God and is really divine is concerned, Melchisedec is a type of the Lord Christ; but as far as the priesthood is concerned, which belongs rather to man than to God, the Lord Christ was made a priest after the order of Melchisedec. For Melchisedec was a high priest of the people, and the Lord Christ for all men has made the right holy offering of salvation. (*Dialogue II,* NPNF 2nd Series, vol. 3, p. 189)

St. Gregory of Nazianzus (*Fourth Theological Oration,* no. xxi) includes Melchisedec among the names of Christ that belong "to the nature He assumed."

Some Jewish writers have found no prophetic or messianic significance in the story of Melchisedec, and have imagined that he was an angel rather than a holy man and priest of God who prefigured Christ (St. Ambrose, *ibid.*). St. John Cassian cites the misuse of the present verse by Nestorians and other heretics in their attempt to prove that Jesus was a mere man (*On the Incarnation of the Lord, Against Nestorius,* Book VII, chap. xiv).

> *v. 4. Now consider how great this man was, unto whom even the patriarch Abraham gave the tenth of the spoils.*

In verses 4-10, we find four evidences of Melchisedec's superiority. First, Abraham the patriarch, the father of the Hebrew race, acknowledged this by the apparently spontaneous act of giving him tithes of his spoils. Since it would be difficult for any Jew to imagine anyone greater than Abraham, the Apostle insists on his point, that the giving of tithes is evidence of Melchisedec's greatness and even of Abraham's inferiority to him (see St. Ambrose, *ibid.*).

> *v. 5. And verily they that are of the sons of Levi, who receive the office of the priesthood, have a commandment to take tithes of the people according to the law, that is, of their brethren, though they came out of the loins of Abraham:*

Now, in speaking of "the sons of Levi who receive the office of the priesthood," he does not mean all the descendants of Levi (as the comma in the English translation would indicate), but rather specifically those of the family of Aaron who inherited the priesthood. The priests of the Hebrew people came from one family of one tribe.

They had a commandment to collect tithes from the people, tithes that were to be used for specific purposes: the support of the priests (Numbers 18:21), a holy offering to God (Leviticus 27:30), and the sustenance of the tribe of Levi (Deuteronomy 18:1-2). This receiving of tithes was regulated by the Law, and was not voluntary. But in Abraham's case, there was no law that required him to pay tithes.

The priests collected only from their brethren, that is, their fellow Israelites, and the latter were obliged to pay them even though they too were descended from Abraham ("came out of the loins of Abraham," St. John Chrysostom, *ibid.*, no. 4).

v. 6. But he whose descent is not counted from them received tithes of Abraham, and blessed him that had the promises.

Melchisedec's superiority to Abraham—the one to whom God had made the promises—is demonstrated not only by his receiving Abraham's tithes, but also because he blessed Abraham. In other words, Abraham himself, the father of the Hebrews, the one reverenced more highly than all others, shows that Melchisedec, who was not of the lineage of Levi, was "to be reverenced more than he" (St. John Chrysostom, *ibid.*).

v. 7. And without all contradiction the less is blessed of [by] the better.

This verse makes the point of the whole exposition. Melchisedec, in accordance with his God-given superior authority ("the better" or "greater") blesses the inferior ("less"). God promised Abraham that all nations would be blessed in his seed ("offspring"), yet Melchisedec could bless him; therefore, Melchisedec's priesthood is superior to that which was still to be born of Abraham himself. This, according to the Apostle, is "without all contradiction" ("beyond all question"). St. Cyril of Alexandria (*Commentary on the Gospel of St. Luke,* Homily 132) summarizes the intent of this passage: "The root and commencement of the very existence of Israel therefore, even the patriarch Abraham, was blessed by the priesthood of Melchisedec; but Melchisedec and his priesthood was a type of Christ the Saviour of us all, Who has been made our High Priest and Apostle."

v. 8. And here men that die receive tithes; but there he receiveth them, of whom it is witnessed that he liveth.

The levitical priests, in spite of their privileges (in being priests, first of all, and in their authority to collect tithes), were still mortal men: they died and were replaced by other mortal men. "Here," of course, means the priests under discussion, but "there," that is,

Melchisedec, who received tithes of Abraham and, through him, of all other priests, is not succeeded by other men. Of this fact we have testimony in Psalm 109/110:4, "a priest for ever after the order of Melchisedec." His continual priesthood can be called his third superiority, but the question of what his "abiding a priest continually" (v. 3) really consists of needs to be answered. Some have concluded that he was immortal, but often it is held that he lives in the One of whom was only the type.

> *vv. 9-10. And as I may so say, Levi also, who receiveth tithes, payed tithes in Abraham. For he was yet in the loins of his father, when Melchisedec met him.*

The fourth superiority of Melchisedec and his priesthood over Levi and his is seen by the Apostle in a certain identity between ancestors and descendants. In that Abraham paid tithes to Melchisedec, those who were "yet in his loins," those who were to be born to his children, by a lineal solidarity, can be said to participate in his activity. Thus, Levi participated in Abraham's offering to the priest and in being blessed by him. The Apostle may have thought that his reasoning would seem strange or at least unusual, so we find the expression "as I may so say" as a kind of preface to it (St. John Chrysostom, *ibid.*).

> *v. 11. If therefore perfection were by the Levitical priesthood, (for under it the people received the law,) what further need was there that another priest should rise after the order of Melchisedec, and be not called after the order of Aaron?*

Continuing his proposition that the New Covenant is superior to the Old and takes its place, the Apostle goes on to talk about their respective priesthoods.

"Perfection" (a translation of the Greek *teleiōsis*) means "completeness" or better, "fulfillment of a purpose." Now, the purpose of the Law, which the people received along with the levitical priesthood, was to bring men to God by sacrificing for their sins and by sanctifying them and cleansing their conscience. This purpose was not fulfilled in any general way, as St. Paul asserts elsewhere (Romans 3 and 4; Galatians 3; see also 10:1 and 9:9 of this Epistle).

Is this tantamount to saying that God was the author of something imperfect? Far from it. As this Epistle explains later (see the two references above), the Law and everything it contained were given as types, figures or shadows of the things that were to come, that is, the New Law and the priesthood of Christ (see St. Gregory of Nazianzus, *Second Oration on Pascha,* no. xiii). Although there were some righteous under the Law, the people in general failed to keep the Law, and it was because of this that the old priesthood failed (St. John Chrysostom, *ibid.* no. 4).

The question the Apostle obviously proposes to answer in the next few verses concerns why another kind of priesthood was needed.

> *v. 12. For the priesthood being changed, there is made of necessity a change also of the law.*

The priesthood was not simply changed in the sense of being adjusted, but replaced (*metatithēmi* in Greek). So if Christ's Melchisedecan priesthood replaces the Aaronic priesthood, it follows that a New Law will take the place of the Old, since the priesthood and the Law were intimately connected, even interwoven. As we shall see later, the transfer of the priesthood from one tribe (of Levi) to another (of Judah), from the priestly tribe to the kingly tribe, is of utmost importance. We must remember too that in Melchisedec, kingship and priesthood were combined.

> *vv. 13-14. For He of whom these things are spoken pertaineth to another tribe, of which no man gave attendance at the altar. For it is evident that our Lord sprang out of Juda; of which tribe Moses spake nothing concerning priesthood.*

Christ, of whom these things are said, was not a descendant of the tribe to which the priesthood belonged, and, according to the

Law, only those who were descended from Aaron could exercise this office. Our Lord "sprang out" of Judah, and Moses said nothing about a priesthood from this tribe. For this reason, it would have been hard for the average Jew to accept the idea of a priest's coming from Judah's descendants. The facts concerning Jesus' ancestry are well known from the records in the Gospels of St. Matthew and St. Luke (see St. Gregory of Nazianzus, *Oration XXXIX,* "On the Holy Lights," no. iii; St. Cyril of Alexandria, *op. cit.,* Homily 1).

The use of the word "Lord" *(Kyrios)* with reference to Jesus Christ is very significant, since it was the title of God Himself in the Greek version of the Old Testament, the one best known among the Jews of the first century. "Sprang out" (from Greek *anatellō*) is another important choice of words. It is not simply the same as "was born," but it is often used with reference to the rising of the sun, a star or even of a cloud, all three of which have been used to indicate God's presence, or as metaphors for God Himself (Malachi 4:2; Revelation 22:16; Exodus 40:34-38, etc.).

v. 15. And it is yet far more evident: for that after the similitude of Melchisedec there ariseth another priest,

While the Gospel has made it clear, as we have seen above, that Jesus Christ was of Judah, the Old Testament prophecies concerning Him generally refer rather to His kingship than to His priesthood: He would be the Law-giver, Judge and Governor for His people (see Genesis 49:10; Psalm 77/78:68; Isaiah 9:6 ff.; 11:1, etc.). In line with the Apostle's reasoning, it is clear that the new Priest was to be after the order of Melchisedec: the work He was to accomplish would require a different kind of priesthood.

Note that the coming of the Priest is described as "arising" (in Greek, *anistatai*). In Psalm 68/69, a prophetic Psalm, the hope for God's intervention to save mankind is expressed in its opening lines, "Let God arise, and let His enemies be scattered." The word is often used to describe such natural phenomena as the rising of the sun and sudden appearances. The emphasis here is on His coming not in the usual priestly succession: thus, the "similitude of Melchisedec" (*homoiotēs* in Greek).

The Nativity troparion makes use of the same idea in its praise of the Savior's appearance on earth: "Thy Nativity, O Christ our God, hath arisen upon the world as the light of wisdom . . . " It also calls Him the "Sun of righteousness," recalling the prophecy of Malachi (4:2), "But unto you that fear my name shall the Sun of righteousness arise with healing in His wings . . . " (Here, as in v. 14 where it reads "sprang out" in translation, the near synonym *anatellō* is used.)

v. 16. Who is made, not after the law of a carnal commandment, but after the power of an endless life.

The priesthood of the Old Covenant was hereditary: one could be a priest only if his father had been a priest and his mother was an Israelite. Such was the commandment (Exodus 28:1), and it was carnal (or "fleshly," *sarkikēs* in Greek), not in any sinful sense, but because the priesthood passed on physically or biologically, from father to son. "Who is made" refers to Christ who became the Priest "from the time that He assumed flesh" (see John 1:14; also, for a discussion of such verbs as "was made," see St. Athanasius, *Second Discourse Against the Arians,* chap. xxi, especially no. 61). His true priestly work consisting of imparting life, which can be done by destroying sin and death. Only the Priest who has "life in Himself" (John 5:26) and who has "all power in heaven and in earth" (Matthew 28:18) can accomplish this. Jesus' life is endless by nature, but the old priesthood was able to continue only in its physical or carnal succession, generation after generation, until it was replaced.

v. 17. For he testifieth, Thou art a priest for ever after the order of Melchisedec.

Again, citing Psalm 109/110, the Apostle now uses its content to establish the fact that the old order is abolished and the new priesthood foretold by the Psalmist has been established. "The Lord hath sworn, and will not repent"—this is His testimony.

> *v. 18. For there is verily a disannulling of the commandment going before for the weakness and unprofitableness thereof.*

The Apostle now says it in the most definite way: the commandment previously given ("going before"), whereby the priesthood was established, has been annulled (*athetēsis* in Greek). The reason is simply that, like the whole law, the priesthood was weak, because it was powerless to give life (Galations 3:21). "He did not say 'for the evil,' nor, 'for the viciousness,' but 'for the weakness and unprofitableness thereof,' yea and in other places also he shows the weakness; as when he says, 'In that it was weak through the flesh' (Romans 8:3). The Law itself then is not weak, but we" (St. John Chrysostom, *ibid.*). In other words, the Law's ineffectiveness, its "weakness and unprofitableness" was the result of the people's disobeying it and fulfilling it only in a formal way. St. John Cassian cites this verse along with Ezekiel 20:25, which reads "So I gave them commandments that were not good, and ordinances in which they should not live." The Saint contrasts the Old Law with the new Law of grace (*First Conference of Abbot Theonas,* chap. xxxiii). The Prophet had reported God's saying concerning the commandments and ordinances He had given His elect. Their observance was to be a sign between God and the house of Israel that they might know that He was the Lord their God (Ezekiel 20:20). Their failures made the commandments and ordinances "not good" and such as "they could not live by" (Ezekiel 20:21,24).

> *v. 19. For the law made nothing perfect, but the bringing in of a better hope did; by the which we draw nigh unto God.*

The Law did not bring men to perfection in that it could not complete or fulfill its purpose. It could not offer the perfect sacrifice, but could only be the type or symbol of that sacrifice which would end all other sacrifice. It could not, therefore, help man to draw near to God. (See St. Athanasius, *First Discourse Against the Arians,* chap. xiii, nos. 59-61 [8-10].)

Another superiority of the new priesthood may be inferred here. By saying that perfection was achieved by the bringing in of a better hope, the Apostle seems to be hinting at a much greater participation for believers. God's plan for His people, promised to Moses, has now been realized; they are now constituted "a royal priesthood, a holy nation" (Exodus 19:6; 1 Peter 2:9; see also St. Ambrose, *On the Christian Faith,* Book III, chap. xi, no. 86; St. Justin Martyr, *Dialogue with Trypho,* chap. cxvii). St. Justin mentions specifically the Eucharist offered by Christians, and the people are active participants along with the priest; while in the Old Covenant, they were passive. Christ's going in behind the veil was on behalf of all people, but, unlike the priests of the Old Covenant, He goes in as a forerunner, as was noted above (6:20).

The hope of the old Law and that of the new were the same in one sense—the realization of God's will for His people. Yet even here there is an importance difference. The hope of the Israel of old was that by pleasing God they might "possess the land" and prosper in this life. The new and "better" hope is for life eternal with God in His heavenly Kingdom (St. John Chrysostom, *ibid.,* no. 5).

There were undoubtedly some who did please God under the Law; St. Paul's words to Timothy seem to imply that: "But we know that the Law is good, if a man use it lawfully." "Lawfully" must indicate that some understood the purpose of the Law: "love out of a pure heart, and of a good conscience, and of faith unfeigned" (I Timothy 1:8,5). Note also what St. John Cassian has said: "And in this way, though it is said of the Mosaic Law that 'the Law brought nothing to perfection,' we read that some of the saints in the Old Testament were perfect because they went beyond the commands of the Law and lived under the perfection of the Gospel . . . " (*op. cit.,* chap. xxix).

vv. 20-21. And inasmuch as not without an oath He was made a priest: (for those priests were made without an oath; but this with an oath by him that said unto Him, The Lord sware and will not repent, Thou art a priest for ever after the order of Melchisedec:)

God did not swear an oath in the installation of the levitical priests. Each, by reason of belonging to the tribe of Levi, simply inherited the office from his father and was no more permanent than he had been. Although God's mere intention or His plan is surety enough, He chose to swear an oath so that it would be understood that Christ's priesthood had a permanent and unending character (St. Cyril of Jerusalem, *Catechetical Lecture X,* no. 14).

The whole Psalm (109/110), of which verse 4 is quoted, is prophetic. The Lord Jesus Christ's ministries are all foretold in it: He will be king, lord, priest and judge, but it is specifically with regard to His priesthood that the oath is made. (The last phrase, "after the order of Melchisedec," is often omitted in critical editions of the Epistle.)

v. 22. By so much was Jesus made a surety of a better testament.

The introductory phrase "by so much" (*kata tosouton* in Greek) indicates that the idea of the above verse (21) is completed in the present one. St. Athanasius (*ibid.,* chap. xiii, no. 59 [8]) points out the importance of the word "better" *(kreittonos)* in this context:

> Both in the verse before us, then, and throughout [twelve times in this Epistle], does he ascribe the word "better" to the Lord, who is better and other than originated [created] things. For better is the sacrifice through Him, better the hope in Him, and also the promises through Him, not merely as great compared with small, but the one differing from the other in nature, because He who conducts [carries out] this economy [dispensation] is "better" than things originated.

Apparently the Arians had misinterpreted the use of "better," and had adduced it as proof of the Son's belonging to the originated or created order. But His being the surety or guarantor (in Greek *eggyos,* a legal term referring to testaments, of which there will be more details in Chapter 9) derives from His being named "priest for ever" (Psalm 109/110) in the timelessness of His being with the Father. "He sware to Him that He should be Priest, which He would not have done, if He were not living" (St. John Chrysostom, *ibid.*). The oath was from all eternity; and thus His priesthood among men is realized in the incarnation, His having become man.

> *v. 23. And they truly were many priests, because they were not suffered to continue by reason of death:*

Being merely mortal men, the priests of the Old Testament were many. No one of them was allowed ("suffered") to continue to be priest because they all, of course, died. No one of them could, therefore, be a priest beyond the extent of his own lifetime.

> *v. 24. But this man, because he continueth ever, hath an unchangeable priesthood.*

The long succession, generation after generation, of priests of the tribe of Levi is contrasted with the priesthood of Jesus, which is to continue forever, because He remains (translated "continueth" from Greek *menein*), and cannot be passed on to another (*aparabaton* means "intransmissible"; "unchangeable" might create an erroneous impression). "But Christ is a High Priest, whose priesthood passes not to another, neither having begun His priesthood in time, nor having any successor in His High Priesthood . . . ever having the dignity of the Priesthood from the Father" (St. Cyril of Jerusalem, *ibid.,* and *Catechetical Lecture XI,* no. 1).

> *v. 25. Wherefore He is able also to save them to the uttermost that come unto God by Him, seeing He ever liveth to make intercession for them,*

The salvation of God's people is the purpose of the priesthood. Now this Priest, who is the ultimate, final Priest, accomplishes the work of salvation. Those who will be saved by Him will be so to all eternity ("to the uttermost," from Greek *eis to panteles,* that is, "completely"). Jesus had said, "No one cometh unto the Father but by me" (John 14:6). So, those who would approach God are led to Him by Jesus Christ.

The permanence and continuity of Christ's priestly activity is summarized in the last clause of the verse: "He ever liveth to make intercession for them." In his *Fourth Theological Oration* (no. xiv), St. Gregory of Nazianzus, refuting the Arian claim that this part of verse 25 supports their doctrine of the Son's inferiority to the Father, explains the Church's traditional understanding of it in these terms:

> . . . it is to plead for us by reason of His Mediatorship, just as the Spirit also is said to make intercession for us [Romans 8:26]. "For there is one God, and one Mediator between God and Man, the Man Christ Jesus" [I Timothy 2:5]. For He still pleads even now as Man for my salvation; for He continues to wear the Body which He assumed, until He make me God ["deifies me"] by the power of His incarnation; although He is no longer known after the flesh [II Corinthians 5:16]—I mean, the passions of the flesh, the same, except sin, as ours. . . . by what He suffered as Man, He as the Word and the Counsellor persuades Him to be patient. I think this is the meaning of His Advocacy.

v. 26. For such an high priest became us, who is holy, harmless, undefiled, separate from sinners, and made higher than the heavens;

Man's condition necessitated a high priest far different from the priests of the Old Law. This Priest is not only human as were they, but He is perfectly so. His characteristics are given: holy (*hosios* in Greek, rather than the usual *hagios;* the word is used frequently in the Old Testament, especially in the Psalms, emphasizing personal piety and worth, and thus its use in the Epistle), harmless (*akakos,* free of any evil), undefiled (*amiantos,* not unclean both personally and, as in the Old Testament, ceremonially), separate from sinners (in the sense of being sinless). All of these qualities refer to Christ's manhood, which was perfect, and they sum up what was said of Him before, "... in all points tempted like as we are yet without sin" (4:15). These things were also required of the priests of the Old Testament in a formal, ritual sense, and were not always fulfilled in a personal way (see Leviticus, 21 and 22). In our Lord's humanity, He became "higher than the heavens" (exalted in His glorified humanity and having entered into the Holy of Holies as our forerunner). "God also hath highly exalted Him, and given Him a name which is above every name" (Philippians 2:9).

> *v. 27. Who needeth not daily, as those high priests, to offer up sacrifice, first for His own sins, and then for the people's; for this He did once, when He offered up Himself.*

The sacrifice of the great High Priest, Jesus Christ, was offered up once and for all (*ephapax* in Greek). He offered up Himself, being the perfect Priest and the perfect Offering or Victim. Unlike "those" high priests, He had no sin of His own, so His offering was made on behalf of His fellow human beings. Further, their offering had to be repeated since none of their sacrifices was sufficient or perfect.

In this verse we find the first mention in our Epistle of Christ's self-sacrifice. This doctrine will be explored in detail in Chapters 9 and 10.

The word "daily" *(kath-hēmeran)* does not mean that the high priests of the Old Law offered sacrifice every day; they did not, for it was on the Day of Atonement that they sacrificed first for themselves, being sinful men, and then for the people (see Leviticus 16). The emphasis seems to be on the need, which indeed was daily. However, the Son of God's intercession, which He makes because of His one complete and all-sufficient sacrifice, is continuous or daily.

v. 28. For the law maketh men high priests which have infir-mity; but the word of the oath, which was since the law, maketh the Son, who is consecrated for evermore.

At the end of this chapter, we find the Apostle again emphasiz-ing the immense difference between the weakness as well as the lim-itations, both inherent and personal, of the men who were made high priests according to the law, and the Son, who is both Son of God and Son of Man, who was made High Priest by the word of God's oath. This oath is not only subsequent to the Law, although eternal in the Divine counsel (see v. 17), but supersedes it. The Son is perfected as the High Priest for the human race, which He repre-sents for evermore. (We have said "perfected" to show that the Greek word translated "consecrated" is *teteleiōmenon*, the term used in the Old Testament for the installation of priests.)

According to St. Epiphanius of Salamis (Cyprus), "He offered Himself in sacrifice in order to abolish the sacrifices of the Old Tes-tament, in offering a perfect and living victim for all—Himself at the same time, Victim, Sacrificial Altar, God, Man, King, High Priest, Flock, Sheep, having done all for us" (*Panarion,* [Heresy] 55, no. 4).

Chapter 8

v. 1. Now of the things which we have spoken this is the sum: We have such an high priest, who is set on the right hand of the throne of the Majesty in the heavens;

Although the kind of high priest we have has been described in the foregoing chapter, especially in the last two verses, the Apostle proposes to speak particularly of what this priesthood comprises. He begins this section by stating the main point of the whole presentation, that this High Priest is "set on the right hand of the throne of the Majesty in the heavens." This he has said at the beginning of this Epistle, when he identifies the Person about whom he is going to speak.

Our great High Priest Jesus Christ is present in heaven, being still both God and Man, having ascended into heaven forty days after His resurrection—that is, with the human nature He had assumed. His high priestly office continues, but both the character of His present priestly office and of His royal dignity are indicated by His "position" with relation to the Father: *seated* at the right hand of the throne of the Majesty in the heavens. While an earthly priest would stand in the performance of his duties, the heavenly Priest is seated, which fact, according to St. Basil the Great (*On the Spirit*, chap. vi), demonstrates the immutability of His office. He also tells us that "the place on the right hand indicates equality of honor." With particular reference to this verse, the Saint assures us that it is by the Holy Spirit that we know these things.

v. 2. A minister of the sanctuary, and of the true tabernacle, which the Lord pitched, and not man.

The word "minister" is a translation of the Greek *leitourgos*, which means the one who does priestly service. This word, along with the noun *leitourgia*, is common in the Greek Old Testament to describe the service of the priest; for example, for the service itself (Numbers 7:5), and for the officiant (IV/II Kings 4:43). Our "liturgist" is the Celebrant of the heavenly liturgy, the liturgist in the sanctuary or Holy of Holies. The Lord, as we have seen, entered into the Holy of Holies as our forerunner (6:20). St. Cyril of Alexandria writes at length about the differences between the two services, the earthly and the heavenly, in his *Commentary on the Gospel of St. Luke*:

> Melchisedec and his priesthood was a type of Christ the Savior of us all, Who has been made our High Priest and Apostle, not bringing near unto God the Father those who believe in Him by means of bloody sacrifices and offerings of incense, but perfecting them unto holiness by a service superior to the Law. (Homily 132)

The sanctuary is now contrasted with the tabernacle (literally "tent"), in which the Old Covenant sacrifices were made. It was a type or symbol of the real tabernacle of heaven itself. It has been "pitched" by God Himself, not by man, as was, of necessity, the earthly tabernacle.

v. 3. For every high priest is ordained to offer gifts and sacrifices: wherefore it is of necessity that this man have somewhat also to offer.

Here we find a repetition of what was said in 5:1, that is, a generalization about the function of a priest. Since Jesus Christ is the Priest, the great High Priest, whatever is said of priests is also said of Him. It was necessary that He offer something. "He became man in the body for our salvation, in order that having somewhat to offer for us He might save us all" (St. Athanasius, *Letter LXI*, "To Maximus," no. 3; see also Theodoret, *Dialogue I*).

His sacrifice has been offered once and for all, having offered Himself, but if He continues to be the Priest of the human race in heaven, what is the meaning of this present priestly office of His?

This question has already been answered in the foregoing chapter (v. 25): His present intercessory office issues from the one final, perfect sacrifice. This point will be studied in more detail later in the Epistle.

v. 4. For if He were on earth, He should not be a priest, seeing that there are priests that offer gifts according to the Law:

The point has been made that our great high Priest is in heaven, "set down on the right hand" of the Father, the "minister of the sanctuary," or Holy of Holies (vv. 1-2). In accordance with the divine plan, He could not be a priest after the order of Aaron. That order had been established to offer sacrifice on earth, and its priesthood had its purpose: it was a way of righteousness, and, more importantly, it symbolized or prefigured what was to come. But the Priest who is the reality of those figures, who offered the ultimate sacrifice, continues to be Priest as a consequence of that one self-oblation. He now and forever exercises His priesthood in heaven, "a priest for ever after the order of Melchisedec," interceding for His brethren who are still on earth.

In this regard, St. John Chrysostom asks, how could He be "a priest on earth?"

> He offered no sacrifice, He ministered not in the Priest's office. And with good reason, for there were the priests [who offered in accordance with the Law]. Moreover he shows that it was impossible that [He] should be a priest on earth. For how [could He be]? There was no rising up against [the appointed priests], he means. (*On Hebrews*, Homily 14, no. 2)

What the Saint seems to be saying is that the Incarnate Son of God did not become one of those who were priests on earth, and that He left the priesthood alone until He abolished it with His sacrifice of Himself, that is, until the reality took the place of the figure.

v. 5. Who serve unto the example and shadow of heavenly things, as Moses was admonished of God when he was about to make the tabernacle: for, See, saith he, that thou make all things according to the pattern shewed to thee in the mount.

Completing the sentence begun in verse 4, the Apostle goes on to describe the very purpose of the service of those priests.

One significant fact about Jewish worship was that it had been given to man from above. God Himself had prescribed the very details of that worship in the tabernacle or temple, specifically for it to be "the example and shadow" of the reality of heavenly worship. "Example" is a translation of *hypodeigma*, properly a "token" or "pattern," which always points to a higher reality, being a type of that reality. Although it was carried out strictly in accordance with what God revealed to Moses—that is, divinely given—it was earthly, performed on earth.

It is not inappropriate to call attention here both to the parallel and the contrast between what was shown to Moses by God and what God Incarnate revealed directly to men in His sojourn on earth. The New Israel also has a divinely prescribed worship, the supper which Christ ordered, saying, "this do in remembrance of me" (Luke 22:19). It makes present all that He has done for men and their salvation as well as the reality of the kingdom to come. In the celebration of the Eucharist, the mystical supper, as St. Paul reminds us, we "do shew the Lord's death till He come" (I Corinthians 11:23-26). Likewise, in connection with the very institution of the Eucharist, the Lord tells the disciples, "I appoint unto you a kingdom, as my Father hath appointed unto me, that ye may eat and drink at my table in my kingdom . . ." (Luke 22:29-30). Thus, we are made to be witnesses of the heavenly priestly office of the great High Priest, and become partakers of the kingdom of the age to come. The Eucharist, then, is a heavenly reality realized on earth.

St John Chrysostom again asks,

What are the heavenly things he speaks of here? The spiritual things. For although they are done on earth, yet nevertheless they are worthy of the Heavens. For when our Lord Jesus Christ lies slain [as a sacrifice], when the Spirit is with us, when He who sitteth on the right hand of the Father is here, when sons are made by the Washing, when they are fellow-citizens of those in Heaven, when we have a country, and a city, and citizenship there, when we are strangers to things here, how can all these things be other than 'heavenly things?' But what! Are not our Hymns heavenly? Do not we also who are below utter in concert with them the same things which the divine choirs of bodiless powers sing above? Is not the altar also heavenly? How? It hath nothing carnal, all spiritual things become the offerings. . . . How again can the rites which we celebrate be other than heavenly? (*ibid.*, no. 3)

v. 6. But now hath He obtained a more excellent ministry, but how much also He is the Mediator of a better covenant, which was established upon better promises.

The superiority of Christ's eternal priesthood, both because of its eternity and its all-embracing effectiveness, has already been emphasized. It is significant in this verse that the term *leitourgias* is used to describe the Lord's present work. The translation "ministry" obscures the precise meaning, since the word's basic content has to do with the service of a priest. And the work or service of that Priest in heaven consists of His continuing to offer intercession for us.

There was a close connection between the Old Covenant and the worship of the covenanted people. Their worship made present for them the nature of their relationship with God. This is true for the New and better Covenant, of which Jesus Christ is the Mediator; He, being the Son of God, is naturally superior to the mediator of the Old Covenant, Moses.

The promises too are superior, for now, among other things, God's people have the assurance of an unending life with Him. The promises of the other covenant were earthly, but we, of the New, in our worship, the Divine Liturgy, have an anticipated participation in the heavenly liturgy; this in addition to the promise of heavenly things.

The word "better," *kreittonos* in Greek, is something like a key word for the entire Epistle, being used about a dozen times with reference to the New Covenant, to the High Priest, and to the new promises. For St. Athanasius (*First Discourse against the Arians*, chap. xiii, no. 59 [8]), this repeated use of "better" is adduced to demonstrate that the Son of God was not of the created order:

> Both in the verse before us, then, and throughout, does he ascribe the word "better" to the Lord, who is better and other than originated things. For better is the sacrifice through Him, better the hope in Him; and also the promises through Him, not merely as great compared with small, but the one differing from the other in nature, because He who conducts this economy, is "better" than things originated.

v. 7. For if that first covenant had been faultless, then should no place have been sought for the second.

Since God instituted the first Covenant, no fault was to be found in it insofar as its purpose was concerned. The fault lay with the people who did not keep the covenant, and it was in this that it was not "faultless." It could also be called "imperfect," in that from the beginning it was designed to be a shadow or type of the covenant that God would perfect with His people. "Wherefore then serveth the law? It was added because of transgressions, till the seed should come to whom the promise was made . . . the law was our schoolmaster to bring us unto Christ, that we might be justified by faith" (Galatians 3:19,24). Thus, St. Paul testifies to the provisional character of the law. So, even while the law was in force, the new law or covenant was anticipated, being "sought."

v. 8. For finding fault with them, he saith, Behold, the days come, saith the Lord, when I will make a new covenant with the house of Israel and with the house of Judah:

Now it is made clear that the fault in the Old Covenant was with "them," the people with whom it was made, as we have indicated above. The Old Testament abounds with references to Israel's and Judah's failure to keep the covenant. "They kept not the covenant of God . . . neither were they steadfast in His covenant" (Psalm 77/78: 10,37). "They have transgressed my covenant, and trespassed against my Law" (Hosea 8:1). "Judah hath dealt treacherously, and an abomination is committed in Israel . . ." (Malachi 2:11). Because of this, one of the prophets revealed that the Lord had proposed or "sought" to make a new covenant with the house of Israel and with the house of Judah; in other words, with both parts of the divided nation. We note also that the New Covenant was to be made or consummated (*synteleō*) with the same people, not with any other, for the Jews were still God's chosen channel for bringing salvation to all men (see St. John Chrysostom, *ibid.,* no. 4).

> *v. 9. Not according to the covenant that I made with their fathers in the day when I took them by the hand to lead them out of the land of Egypt; because they continued not in my covenant, and I regarded them not, saith the Lord.*

The quote from that prophet, Jeremiah, begun in verse 8, continues in verses 9-12 (see Jeremiah 31:31-34 [38:31-34 LXX]). This passage is, by the way, the only place in the Old Testament where the New Covenant is mentioned specifically.

The Lord, speaking through the Prophet, declares that the New Covenant which He will make will be different from the First, which was made when He led them to safety out of Egypt and toward the promised land. The Lord's saying "by the hand" recalls His loving care for this rescued people, so graphically described in Deuteronomy 1 (vv. 31-33):

> And in the wilderness, where thou hast seen how that the Lord thy God bare thee, as a man doth bear his son, in all the way that ye went, until ye came into this place . . . who went in the way before you, to search you out a place to pitch your tents, in fire by night, to shew you by what way ye should go, and in a cloud by day.

Their fault is made clear again: they were not true to nor did they abide in the covenant. St. John Chrysostom *(ibid.)* is not reluctant to warn the Christians of his time of the consequences of disobedience, recalling what happened to the Jews: "Thou seest that the evils begin first from ourselves ('they' themselves first, saith he, 'continued not in [the covenant]' and the negligence is from ourselves, but the good things from Him, I mean the [acts] of bounty." The chosen people's hardships and especially the Babylonian Captivity may be seen as evidences of His forsaking them ("I regarded them not"). Apparently some Jews regard the "new covenant" of Jeremiah's prophecy as a renewal of the Old Covenant, after the return from captivity, but this is obviously not what the Apostle intends here.

> *v. 10. For this is the covenant that I will make with the house of Israel after those days, saith the Lord; and I will put my laws into their mind, and write them in their hearts: and I will be to them a God, and they shall be to me a people:*

The finality of the New Covenant is hinted at in the choice of verb, "I will make." It is the verbal form of the word "covenant" (*ē diathēkē ēn diathēsomai*, or literally, "the covenant which I shall covenant" with them). This time the covenant will not be written on tables of stone, but He will write the new laws in their minds and hearts. In other words, the new Israelite will be one who is truly converted, not one who simply inherits the covenant or who only externally keeps commandments and laws. St. John Chrysostom anticipates the objection of those who might say that the only difference between the covenants was the manner in which they were given:

> Now if any person should say that the difference is not in this respect [a new law replacing the old], but in respect to its being put into their hearts; He makes no mention of any difference of ordinances, but points out the mode of its being given . . . ; let the Jew in that case show that this was ever carried into effect; but he could

not, for it was made a second time in writings after the return from Babylon. But I show that the Apostles received nothing in writing, but received [it] in their hearts through the Holy Spirit. Wherefore also Christ said, "When He cometh, He will bring all things to your remembrance, and He shall teach you" [John 14:26]. (*ibid.,* no. 5).

When the New Covenant would be made—the relationship between God and man: the reconciliation effected in Christ, for which purpose it would be made—it would be perfect. He would indeed, then, be their God, and they would be His people, for they would continue in the covenant.

v. 11. And they shall not teach every man his neighbor, and every man his brother, saying, Know the Lord: for all shall know me, from the least to the greatest.

The New Covenant, further, will call for a personal relationship with God. No privileged class will hold the knowledge of Him like some possession which they impart to others. From this, no one is to be excused, from the least to the greatest in the body of believers. It may be noted that the word translated "neighbor" (*plēsion* in Greek) in this Epistle could be understood in its usual Jewish sense, that is, a fellow-member of the people of the covenant. In the Septuagint, however, the Prophecy of Jeremiah has another word, *politēn,* literally, "citizen" or "fellow-citizen" of a kingdom. Both are appropriate, in that our Lord gave a new sense to "neighbor," and those who follow Him are citizens of His kingdom.

The Lord's promise of deliverance and redemption, which is the subject of Isaiah 54, helps us to understand what the Psalmist means when he says the Lord "will not always be chiding, neither keepeth He His anger for ever" (102/103:9). The Prophet Isaiah refers to the "forsaking" of the chosen people, which the Prophet Jeremiah mentions (see v. 9 above): "For a small moment have I forgotten thee; ... in a little wrath, I hid my face from thee for a moment; but with everlasting kindness will I have mercy on thee, saith the Lord thy

Redeemer." One of the results of this new relationship with His people is that "All thy children shall be taught of the Lord" (Isaiah
54:13). In the present verse, the Apostle confirms that this has come
to pass; and St. John the Apostle (I John 2:27) elaborates this fact and
explains how it is possible: "But the anointing which ye have received
of Him abideth in you, and ye need not that any man teach you, but
as the same anointing teacheth you of all things, and is truth . . . ye
shall abide in Him." This is a direct reference to the Mystery of Chrismation, in which "the seal of the gift of the Holy Spirit," the Spirit of
truth, is given to all. St. John had prefaced his reminder with the
warning that there are many seducers who teach something other
than what the Holy Spirit teaches.

Clement of Alexandria, writing toward the close of the second
century, provides us with another important application of the present verse: he demonstrates the folly of depending on human reason
for arriving at a knowledge of God, since "we have the Teacher
[Christ] from whom all instruction comes . . . and that which the
chiefs of philosophy only guessed at, the disciples of Christ have
both apprehended and proclaimed" (*Exhortation to the Heathen*,
chapter xi).

*v. 12. I will be merciful to their unrighteousness, and their sins
and their iniquities will I remember no more.*

The New Covenant, sealed by the death of Christ on the Cross,
brings forgiveness of sins, because He took upon Himself the sins of
the whole world. "Being justified freely by His grace through the
redemption that is in Christ Jesus; whom God hath set forth to be a
propitiation through faith in His blood, to declare His righteousness
for the remission of sins that are past" (Romans 3:24-25). The
believer, the new Israelite, even if he falls into unrighteousness and
sin, may still have his sins forgiven by Christ's great sacrifice. For
this, he must repent: "I rejoice, not that ye were made sorry, but that
ye sorrowed to repentance . . ." (II Corinthians 7:9). When confession is made, the forgiveness that is pronounced in God's name is the

forgiveness made possible by the Cross. For St. Cyril of Alexandria, a very great example of repentance is that of the woman who washed Jesus' feet with her tears and wiped them with her hair. "Thus, a woman, who before had been lewd, and guilty of sensuality, a sin difficult to wash away, missed not the path of salvation; for she fled for refuge to Him who knoweth how to save, and is able to raise from the depths of iniquity" (*op. cit.*, Homily 40 on Luke 7:36-50).

It is obvious that the Lord's promise through the Prophet Isaiah (see our comments on verse 11) was addressed to the descendants of those who "continued not in His covenant." And since it is made clear in verse 8 that the New Covenant was still to be made with the Jews, even the two parts of the divided nation being mentioned, the house of Israel and the house of Judah, these children of Abraham were to have the first opportunity for reconciliation and the forgiveness of the sins of their fathers. But, it is also evident that even if very few of them respond to His new call, He will raise up other children from among the Gentiles. Such is the point of the Parables of the Marriage Feast of the King's Son (Matthew 22:1-14) and of the Great Supper (Luke 14:16-24). (See also Matthew 3:9; 8:11; Luke 3:8.)

v. 13. In that he saith, A new covenant, he hath made the first old. Now that which decayeth and waxeth old is ready to vanish away.

Now the Apostle declares that the New Covenant has made the first one old, in the sense of its no longer being in effect: it has been replaced. He sees the fulfillment of Jeremiah's prophecy in the New Covenant and in the Church, where the knowledge of God is experienced, sins are forgiven and the people participate in the Kingdom of Heaven.

St. Gregory of Nyssa (*Against Eunomius*, Book II, no. 8) applies the language of the second part of this verse, "decay and wax old, and vanish away," to the old creation insofar as it is replaced by the new creation. He says:

The mighty Paul, knowing that the Only-begotten God, Who has the pre-eminence in all things [Colossians 1:18], is the Author and Cause of all good, bears witness to Him that not only was the creation of all existent things wrought by Him, but that when the original creation of man had decayed and vanished away, to use his own language, and another new creation was wrought in Christ, in this too no other than He took the lead, but He is Himself the first-born of all that new creation of men which is effected by the Gospel.

Chapter 9

v. 1. Then verily the first covenant had also ordinances of divine service, and a worldly sanctuary.

The first part of this chapter (vv. 1-10) contains a summary of the worship prescribed in the Old Covenant or Testament and a contrast between it and the high priestly work of Jesus Christ in the heavenly sanctuary.

To begin with, the Apostle calls his readers' attention to a fact of which they were, of course, familiar. There was a prescribed system or order of worship with its ordinances or regulations (in Greek, *dikaiōmata*). The word translated "divine services" is *latreia*, which means simply worship, but it is used exclusively for the worship due God alone.

There was also a specific place on earth for this worship. For this reason, this holy place or sanctuary is called "worldly" (*kosmikon* in Greek), without any evil connotation. The writer's intention is to show that the worldly sanctuary was typical or symbolic of the heavenly sanctuary.

It should be noted that the Apostle reading for certain feasts of the All-holy Virgin (the Entry into the Temple, for example) is taken from this chapter of Hebrews (verses 1-7, verses 2 and 4, especially).

v. 2. For there was a tabernacle made; the first, wherein was the candlestick, and the table, and the shewbread; which is called the sanctuary.

The tabernacle or "tent" described is the one the Lord commanded to be raised in the wilderness (see Exodus 25 and 26). The purpose of the tabernacle is specified in Exodus 25:8: "And let them make me a sanctuary; that I may dwell among them." The Greek word for tabernacle or tent is *skēnē* and the word to pitch a tent or make a tabernacle is the related word *skēnoō*; the first indicates a

131

dwelling, and the second, to make one's dwelling. In the prologue of St. John's Gospel (v. 14) we find: "And the Word was made flesh, and dwelt among us," where *eskēnōsen* is used to indicate "He took up His dwelling among us."

One troparion for the feast of the Entry of the All-holy Theotokos says (Second Canon, Ode 3), "We sing thy praises as the Tabernacle that held God." Thus understood, the tabernacle in the wilderness was a figure of the dwelling place that God prepared for Himself, so that He could dwell among men: and that dwelling place was the All-holy Virgin Mary.

The tabernacle was a single tent with a veil inside dividing it into two parts, although here it is described as if there were two tents. The first tent (or first part of the tent) contained the candlestick or lamp stand of pure gold with seven branches (Exodus 25:31-37). Also in this outer chamber was the table on which was placed the bread (loaves) of the Presence, the Shewbread, twelve loaves in all, representing the twelve tribes of Israel (see Leviticus 24:5-6). This was the holy place or sanctuary (*hagia* in Greek).

> *v. 3. And after the second veil, the tabernacle which is called the Holiest of all;*

There were also two veils (their measurements and colors were strictly prescribed—see Exodus 26), the first covering the entrance to the first part of the tabernacle, and the second inside in front of the second part. Thus, the "holy place" was separated from the "Holiest of all" (in Greek, *Hagia Hagiōn* or "Holy of Holies"). The significance of this inner chamber will receive special emphasis in the second part of this chapter.

> *v. 4. Which had the golden censer, and the ark of the covenant overlaid round about with gold, wherein was the golden pot that had manna, and Aaron's rod that budded, and the tables of the covenant;*

Now we find a description of the furnishings of the Holy of

Holies. The golden censer is actually the golden "altar of incense" (*thymiatērion* in Greek), and really stood just before the second veil in the outer tabernacle (Exodus 30:6). However, a golden censer which contained burning incense was taken from this altar into the Holy of Holies on the day of atonement (Leviticus 16:12).

The ark (chest) of the covenant was the main item of furniture in the inner sanctuary. It contained only the stone tablets of the covenant, on which were written the ten commandments. The Apostle indicates that it also held the golden pot or urn in which was a portion of the heavenly manna from the wilderness miracle (Exodus 16:32-34), and Aaron's rod which sprouted—the divine testimony to his exclusive right to the priesthood (Numbers 17:1-11; see also Exodus 25:16,21; 40:20; Numbers 17:10; Deuteronomy 10:5; III/I Kings 8:9).

The liturgical texts abound in references to these furnishings, and it is evident that our Tradition holds them to be figures of the Ever-virgin Mary, they being assurances of God's presence, and she being the chosen vessel to receive God in her womb and His chosen meeting place with His people. (For example, Third Sunday of the Great Fast, Matins Canon, Ode 7; Saturday of the Akathist Hymn, Vespers, stichera on "Lord, I have cried"; Nativity of the All-holy Virgin, Matins, Second Canon, Ode 6). "The prophets proclaimed thee in ages past, speaking of thee as ark of holiness, golden censer, candlestick, and table . . ." (Entry of the All-holy Theotokos into the Temple, Matins, second Canon, Ode 3).

v. 5. And over it the cherubims of glory shadowing the mercy seat; of which we cannot now speak particularly.

Placed over or upon the ark was the mercy seat, a sort of lid or cover (*epithēma* in Greek). The word translated "mercy seat" is *hilastērion* from the verb *hilaskomai*, meaning "reconcile oneself," "propitiate," "atone for," or "expiate." There were images of cherubim, one on each end, and their wings overshadowed the mercy seat. They are called "of glory" or of God, since the space between them was the place where God promised to meet Moses and commune with him (Exodus 25:22), and, after the establishment of the priesthood, with Aaron and his successors (Leviticus 16:2). In both Odes 3 and 4 of the Akathist Hymn, Saturday of the Fifth Week of the Fast, the All-holy Virgin is addressed as the "mercy seat," again, the one chosen by God as the place of His meeting with His people, "Hail, Mercy Seat, our fervent intercessor" and "Hail, Mercy Seat of the world."

We should take note of the fact that the holy Fathers, particularly St. John of Damascus (*On the Divine Images*, "Third Apology," no. 24, for example) cite God's commanding Moses to make images of the Cherubim both over the mercy seat and on the veil as support for the propriety of images. Similar reference is also made in the prayers for the consecration of icons.

The last clause, "of which we cannot now speak particularly" (more literally, "it is not now time to speak particularly"), can be understood as indicating the Apostle's eagerness to get back to his principal line of thought. He may feel that the details, the symbolisms and allegorical interpretations, are not necessary for his readers to dwell upon at the present. "In these words he hints that these were not merely what was seen, but were a sort of types [or figures] ... perhaps because they needed a long discourse" (St. John Chrysostom, *On Hebrews*, Homily 15, no. 1).

v. 6. Now when these things were thus ordained, the priests went always into the first tabernacle, accomplishing the service of God.

Having described the various objects of the Old Covenant worship, the Apostle goes on to explain the rites themselves. The articles and furnishings of the first tent had been "ordained" (in Greek *kateskevasmenōn*, or "arranged," "prepared") for the purpose of the "daily" (*dia pantos*, translated "always," but literally "continually") "service of God" (literally, simply "worship," *latreia*, in Greek, but exclusively that due God alone, thus the translators' insertion of the name "God"), which the priests carried out or celebrated. The priests' right and duty to perform these ceremonies only in the first tabernacle seems to be emphasized here. They were actually forbidden to enter into the second tent (see Numbers 18:3-7).

St. John Chrysostom seems not to see a type or prefigure in this worship in the outer tabernacle, but will stress the symbolic character of that of the Holy of Holies. "That is, these things indeed were there, but the Jews did not enjoy them: they saw them not. So that they were no more theirs than ours for whom they prophesied" (*ibid.*, no. 2).

> *v. 7. But into the second went the high priest alone once every year, not without blood, which he offered for himself, and for the errors of the people:*

Now if those ceremonies of the outer tabernacle were not seen by the people, those within the inner chamber were far more inaccessible. "So far was the Holy of Holies removed from presumptuous access, that it might be entered by one man only once a year; so far were the veil, and the mercy-seat, and the ark, and the Cherubim, from the general gaze and touch" (St. Gregory of Nazianzus, *In Defense of His Flight to Pontus*, no. 94).

It was only the high priest who could go into the Holy of Holies, and only on the day of Atonement, the tenth day of the seventh month (Leviticus 16). On that day he entered three times (the "once" refers to the one occasion in the year): first, with the incense (Leviticus 16:13); second, to make atonement or expiation for himself and his household (16:17); and the third, to atone for the "errors" ("sins of ignorance," *agnoēmatōn* in Greek) of the people (16:30).

We note, however, that after the preliminary offering of incense, it was necessary for him to enter "with blood," the blood of sacrificed animals (the second entry with that of a bullock, and the third with that of a goat). To enter that sacred place without blood of sacrifice was punishable by death (Leviticus 16:2). The theme of "blood offering" has now been introduced, and, as the chapter proceeds, we shall understand that this animal blood was symbolic of the blood of Christ, offered for the sins of mankind (St. John Chrysostom, *ibid.*).

Perhaps the use of "sins of ignorance" points up the fact that deliberate sins were not forgivable (Numbers 15:27-31), so as to make a contrast with the effectiveness of the sacrifice of Christ, which would cover all of man's sins: "... the blood of Jesus Christ His Son cleanseth us from all sin" (I John 1:7).

v. 8. The Holy Ghost this signifying, that the way into the holiest of all was not yet made manifest, while as the first tabernacle was yet standing:

As the first mention (2:4) of the Holy Spirit in this Epistle indicates, it is He that reveals to men the true meaning of the signs performed by the Son of God; further, it is He who calls them to give earnest heed to the voice of God that they not continue in the rebellion of their fathers (3:7). Now we are told that it was His function to make the people of God, even in the days of Moses and Aaron, understand that all things prescribed for worship and purification were types and therefore temporary. His inspiration was designed to make them know the reasons why access to the Holy of Holies was denied to all except the high priest. It is also true that the priests who performed divine service on behalf of the people were confined to the first tabernacle; only the high priest could go beyond the veil and come into the presence of God—to "draw nigh unto God" (7:19)— and that he could do only one day of the year. As long as the first tabernacle existed the way was not open to all; its very existence showed that perfect communion with Him was not yet available. The One who would provide that access is He who called Himself "the Way, the Truth, and the Life" and declared that "no man cometh unto the Father but by me" (John 14:6).

v. 9. Which was a figure for the time then present, in which were offered both gifts and sacrifices, that could not make him that did the service perfect, as pertaining to the conscience;

The first tabernacle was a figure ("comparison" or "symbol," *parabolē* in Greek) for "the time then present," that is, the time before Christ, and whatever sacrifices were made in it could cover or atone for the sins of ignorance referred to above. Those who gave the gifts and even the one who performed the services, the high priest, could not have their consciences cleansed by them. Thus they were incomplete, not perfect ("not able to be perfect," Greek *teleiōsai*). We understand, by the Holy Spirit, that the time referred to is the time before the coming of Christ, a time of expectation of His coming and the perfect sacrifice. These things were obviously effective for a time only, since they had to be repeated (see 7:19; 8:7; Galatians 3:21):

> "As pertaining to the conscience [*kata syneidēsin*]." For the sacrifices did not put away [forgive] the defilement from the soul, but still were concerned with the body: "after the law of a carnal commandment" [Hebrews 7:16]. For they certainly could not put away [forgive] adultery, nor murder, nor sacrilege. (St. John Chrysostom, *ibid.*, no. 3)

v. 10. Which stood only in meats and drinks, and divers washings, and carnal ordinances, imposed on them until the time of reformation.

We are now shown that the effectiveness of the rites in the outer tent extended only to those regulations that concerned the body—eating and drinking laws (Leviticus 11; Deuteronomy 14 and Numbers 6:3,15) and ritual washings (Leviticus 11:25; 15:5; Numbers 8 and 19). These were all carnal (fleshly or bodily) ordinances, that had to do with violations of a ritual nature. They had been laid upon the people of Israel for a time only, as a kind of preparation, until the time of reformation (that is, "the time of setting things straight," *mechri kairou diorthōseōs* in Greek), when the New Covenant would take the place of the Old. (See St. John Chrysostom, *ibid.;* St. Gregory of Nazianzus, *Panegyric on St. Basil*, no. 43; and St. Athanasius, *Paschal Letter XIX*, no. 3, in which he disputes the claim of the Marcionites that the Old Testament had nothing to do with the New.)

> *v. 11. But Christ being come an high priest of good things to come, by a greater and more perfect tabernacle, not made with hands, that is to say, not of this building;*

Now that the worship of the Tabernacle (or the Temple) according to the Old Covenant have been reviewed—its meaning, its purpose, and its limitations—we come to the matter toward which the whole preceding part of the Epistle is directed: the priesthood of Christ and its meaning and effectiveness. A series of contrasts between the Old and the New Covenants will be made.

We note, first of all, that Christ came (*paragenomenos* in Greek, "came forth" or "appeared") already the High Priest. "For this cause came I unto this hour" (John 12:27). "He did not first come and then become High Priest, but He came and became at the same time" (St. John Chrysostom, *ibid.*, no. 4). He is the High Priest of the "good things," the redemption and deliverance, which was to come, and has, indeed, already come. Further, in that Christians have a foretaste of the Kingdom to come, He is the High Priest of the good things yet to come, life in the eternal Kingdom. The service of the levitical priests was limited in effectiveness to their own time; Christ's priesthood and the exercise of it are forever.

His tabernacle is not of this creation (rather than "building," Greek *ktiseōs*). It is both His body and the heavenly tabernacle, and it is greater and more perfect precisely because, as in all other things, the heavenly is superior to the earthly, the latter being only a copy or symbol of the former. The expression "not made with hands" refers to the building of the tabernacle itself by men and emphasizes the fact that no human effort was involved in building the "great and more perfect tabernacle." The false witnesses at the Lord's trial testified: "We heard Him say, I will destroy this temple that is made with hands, and within three days I will build another not made with hands" (Mark 14:58). And, further, at His cleansing of the temple, when the Jews demanded a sign, He indeed said, "Destroy this temple, and in three days I will raise it up. . . . He spake of the temple of His body" (John 2:18-21).

v. 12. Neither by the blood of goats and calves, but by his own blood he entered in once into the holy place, having obtained eternal redemption for us.

As we have seen above, the priests of the Old Covenant entered the earthly Holy of Holies "not without blood," that is, the blood of sacrificed goats, in expiation for the sins of the people, and of calves, for his own sins and those of the priests. This entry was made once a year on the Day of Atonement, but it had to be repeated year after year.

The contrast between the great High Priest's entry and theirs is this: it was by His own blood that He entered the heavenly Tabernacle, of which the earthly was but a type. And His entry, that is, His sacrifice, does not have to be repeated—it was but once and for all men and for all times. As will be pointed out later, the real contrast was in the person of the High Priest Himself: He had no sins of His own for which to atone; His work was on behalf of His fellows, all human beings, who became His brothers in the Incarnation. And what He obtained for us was eternal redemption (*lytrōsin* in Greek, "deliverance" or "liberation"). "The mystery has been fulfilled; the things that are written have been accomplished; sins are forgiven" (St. Cyril of Jerusalem, *Catechetical Lecture XIII*, no. 32).

What sacrifice remains for us? Since our Forerunner Jesus has entered the holy place for us, according to St. Athanasius, our response must be "to take up our sacrifices, observing distribution to the poor, and thus, enter into the holy place . . ." (*Paschal Letter XLV*).

This idea finds liturgical expression in the Canon to the Cross and Resurrection sung at Sunday Matins in tone 1: "Christ, having appeared an high priest of the good things to come, put our sins to flight, and having shown through His own blood a strange way unto a better and more perfect tabernacle, He entered as our Forerunner into the holy place" (see Hebrews 7:17-20).

vv. 13-14. For if the blood of bulls and of goats, and the ashes of an heifer sprinkling the unclean, sanctifieth to the purifying of the flesh: how much more shall the blood of Christ, who through the eternal Spirit offered himself without spot to God, purge your conscience from dead works to serve the living God?

If the ritual sacrifices were effective for restoring external purity, then, the Apostle asks, how much more effective must be the blood of the only sinless One, who offers not the blood of other living creatures on behalf of sinful men, but Himself: the blood of Christ efficacious for the cleansing of the defilements of the soul, not just the purifying of the flesh. St. Athanasius (*Paschal Letter XIV*, no. 2), quoting this verse, adds, "but now, through the grace of God the Word, every man is thoroughly cleansed."

The full and perfect manhood or humanity of Christ was offered in self-sacrifice. But since He is eternal by nature, the redemption that He obtained for us is also eternal. The holy Fathers always stress the cooperation of the three Persons of the Holy Trinity in the work of redemption. It was "through the eternal Spirit" that Christ offered the sacrifice, and thus we also learn of the eternity of the Holy Spirit (see St. Ambrose, *On the Holy Spirit*, Book I, chap. 8, no. 99). The Evangelists St. Matthew and St. Luke tell us that the Saviour's body was prepared for sacrifice by the Holy Spirit (Matthew 1:18-20; Luke 1:35; see also St. John Chrysostom, *ibid.*, no. 5).

Works are described as dead first because of their limited effectiveness, and secondly because of the perfunctory performance of them. Now, given that some uncleanness could have been produced accidentally, the rites were powerless to cleanse anyone's conscience, even of those who had willfully contracted the impurity. Further, since the "sprinkling of ashes of an heifer" was a rite specifically designed for the purification of one who had touched a dead body (Numbers 19), its mention here can only emphasize the deadness of such rites. St. John Chrysostom (*ibid.,* nos. 5-6) applies this reference in this way:

> "Shall purge your conscience from dead works." And well said he "from dead works"; if any man touched a dead body, he was polluted; and here, if any man touch a "dead work," he is defiled through his conscience. . . . Here he declared that it is not possible while one has "dead works to serve the living God," for they are both dead and false. . . . Let no man then enter in here with "dead works." For it was not fit that one should enter in who had touched a dead body, much more one that has "dead works."

By the offering of the blood of Christ, the conscience (or soul) of man is purged from dead works. This is the second reference to dead works (see 6:1). They are dead, because they did not free man's conscience from the hold of death; on the other hand, those ritual cleansings were external signs of the inner cleansing that came with the redemption obtained by Christ. Henceforth, however, the character of the works—good works—performed by man is changed: Christ's sacrifice transforms the works of the believer so that they become living works.

The effect of this purging is man's being enabled to "serve the living God," the God who is life and gives life (see John 6:57). To "serve the living God" (in Greek, *latrevein*) means two things: to worship God and to serve Him or do His will in life. Those who are now reborn in Christ serve the living God by their participation in the worship in the heavenly sanctuary, into which they enter in Christ, and to minister to all who are in need.

v. 15. And for this cause he is the Mediator of the new testament, that by means of death, for the redemption of the transgressions that were under the first testament, they which are called might receive the promise of eternal inheritance.

The priestly work of Christ, as just described, established Him as the Mediator of the New Covenant or Testament (see 8:6) He is both

God and Man; as such He is the surety and guarantor (in Greek, *eggyos* [*engyos*]) of the covenant and its mediator (*mesitēs*), representing all men.

> How did He become Mediator? He brought words from the Father and brought them to us, conveying over what came from the Father to us, and adding His own death thereto. We had offended: we ought to have died: He died for us and made us worthy of the Testament. By this is the Testament secure, in that henceforward it is not made for the unworthy. (St. John Chrysostom, *op. cit.,* Homily 16, no. 2; see also 7:22)

Again we recall that it was Jeremiah the Prophet who foretold the giving of the New Covenant (31:31-34 [38:31-34 LXX]).

The word for testament in Greek is *diathēkē*. It can mean both testament in the sense of a last will and a pact or agreement. While God made a pact with the Hebrews originally, His new pact extends to all who believe in Him. The Apostle states that for the inheritance redemption (*apolytrōsis* in Greek), to be effective, the One who makes the will has to die (see v. 16).

The effect of Christ's redemption extends not only to those who have believed in Him since His coming in the flesh, but it also goes back to cover the sins of those righteous who transgressed under the old Law (I Peter 3:18-19). They too were called and will receive the inheritance promised to the new people of God (see 11:39-40). On the Sunday of the Holy Forefathers, we sing: "O thou who wast willing to become, like us, of their [the Forefathers'] seed, that thou mightest save our Forefathers who fell of old . . ." (Vespers, stichera on "Lord, I have cried").

> *vv. 16-17. For where a testament is, there must also of necessity be the death of the testator. For a testament is of force after men are dead: otherwise it is of no strength at all while the testator liveth.*

The meaning of *diathēkē* as a last will and testament is stressed here: it goes into effect with the death of the testator. As in human affairs, the will is operative only on the death of the one who makes it, so likewise Christ's bequest of eternal salvation to the sinner is effective because of His death.

> *vv. 18-20. Whereupon neither the first testament was dedicated without blood. For when Moses had spoken every precept to all the people according to the law, he took the blood of calves and of goats, with water, and scarlet wool, and hyssop, and sprinkled both the book, and all the people, saying, This is the blood of the testament which God hath enjoined unto* [upon] *you.*

The first covenant, as we have been reminded in the foregoing part of this chapter, was sealed, ratified, sanctified with blood, that is, death. Reference is made here to the sacrificial ceremony at which the covenant was inaugurated, as recorded in Exodus 24. Moses went up alone on Mt. Sinai to the presence of God, and the others with him worshipped from afar (24:1). Moses wrote down all the words of the Lord (24:4), and this writing is the book or scroll of the covenant which he read to all the people (24:7). The blood of the sacrificed animals was sprinkled on the altar on which lay the book and then on all the people; their acceptance of the covenant is attested to: "They said, All that the Lord hath said will we do, and be obedient" (24:7-8).

The "water, scarlet wool, and hyssop" mentioned here are all things used in the purification rites: water with the ashes of a heifer, or alone for washing; wool, symbolic of purity, dyed scarlet red; and hyssop, a plant native to the area, the branches of which were used for ceremonial sprinkling. Scarlet was originally the name of a fine cloth which became a descriptive adjective because of its color: it was the color of the tabernacle hangings (Exodus 25:4) and the high priest's garments (Exodus 39:1).

All of these are symbolic, for when the new covenant was ratified on the cross, they all have their part in the events that took place: the soldiers, in their mockery of the royalty of the great High Priest, put a scarlet robe on Him (Matthew 27:28), and they "filled a sponge with vinegar, and put it upon hyssop, and put it to His mouth" (John 19:29); and finally, "they pierced His side with a spear, and forthwith came there out blood and water" (John 19:34). As one of the verses on the Beatitudes sung at the Passion Service of Holy Friday states, "His side was pierced with a spear, that it might cause rivers of life to flow for me," that is, the blood and water are figures of the life-giving mysteries of baptism and the eucharist (see St. Cyril of Jerusalem, *Catechetical Lecture III*, no. 5). "Tell me then why the book of the testament is sprinkled, and also the people, except on account of the precious blood, prefigured by the first?" (St. John Chrysostom, *ibid.*, no. 3).

When the Lord by anticipation sealed the New Covenant at the Supper with "This is my blood of the New Testament, which is shed for many," we may recall the words of Moses at the sealing of the Old Covenant: "This is the blood of the covenant which the Lord hath made with you, concerning these words" (Exodus 24:8).

God gave the Law to Moses, but since the time for His taking flesh that He might give His life on behalf of all mankind had not yet come, He prescribed a substitute as a figure, an innocent animal, since He would not require that a human being sacrifice himself, even were there one pure enough for that purpose. All men were corrupted by sin; the animal was spotless and innocent. St. John Chrysostom (*ibid.*, no 3), completing his explanation of the sacrificial system, adds:

> There was no one [human being] who died there: how then could that Testament be firm? In the same way (he says). How? For blood was there also, as there is blood here. And if it was not the blood of Christ, do not be surprised; for it was a type. "Whereupon," he says, "neither was the first Testament dedicated without blood" [see also our comments on v. 15, above].

vv. 21-22. Moreover he sprinkled with blood both the tabernacle, and all the vessels of the ministry. And almost all things are

by the law purged with blood; and without shedding of blood
[there] is no remission.

Some of the details mentioned in verse 21, as well as in verses 18-20—the sacrificing of goats, the use of water, scarlet wool and hyssop—are not included in the Exodus account of the inaugural sacrificial rite celebrated by Moses (see Exodus 24:3-8). These additions are borrowed from other rites of cleansing: goats were sacrificed on the Day of Atonement (Exodus 9:13); lepers were cleansed with water, scarlet wool and hyssop (Leviticus 14:4-7). The Apostle has replaced in his account here the altar with the book or the scroll, and it may be assumed that the book was laid upon the altar. Further, the tabernacle was not yet built when Moses set up his first altar, and when it was, both the tent and the vessels of divine service or liturgy (in Greek, *leitourgias*, here translated as "the ministry") were consecrated with oil (Exodus 30:22-29).

The Apostle was obviously too familiar with the tradition and history to make any error in this regard, and he certainly does not falsify the record. His point is to generalize and to emphasize the fact that everything connected with the Old Covenant bore the mark of blood. The Covenant itself was sealed by blood.

The word "almost" (*schedon* in Greek) is introduced perhaps to indicate that some of the things employed in the blood sacrifices were consecrated by a holy oil. But the Apostle's point is still that the sacrifices themselves were of limited effectiveness. Again, the forgiveness obtained through them was for ritual transgressions and for purification of the body (St. John Chrysostom, *ibid.*, nos. 3-5). The fact that he leaves firmly established is that the shedding of blood—the sacrifice of life—was necessary for forgiveness. But, the forgiveness he is about to discuss is complete, totally effective, since it is the cleansing, not just of the body, but of the conscience (see vv. 13-14, above).

v. 23. It was therefore necessary that the patterns of things in the heavens should be purified with these; but the heavenly things themselves with better sacrifices than these.

As we know, the things of the worship of the Hebrews (the tabernacle and all its vessels, the rites, etc.) were patterns (or "examples" or "signs") of those in heaven, where the worship of God continues without interruption. The purification or sanctification of earthly things that were patterns of the heavenly was necessary because of the fact that they belonged to sinful man, were, indeed, part of the physical world corrupted by man's sin. The heavenly originals, of course, are not in need of purification, but it is important to understand what is meant by "the heavenly things themselves." Note what St. John Chrysostom (*ibid.,* no. 6) has to say on this subject: "And what does he mean by 'the things in the heavens?' Is it Heaven? Or is it the Angels? None of these, but what is ours. It follows then that our things are in Heaven, and heavenly things are ours, even though they are accomplished on earth." Thus, it appears that man, who will follow the Forerunner into the heavenly sanctuary, who will be made "heavenly things," has need of being purified in his life and his sacrifice of himself by the "better sacrifice," which is that of Christ Himself. For Christians, heaven is the place of their real citizenship, while they live as citizens on earth. St. Paul says, "Our conversation [way of life] is in heaven," and in this way of life they are "heavenly" (Philippians 3:20).

It must be remembered that Jesus Christ came as the great High Priest to mediate between God and man, and, finally, to offer the sacrifice necessary to crown that mediation. Man must enter the heavenly sanctuary, and it was in order to prepare him for that entry that Christ made the "better" sacrifice, that is, the perfect and final sacrifice. Man's calling is heaven: the presence of God and union with Him. As the one created in the image of God, he participates in heaven, but he is in need of purification from his sins. This is accomplished by Christ's shedding His own blood, and, when He ascended into heaven after His resurrection, His taking up with Himself the very human nature He had assumed, and thereby all men who believe in Him and follow Him. It is men that have been purified to become "heavenly things," by the "better sacrifices," so that they may enter the heavenly sanctuary.

> *v. 24. For Christ is not entered into the holy places made with hands, which are the figures of the true; but into heaven itself, now to appear in the presence of God for us:*

Here we find the whole argument summarized, and the contrast is once again made between the earthly tabernacle with its sanctuary made by men and the one in heaven, of which the first is a figure. Now Christ has entered the sanctuary symbolized by the earthly one to appear before God. He had come from there to begin with, and He now returns with His own glorified human nature, after having made man worthy by His sacrifice; thus we may enter in with Him.

St. Athanasius makes reference to this verse in his exposition of the true meaning of Philippians 2:9, in which the Apostle declares that "God also hath highly exalted Him, and given Him a name that is above every name." The Arians understood this exaltation to prove that Christ was in need of moral advancement or reward for accomplishments, and, therefore, not of the same essence with the Father. St. Athanasius insists that this exaltation refers to His humanity and that He was exalted precisely for the same reason that He entered into the heavenly sanctuary: to appear in the presence of God *for us.* He explains: "He is said *because of us* and *for us [italics added]* to be highly exalted, that as by His death we all died in Christ, so again in the Christ Himself we might be highly exalted, being raised from the dead, and ascending into heaven . . ." (*First Discourse Against the Arians*, chap. xi, no. 41).

v. 25. Nor yet that He should offer Himself often, as the high priest entereth into the holy place every year with blood of others;

Having made a point of the fact that Christ did not enter the holy place made with hands, the earthly tabernacle, but rather into the heavenly tabernacle, to appear in the presence of God on our behalf, the Apostle now shows that Christ, the great High Priest, unlike the earthly high priest, does not need to repeat the offering. "Often" (in Greek, *pollakis*) refers to the yearly renewal of the sacrifice, since no one of those offerings was permanently efficacious. And, since sacrifice calls for the giving of life—the shedding of blood—the high priest could not enter the Holy of Holies without blood, and this he did with that of other creatures, lambs, goats, calves, etc. Thus, according to this principle, even the great High Priest enters the Holy of Holies, the heavenly sanctuary, with blood, but it was His own. "Great is the distance [between the two sacrifices]. He is Himself then both victim and Priest and sacrifice" (St. John Chrysostom, *op. cit.*, Homily 17, no. 3).

v. 26. For then must he often have suffered since the foundation of the world: but now once in the end of the world hath he appeared to put away sin by the sacrifice of himself.

If He had had to enter the Holy of Holies to sacrifice repeatedly, He would have had to undergo the corresponding suffering. And since His sacrifice covers the sins of all, even from the foundation (creation) of the world, He would have had to suffer in each generation from the beginning. But now He has entered only once, and that one sacrifice is effective for all generations, those already past, those present and those of the future. "Seest thou how many are the differences? The 'often' for the 'once'; 'the blood of others' for 'His own.' . . . For if it had not been so, and it had been necessary to offer many sacrifices, He must have been many times crucified" (*ibid.*).

The expression "in the end of the world" (more literally "the consummation of the ages," *synteleia tōn aiōnōn* in Greek) has been understood in various ways. It may refer to the end of the old age of types and figures, in which the levitical priesthood was obliged to repeat its sacrifices. Its end was signaled with the appearance or manifestation of the great High Priest, who put away sin ("for the putting away," from Greek *eis athetēsin*, "nullification" or "remission") by the sacrifice of Himself. In a larger sense, the word "consummation" indicates a summation, bringing together, accomplishment or completion, and would therefore refer to the "fullness of time" according to God's design for the redemption of the human race. This idea is brought against the distortion by the Arians of the Incarnation of the Son of God in a letter of St. Athanasius (*Letter LXI*, "To Maximus," no. 2): "Accordingly it is no good venture of theirs [the Arians] to say that the Word of God came into a certain holy man; for this was true of each of the prophets and of the other saints, and on that assumption He would clearly be born and die in the case of each one of them."

St. Cyril of Jerusalem explains the opening verse of St. Matthew's Gospel: " 'The book of the generation of Jesus Christ, the Son of David, the Son of Abraham,' which is to be understood 'according to the flesh,' for He is the Son of David 'in the end of the ages,' but the Son of God 'before all ages,' without beginning" (*Catechetical Lecture XI*, no. 5).

Finally, it may be said with reference to "the consummation of the ages" that, just as the "fullness of time" corresponded to the time of God's acting to bring about the redemption of man, so it also answered to the progressive deterioration of the fallen human race (see St. Athanasius, *The Incarnation of the Word of God*, chap. i, no. 5). Even after the Law was given, designed to help man overcome sin, his sinfulness got worse, as if once man had learned what sin was, he delighted in turning away from God and giving himself over completely to sin (see Romans 1 and 5). In Athanasius' words, "they had gone on gradually from bad to worse, not stopping at any one kind of evil, but continually, as with insatiable appetite, devising new kinds of sins" (*ibid.*).

vv. 27-28. And as it is appointed unto men once to die, but after this the judgment: so Christ was once offered to bear the sins of many; and unto them that look for him shall he appear the second time without sin unto salvation.

Here the Apostle refers to the consequence of man's sin, that they all have to die, as elsewhere he says, "the wages of sin is death" (Romans 6:23). And they die but once, but since "the gift of God is eternal life through Jesus Christ our Lord," the tyranny of death has been broken.

> What then? Do we no longer die that death? We do indeed die, but we do not continue in it: which is not to die at all. For the tyranny of death, and death indeed, is when he who dies is never more allowed to return to life. But when after dying is living, and that a better life, this is not death, but sleep. Since then death was to have possession of all, therefore He died that He might deliver us. (St. John Chrysostom, *ibid.,* no. 4)

So Christ died once like all men, but He is not subject to the judgment, but He Himself will be the Judge of all.

After death all men are subject to judgment, but Christ, after His death, rose from the dead and offers that same resurrection to all who believe in Him. He was once offered, or rather, offered Himself, to bear the sins of many: here the Apostle says not "all" but many, because not all were willing to accept His salvation. Christ will come a second time, but as Judge, and in His second coming, no longer to condemn sin—for He did away with its tyranny and finality, once and for all, in the first coming. He will come with the fruit of His sacrifice, with salvation, for those who await Him in faith and hope (*ibid.*).

Chapter 10

v. 1. For the law having a shadow of good things to come, and not the very image of the things, can never with those sacrifices which they offered year by year continually make the comers thereunto perfect.

The law contained but a shadow (in Greek, *skian*) of the good things to come (the hope of salvation), that is, it only suggested or gave an idea of the realities to be revealed. We find a similar use of the word "shadow" in Colossians 2:17 where reference is made to "meat and drink, respect of a holy day, of the new moon, or of the sabbath," which are called by St. Cyril of Jerusalem "burdens of the law grievous to be borne . . . which, when the truth had come were rightly withdrawn" (*Catechetical Lecture XVII*, no. 29). And as St. Symeon the New Theologian says (*Discourse XXVIII*, no. 4), "Those who lived before grace, since they were under the Law, found themselves sitting under its shadow." The prologue of St. John's Gospel sums it up: "The Law was given by Moses, but grace and truth came by Jesus Christ" (1:17).

The law did not have the image (*eikōn* in Greek) of the realities, that is, a true form of them. In his *Duties of the Clergy*, St. Ambrose says, "The shadow is in the Law, the image in the Gospel, the truth in heaven" (Book I, chap. xlviii, no. 248).

Such was the nature of the law: it was neither intended for, nor capable of, bringing the "comers thereunto" (the worshippers and participants in them) to perfection. The inability of those sacrifices to do that is obvious from their continual, year by year, repetition. St. John Chrysostom calls them an "arraignment of sins rather than a release from them, an arraignment of weakness, rather than an evidence of power" (*On Hebrews,* Homily 17, no. 5). Their usefulness, according to St. Gregory of Nazianzus, consisted in bringing

151

those "of a denseness of a material body and of an imprisoned mind into consciousness of God" (*Second Oration on Pascha,* no. xi).

> *v. 2. For then would they not have ceased to be offered? because that the worshippers once purged should have had no more conscience of sins.*

If the sacrifices had been able to perfect the worshippers, they would have ceased to be offered. There would have been no further need for sacrifice, since men's consciences would have been cleansed:

> For as a medicine, when it is powerful and productive of health, and able to remove the disease entirely, effects all after one application; as, therefore, if being once applied it accomplishes the whole, it proves its own strength in being no more applied, and this is its business, to be no more applied; whereas if it is applied continually, this is a plain proof of its not having strength. For it is the excellence of a medicine to be applied once, and not often. (St. John Chrysostom, *ibid.*)

We call our readers' attention to verses 9 and 14 of the preceding chapter, in which the same word "conscience" is used. It has to do with one's awareness of and feeling of guilt for his sins.

> *v. 3. But in those sacrifices there is a remembrance again made of sins every year.*

The yearly sacrifices on the Day of Atonement were more a reminder of sins committed than a means for their remission. St. John Chrysostom's assessment of their character, cited above, makes good sense in light of this verse. The same Saint goes on to add, "He ordained offerings 'continually,' because of their want of power, and that a remembrance of sins might be made" (*ibid.*). Now, this remembrance (*anamnēsis* in Greek) could perhaps have two purposes: first, it reminded those worshippers that their sins were a hindrance to their perfect communion with God; and, second, it might also point to the all-effective sacrifice of Christ, by which all sins, even those of the past, were (so to say) gathered up and remitted. St. John Chrysostom did say, "This is a figure of that [sacrifice], and this remembrance [a figure] of that" (*ibid.*, no. 6). His second "that" is, in other words, Christ's remembering all sins and forgiving them all in His once-and-for-all sacrifice. The holy Fathers have emphasized the fact that those who lived before the coming of Christ and were faithful and obedient were also saved by His offering of Himself (see our comments on 9:15, above).

v. 4. For it is not possible that the blood of bulls and of goats should take away sins.

The Apostle concludes this four-verse summary of the inferiority and inadequacy of the Old Covenant with the declaration that there is no relation between the blood of animals—be they bulls, goats or lambs—and man's moral offenses (see St. Cyril of Alexandria, *Commentary on the Gospel of St. Luke*, Homily 46).

Considering the content of this verse, St. Gregory of Nazianzus illustrates his teaching on holy Baptism:

> Let us then be baptized that we may win the victory; let us partake of the cleansing waters, more purifying than hyssop, purer than the legal blood, more sacred than the ashes of the heifer sprinkling the unclean, and providing a temporary cleansing of the body, but not a complete taking away of sins; for if once purged, why should they need further purification? (*Oration on Holy Baptism*, no. xi)

vv. 5-7. Wherefore when He cometh into the world, He saith, Sacrifice and offering thou wouldest not, but a body hast thou prepared [for] me: in burnt offerings and sacrifices for sin thou hast had no pleasure. Then said I, Lo, I come (in the volume of the book it is written of me,) to do thy will, O God.

Now attention is turned to the One who would truly bring back to God those who were alienated from Him by sin. The words of

Psalm 39/40 are quoted and shown to be prophetically those of the Son of God Himself on coming into this world. They repudiate animal sacrifices as being unacceptable to God for a propitiation for man's sins. Jesus told the Pharisees who questioned His care for the many publicans and sinners who came to Him, "Go ye and learn what that meaneth, I will have mercy and not sacrifice" (Matthew 9:10-13).

The divine Son's words in the Psalm show that He, in obedience to the Father, comes into the world to do the paternal will. He Himself said: "My meat is to do the will of Him that sent me, and to finish His work" (John 4:34), and "I seek not mine own will, but the will of the Father which hath sent me" (John 5:30).

The last clause of verse 5, as quoted from the Septuagint, refers to the body of the Incarnate Son of God prepared specifically (in view of verse 10 below) for His supreme sacrifice, which would take away the sins of the world. Concerning this, Theodoret of Cyprus says:

> Joseph, ignorant of the mystery [of Christ's conception], was suspicious of adultery; he was therefore plainly taught the formation by the Spirit. It is this which He signified through the prophet when He said, "a body hast thou prepared me" [Psalm 15:7 LXX], for the divine Apostle being full of the Spirit interpreted the prediction. If then the offering of gifts is the special function of priests and Christ in His humanity was called priest and offered no other sacrifice but His own body, then the Lord Christ had a body. (*Dialogue I,* "The Immutable" [NPNF 2*nd* Series, vol. 3, p. 169])

Further, through the Prophet Christ speaks of the reason for His coming into the world, that is, to do God's will, which ultimately is to give His body in sacrifice for sinful man. "In the volume of the book it is written of me" shows us that the whole Old Testament speaks of Christ, and, certainly, of His obedience to the Father's will. (For an extended treatment of this point, see St. Irenaeus, *Against Heresies,* Book IV, chap. xxvi.)

vv. 8-9. Above when He said, Sacrifice and offering and burnt offerings and offering for sin thou wouldest not, neither hadst pleasure therein; which are offered by the Law; then said He, Lo, I come to do thy will, O God. He taketh away the first, that He may establish the second.

Now, those offerings, in all their variety, were made according to the Law, but our Lord Jesus Christ came to replace all of them by His own self-sacrifice. It was God's will that man be saved, cleansed and redeemed; He "will have all men to be saved and come to the knowledge of the truth" (I Timothy 2:4). For this, God took the initiative and sent His Son to do His will. In so doing, the Son abolishes the First Covenant and establishes the Second. St. Irenaeus wrote at length about the reasons for the formation of the Old Covenant and its replacement by the New (*op. cit.,* chaps. 17 and 18).

v. 10. By the which will we are sanctified through the offering of the body of Jesus Christ once for all.

It is then by the will of the Father and of the Son and by the accomplishment of that will by the Son in His God-Manhood that we are sanctified, that is, our sins are forgiven, our consciences cleansed, and our reconciliation with God is effected. This was realized through the voluntary sacrifice of that body which God prepared for the Son. That sacrifice was offered once and for all, that is, it is effective for all men, for all their sins and for all times.

Concerning the will of the Father and the Son, St. Ambrose instructs us:

Not without the Father does He [the Son] work; not without His Father's will did He offer Himself for that most holy Passion, the Victim slain for the salvation of the whole world; not without His Father's will concurring did He raise the dead to life. For example, when He was at the point to raise Lazarus to life, He lifted up His eyes and said, "Father, I thank thee, for that thou hast heard me. And I knew that thou dost always hear me, but for the sake of the multitude that standeth round I spake, that they may believe that thou hast sent me" [John 11:40], in order that, through speaking agreeably to His assumed character of man in the flesh, He might still express His oneness with the Father in will and operation, in that the Father hears all and sees all that the Son wills, and therefore also the Father sees the Son's doings, hears the utterances of His will, for the Son made no request and yet said that He had been heard. (*On the Christian Faith*, Book IV, chap. vi, no. 70)

vv. 11-12. And every priest standeth daily ministering and offering oftentimes the same sacrifices, which can never take away sins: but this man, after He had offered one sacrifice for sins for ever, sat down on the right hand of God;

The ineffectiveness for the forgiveness of sins of the priests' daily celebrating divine services ("ministering" is here the translation of Greek *leitourgōn*) as well as the yearly repetition of the sacrifices has already been dealt with in detail. Likewise the all-sufficient sacrifice of Christ for the sins of all men has been emphasized.

Even though, as it seems, the sacrifices were still being made at the time of the composition of this Epistle, what the Apostle says here is no doubt a generalization that may apply to such services at any time in Israel's history. Their being offered in his time certainly means that this letter was written before 70 A.D., the year the temple was destroyed and all sacrifice literally ceased. In a sense, however, they had already ceased in that there existed the consciousness of their being unacceptable to God (see St. John Chrysostom, *op. cit.*, Homily 18, no. 1).

The contrast between the work of those priests and that of the great High Priest is illustrated by the two verbs "stand" and "sit." Their work was never complete; His, on the other hand, is shown to be complete in that He sat down, rested from all His work, and assumed His place at the right hand of the Father (see Matthew 26:64; Mark 16:19: Romans 8:34; Colossians 3:1; I Peter 3:22, etc.). The idea expressed in verse 10 is again stressed: that

Christ's sacrifice was offered once and for all—for all men, for all their sins, and for all times.

At the feast of the Lord's Ascension, the hymns and verses praise His fulfillment of the divine economy, His sacrifice on behalf of all mankind, His taking His human nature and ours with Him into heaven, and His sitting down on the right hand of the Father, from which He was never separated (see the stichera on "Lord, I have cried" in Vespers for that feast).

v. 13. From henceforth expecting till His enemies be made His footstool.

The last part of the prophecy in Psalm 109/110:1 is again recalled: "Sit thou at my right hand till I make thine enemies thy footstool." Thus, the Divine-Human Mediator rests from His work, although "He ever liveth to make intercession for us" (7:25), and waits (in Greek, *ekdechomenos*) for His enemies to be subjected to Him. Although the power of the chief enemy, the Devil, has been broken by the death and resurrection of the Savior, there remain enemies who continue to do the Evil One's will and work to draw men away from Christ. "For He must reign, till He hath put all enemies under His feet. The last enemy that shall be destroyed is death" (I Corinthians 15:25-26).

v. 14. For by one offering He hath perfected for ever them that are sanctified.

Here we have another of the Apostle's conclusions or summations of the arguments contained in preceding verses; similar ones are found in 4:16, 7:28, and 9:28.

Those who are sanctified—that is, those who believe in Christ, put all their trust in Him, repent of their sins, and follow Him in humble obedience—are "perfected" by His one sacrifice (St. John Chrysostom, *ibid.*, no. 2). Again, the word translated "perfected" is *teteleiōken* in Greek. It is used by the Lord in reference to His work of redemption (Luke 13:32), which He is to complete on the third day. When applied to those who have been sanctified or set apart, separated for God, it must mean that they are to have their sanctification, salvation, and reconciliation completed "for ever" (in Greek, *eis to diēnekes*) that is, continually and without interruption. In other words, they will have eternal life as the end of their sanctification. Thus, the one offering of the Incarnate Word accomplishes what countless offerings under the Old Covenant could never bring about.

> *vv. 15-17. Whereof the Holy Spirit also is a witness to us: for after that He had said before, This is the covenant that I will make with them after those days, saith the Lord, I will put my laws into their hearts, and in their minds will I write them; and their sins and iniquities will I remember no more.*

It was the Holy Spirit who had inspired the Prophet Jeremiah (31:33-34 [38:33-34 LXX]) to foretell the establishment of the New Covenant, which would call, not for outward observance, but for inner conversion. God's laws—His will for us—will be written in our hearts and minds, while the first law was written upon tables of stone (see also II Corinthians 3:3). The consequence of this conversion is given in the prophecy, but not included in the quotation in the present Epistle: "and I will be their God, and they shall be my people."

St. Cyril of Jerusalem (*Catechetical Lecture XVII*, no. 33) makes use of this mention of the Holy Spirit along with others of St. Paul as evidence of the Spirit's existence and of His activity in the period of the Old Testament.

The forgiveness of sins obtained by the Lord Jesus Christ for mankind in His sacrifice is complete, and therefore, the Lord's words expressed by the Prophet tell us that He will even erase from His memory the sins and iniquities of those who repent and put their faith in Christ, and along with them, the just and righteous of the Old Testament (see Romans 3:25).

v. 18. Now where remission of these is, there is no more offering for sin.

St. John Chrysostom says, "So then He forgave their sins, when He gave the Covenant, and He gave the Covenant by sacrifice. If therefore He forgave the sins through the one sacrifice, there is no longer need of a second" (*ibid.*, no. 3).

There is but one effective sacrifice, that made by Christ, and the sacrifices apparently still being offered by the priests, as the Apostle points out, are useless and vain, because they perpetuate the "shadow" of the reality, when the reality has already come. Again, we recall that in the early part of the Epistle, concern was expressed that some of the Hebrews who had professed belief in Christ still felt some attraction to the old ways, and were constantly being tempted to return to the temple and its sacrifices.

v. 19. Having therefore, brethren, boldness to enter into the holiest by the blood of Jesus,

The dogmatic exposition of the Epistle is now being completed (in this and the two following verses), and the Apostle, convinced that the very truth he has explained in great detail must evoke a response, will proceed to exhort the Hebrew Christians to remain faithful.

The sacrificial work of Jesus Christ, as the final priest, has given them access to the heavenly sanctuary (9:7-12). They can have boldness or confidence (see 4:16 and 10:35), because of the fact that they have a High Priest, who is like them in every way except that He is sinless. The shame of sin has been taken away, all things forgiven, and "being made fellow-heirs, and enjoying so great love, produces boldness" (St. John Chrysostom, *op. cit.*, Homily 19, no. 2).

"Christ having appeared an High Priest of the good things to come, He put our sins to flight, and having shown through His own blood a strange way unto a better and more perfect tabernacle, He entered as our forerunner into the holy place" (Sunday Matins for Tone 1, Canon to the Cross and Resurrection, Ode 4).

Some of the Hebrews, as well as others, were tempted to abandon their new faith because they found that it was even more difficult to follow the Gospel, and to live up to the things that were expected of them, than it was to follow the Law. St. Symeon the New Theologian sees this same danger in Christians of his time, and calls this reaction a "new heresy." Those who claim that it is impossible to keep the commandments of the Gospel and become like the holy Fathers, "shut up the heaven that Christ opened for us, and cut off the way to it that He inaugurated for us" (*Discourse XIX*, no 4).

> *v. 20. By a new and living way, which He hath consecrated for us, through the veil, that is to say, His flesh;*

The new and living way is Jesus Himself, who declared Himself to be "the Way, the Truth, and the Life" (John 14:6). His way is new, for it has replaced the old way. His way is living, because He, having life in Himself (John 5:26), rose from the dead and lives forever. "For the first way being destroyed, there must needs again be consecrated for the wanderers a new and living way, even I myself, Who am the way," as St. Gregory of Nyssa has the Lord say when He calls Himself "the way" (*Against Eunomius*, Book III, no. 2).

The way He consecrated (*enekainisen*, in Greek: "to inaugurate by sacrifice," as when a temple or altar was consecrated, from the root verb *kainoō*, to "make new"), through the veil (or curtain) of His flesh: the veil through which the Old Covenant priest passed to enter the sanctuary was a figure of the veil of His own flesh-and-blood humanity, by which all now have access to the heavenly or true sanctuary. "And because His flesh, this veil was dishonored, there the typical veil of the temple was rent asunder, as it is written, 'And behold, the veil of the temple was rent in twain from the top to the bottom . . . '" (St. Cyril of Jerusalem, *Catechetical Lecture XIII*, no. 32, quoting Matthew 27:51; see also Blessed Theophylact,

Explanation of the Holy Gospel According to St. Matthew, on vv. 50-53). This happened at the very moment of the Lord's death on the cross.

v. 21. And having an high priest over the house of God;

Since the Apostle will begin, in verse 22, his exhortation to the Hebrews to have faith, remain steadfast, and be united one to another, verse 20 gives the first reason for heeding his call; the second reason is stated here: we have a high priest over the house of God, that is, the house of Israel. The sense is that the high priesthood of Jesus Christ is a present and permanent reality, being a priest for ever after the order of Melchisedec. After the once-and-for-all sacrifice, His present and continual priestly work consists of the fact that "He ever liveth to make intercession for us" (7:25).

v. 22. Let us draw near with a true heart in full assurance of faith, having our hearts sprinkled from an evil conscience, and our bodies washed with pure water.

The first point in the exhortation is that God's people must approach Him through worship in their continuing earthly life with sincerity of heart, with full confidence that their sins have been forgiven, and with the full assurance which comes through faith. Further, he reminds them of their baptism: while their bodies had been washed with water, their hearts and minds were sprinkled with the blood of Jesus. Elsewhere it is said: "Know ye not that so many of us as were baptized into Jesus Christ were baptized into His death," and "We were buried with Him in baptism into His death" (Romans 6:3-4). The language here used recalls the sprinkling with blood in the Old Testament sacrifices (Exodus 24:8).

v. 23. Let us hold fast the profession of our faith without wavering; (for He is faithful that promised;)

The Apostle is urging the Hebrew Christians to remain faithful to that solemn profession of faith in Christ that has always been required in Baptism (see the *Catechetical Lectures* of St. Cyril of Jerusalem, especially Lectures III and IV of the "procatechesis" series). The reason why this must be done is that the One who made the promises of eternal life in the kingdom of God, that is, Christ, is faithful (I Thessalonians 5:24). St. Paul charges Timothy, in view of the profession he had made to "keep this commandment without spot, unrebukeable, until the appearing of our Lord Jesus Christ" (I Timothy 6:11-14).

> *v. 24. And let us consider one another to provoke unto love and to good works:*

One of the characteristic elements of the life in Christ is concern for others. Love and good works are products of this concern within the Christian community, and from there it must extend to all people. Consideration of the members of the Body for one another is the response to God's manifest love for us, to the Lord's "new commandment," that "Ye love one another." St. Symeon the New Theologian bases his exhortation to his community in the first week of the Great Fast on this verse. He says, in part, "You have tasted of the true life and have obtained compassion for your neighbors from God who is compassionate. . . . Therefore do not fail to stir up, to encourage, to instruct your neighbors . . . to stir up your brother to increased effort of love and good works . . ." (*Discourse XI,* "On Fasting," no. 6).

> *v. 25. Not forsaking the assembling of ourselves together, as the manner of some is; but exhorting one another: and so much the more, as ye see the day approaching.*

Apparently some members of the community were guilty of "rejecting the assembly." The term translated by "assembling" was very frequently used for the gathering of the faithful for the Eucharist (in Greek, *episynagōgēn*). Their absence will result in the loss of concern for the other members. The coming together so as to constitute the body of the Church is not an optional feature of the Christian life, but an essential one: no one is a Christian alone, rejecting the company of fellow Christians; above all, he must participate in the feast of God's love for us, the Eucharist. St. Ignatius of Antioch makes a point of this in several of his epistles. "He, therefore, that does not assemble with the Church, has even by this manifested his pride, and condemned himself. For it is written, 'God resisteth the proud'" (*Epistle to the Ephesians,* chap. v). The unity manifested in the assembly is the Church's greatest weapon against Satan: "For when ye assemble frequently in the same place, the powers of Satan are destroyed, and the destruction at which he aims is prevented by the unity of your faith" (*ibid.,* chap. xiii).

It is of special urgency that this bond of love be maintained by the followers of Christ, since the Day (meaning the "the Day of the Lord," the Second Coming—I Corinthians 3:13 and I Thessalonians 5:4) must always be remembered. For it is that Day that is anticipated by the Church, indeed, is eagerly awaited. In the Eucharistic assembly, the kingdom to come is manifested and made present. The loss of hope in Christ's coming again can only produce wavering and laxness in the observance of the greatest of the commandments, love of God and love of one's neighbor. That hope is kept lively in the assembly. (See also St. Augustine, *On the First Epistle of St. John,* Homily 4, no. 2.)

> *v. 26. For if we sin wilfully after that we have received the knowledge of the truth, there remaineth no more sacrifice for sins;*

St. John Chrysostom (*op. cit.,* Homily 20, nos. 1-3) is convinced that the Apostle is still concerned here with what happens to those who reject the assembly of the Christian community for the Eucharist. The Hebrew Christians are reminded that they received "the knowledge of the truth" on being baptized and becoming members of the Body of Christ. Like trees, they have been planted and watered by the Spirit, and if they do not live in accordance with their calling or they try to lead a double life, they are guilty of squandering their gift and they sin deliberately.

They cannot be baptized a second time; just as there was one sacrificial death of the Savior, there is only one baptism into that death. St. John, however, is quick to remind his audience that there is still repentance and remission of sins even for the chronic sinner, although earlier, in the second century, there was a much harsher attitude toward repeated repentances (*The Shepherd of Hermas,* Book II, Commandment IV, chap. iii; see also Clement of Alexandria, *Stromata,* Book II, chap. xiii). Since both of these make reference to the present verse from Hebrews, it may be assumed that what is meant is repentance from the sin of apostasy. St. John points directly to the error of the Novatians, who denied repentance and the mysteries to those who had fallen into deadly sin after baptism.

v. 27. But a certain fearful looking for of judgment and fiery indignation, which shall devour the adversaries.

Since the Apostle is attempting to combat the fairly common sin of apostasy, he rather conscientiously warns those who have fallen away of the consequences and points out what they have to look forward to: "a fearful expectation of judgment" and a "fiery jealousy" (*pyros zēlos* in Greek). St. Paul elsewhere calls his own jealousy over those whom he had brought to faith in Christ and have fallen away "a jealousy of God" (II Corinthians 11:2). That God Himself should be jealous for those who became His adopted children in baptism is not surprising, because the same was attributed to Him in the case of Israel (see Nahum 1:2; Zechariah 1:14, etc.). This fire will consume them that have become His adversaries. The apostate is thus in a condition much worse than that of the unbeliever (6:8; see also St. John Chrysostom, *ibid.,* no. 2).

v. 28. He that despised Moses' law died without mercy under two or three witnesses:

As in other places in this Epistle, the writer brings into his argument examples from the Law under which the Hebrews lived until the coming of grace. To "despise Moses' law" (*athetēsas*, from *atheteō nomon Mōseōs*) was not as much to violate specific commandments as it was to deny the very authority of the Law, disregard it completely, and to live without reference to it. Jesus condemned those scribes and Pharisees who "bound heavy burdens on those who were under the law, commanding that the ordinances of Moses should be kept inviolate, and passing sentence of death upon any who despise it, while they themselves paid not the slightest heed to the duty of performing its precepts" (St. Cyril of Alexandria, *op. cit.,* Homily 85). The hypocrisy of the Keepers of the Law notwithstanding, the Law did provide that certain offenses were punishable by death with no pardon ("without compassion," in Greek *chōris oiktirmōn*), but with the testimony of more than one witness (Numbers 35:30). It was the most severe of all offenses, the rejection of the whole law and turning to other gods, that the Apostle has in mind here (Deuteronomy 13:6 ff.), since he is dealing with a parallel offense in the apostasy of some Hebrew Christians.

> *v. 29. Of how much sorer punishment, suppose ye, shall he be thought worthy, who hath trodden under foot the Son of God, and hath counted the blood of the covenant, wherewith he was sanctified, an unholy thing, and hath done despite unto the Spirit of grace?*

Since the Law was only a shadow or figure of the New Law of Christ, its punishments were primarily of an earthly or temporal nature. Greater penalties, "sorer punishments," ("sorer" is used for *cheironos,* "worse," comparative of *kakos*) appropriate to the New Law, those of an eternal nature, must await those who willfully reject ("trample under foot") Him who is Christ, the Son of God. If death was the punishment according to the Old Law, because of certain violations, it was not as severe as that punishment that is due because of rejection of the Savior, for it is eternal.

With "forsaking the assembling of ourselves together" (v. 25) still in mind, the Apostle brings forth the same kind of warning we find in I Corinthians (11:27-30) concerning the unworthy reception of the Body and Blood of Christ in the Eucharist. He who considers the eucharistic elements as merely common bread and wine rather than the consecrated body and blood have insulted, "done despite unto" *(enybrisas)*, the Spirit of grace. That the Eucharist is referred to here is taken for granted by the holy Fathers. St. John Chrysostom asks: "And how does a man 'tread under foot the Son of God?' When partaking of Him in the mysteries he has wrought sin, has he not trodden Him under foot? Has he not despised Him?" (*ibid.*, no. 3). It is the Holy Spirit who has given us this benefit of receiving Christ in the Eucharist, but he who "accepts not a benefit does despite to the Benefactor" (*ibid.*). Earlier St. Athanasius has explained the meaning of this passage in similar terms:

> Now he who has been counted worthy of the heavenly calling, and by this calling has been sanctified, if he grow negligent in it, although washed becomes defiled: "counting the blood of the covenant by which he was sanctified a profane thing, and despising the Spirit of grace," he hears the words, "Friend, how camest thou in hither, not having wedding garments?" (*Paschal Letter VII*, no. 9)

The very cause for the rejection of the assembly was evidently the rejection of the Eucharist itself. Apparently this sin was still found among some Christians in the time of St. Ignatius: "They abstain from the Eucharist ... because they confess not the Eucharist to be the flesh of our Savior Jesus Christ" (*Epistle to the Smyrneans*, chap. vii).

> *v. 30. For we know Him that hath said, vengeance belongeth unto me, I will recompense, saith the Lord. And again, The Lord shall judge His people.*

By beginning with "we know" the Apostle shows that he assumes the familiarity of the people he is addressing with what their Scriptures say concerning God's vengeance and His judgment. He quotes Deuteronomy 32:35-36 and Psalm 49/50:4, as evidences that the consequences of willful turning away from God are inevitable. Terms such as vengeance, punishment, and judgment are human expressions designed to capture the sense of this inevitability, for God's justice is not capricious, nor is it the result of favoritism or partiality. "Vengeance is mine; I will repay" is also found in Romans 12:19, but in this case it teaches that it is wrong for Christians to avenge themselves or to take revenge into their own hands. Schismatics, who are themselves under God's judgment for separating themselves from the Church, such as the followers of Novatian, are reminded of their error and guilt when they judge those who remain faithful and whom they seek to entice (*Treatise Against the Heretic Novatian,* no. 7 [ANF vol. 5, p. 659]).

v. 31. It is a fearful thing to fall into the hands of the living God.

Surely it is comforting to those who believe and remain obedient and faithful to God to "fall into His hands." This is what it means to David the Prophet, for unlike what will happen to him if he falls into the hand of man, from God he will receive many mercies (II Kings/II Samuel 24:14). On the other hand, it is terrifying for the apostate or the idolater to fall into His hands, for, as His mercy is great, so is His justice. For St. Ephraim the Syrian, this verse applies directly to those whom St. Paul warns (in II Thessalonians 1:7-8), those that "know not God, and that obey not the gospel of our Lord Jesus Christ," of the second coming of the Lord, in "flaming fire and taking vengeance" (*Homily on our Lord,* no. 22).

In all of what is said above, we may conclude that for the Apostle the apostasy of his times is equivalent to the idolatry of the Israelites in Old Testament times. This may be the reason for there being no definite article in the Greek text (*theou zōntos*); a more literal translation would be "a living God," so as to contrast Him with the lifeless gods of idolatry.

v. 32. But call to remembrance the former days, in which, after ye were illuminated, ye endured a great fight of afflictions;

After having warned his readers of the terrible consequences of apostasy, he now turns to a gentle, fatherly, even soothing exhortation, and praises them for the witness they gave formerly to their faith (see Clement of Alexandria, *Stromata,* Book IV, chap. xiii). He reminds them of how dedicated and brave they had been after their baptism. Such is the meaning of "illumination," as here in the verb "were illuminated," *phōtisthentes* (see St. John Chrysostom, *First Instruction to Catechumens,* no. 2). He tries to encourage them from their own example, praising them for the great fight they waged with their tormentors and persecutors. "Great fight" translates *athlēsin,* used of athletic contests, a term that will be used in later years in connection with the trials and sufferings of the martyrs.

v. 33. And partly, whilst ye were made a gazing-stock both by reproaches and afflictions; and partly, whilst ye became companions of them that were so used.

The results of their becoming followers of Christ and being baptized were, on the one hand ("partly"), that they became a public spectacle (here the word translated "gazing stock" is elsewhere translated "spectacle," for example, I Corinthians 4:9), as in a stadium or theater (*theatrizomenoi,* related to our word "theater," means "to bring on stage," and often "to hold up to ridicule"). Being made fun of or mocked by their former co-religionists, they were victims of taunts or contempt ("reproaches") as well as of physical harm ("afflictions"). On the other hand ("partly"), they are to he encouraged by all that has happened to them, since they have joined the company of the great contenders for the faith, the Apostles (St. John Chrysostom, *On Hebrews,* Homily 21, no. 2; see also Philippians 1:7).

v. 34. For ye had compassion of me in my bonds, and took joy-fully the spoiling of your goods, knowing in yourselves that ye have in heaven a better and an enduring substance.

Although the more widely accepted text of this Epistle omits "me" and "my" and translates the opening clause, "for ye had com-passion of those in bonds," and while St. John Chrysostom does not include them in his quotation of the verse, he adds: "Thou seest that he is speaking of himself and the rest who were in prison" (*ibid.*).

Some of the believers had undoubtedly been put into prison ("bonds"), and some had had their possessions seized ("spoiling of your possessions," from Greek *harpagēn tōn hyparchontōn hymōn*), either by the authorities or by angry former companions who looted their homes when they were imprisoned. All Christians, even those who were still free, suffered with those in jail. Thus, they had will-ingly, even joyfully, accepted the seizure of their earthly property, since they knew that they had the promise of Christ of a greater and imperishable possession in heaven for their endurance. This conso-lation echoes the Lord's teaching at the beginning of His public work: "Rejoice and be exceeding glad: for great is your reward in heaven: for so persecuted they the prophets which were before you" (Matthew 5:12; see also 6:20).

v. 35. Cast not away therefore your confidence, which hath great recompense of reward.

In other places in this Epistle (6:10, for example), those who are apparently getting impatient for the realization of the promise are encouraged to persevere until the end:

> It is as if one should speak of an athlete who had overthrown all, and had no antagonist, and was then to be crowned, and yet endured not that time, during which the president of the games comes, and places the crown upon him; and he impatient, should wish to go out, and escape as though he could not bear the thirst and the heat. (St. John Chrysostom, *ibid.,* no. 3)

"Recompense of reward" translates the compound Greek word *misthapodosian,* that is, "one's wages," or "what is due" (see also 2:2 and 11:26).

v. 36. For ye have need of patience, that, after ye have done the will of God, ye might receive the promise.

"Patience, and an enduring and courageous mind, form the impenetrable armor of the saints; for they render them approved and resplendent with the praises of piety," so St. Cyril of Alexandria is moved to say with reference to this verse (*op. cit.,* Homily 87). In numerous places in his epistles, St. Paul exhorts his people to have patience; he praises some who have this virtue, because it is a consequence of their faith. The experience of persecutions and tribulations make both faith and patience increase (II Thessalonians 1:3-5).

Here the Apostle tells them that, since they have already done the will of God, enduring all kinds of afflictions, combat, and the loss of their earthly freedom and their material possessions, they now need only one thing: patience. They cannot let their feelings of weakness make them lose their steadfastness, for Holy Scripture teaches that for the faithful weakness becomes strength (Joel 3:10,11; Zechariah 12:8). St. John Cassian finds these Old Testament calls to make strength out of weakness applicable to Christians. He quotes St. Paul's boast concerning how the Lord has turned his own weakness into strength (*First Conference of Abbot Serenus,* chap. v).

vv. 37-38. For yet a little while, and He that shall come will come, and will not tarry. Now the just shall live by faith: but if any man draw back, my soul shall have no pleasure in him.

These two verses are quoted from the Prophet Habakkuk (2:3-4 LXX), with the addition of a phrase from Isaiah (26:20), "yet a little while" (*mikron hoson hoson*).

The Fathers of the Church testify to the appropriateness of its use here by the Apostle to strengthen and encourage the discouraged

Hebrew Christians to have patience and to remind them that their patience will be rewarded with the coming of the One who has promised to come again. St. Cyril of Alexandria, for example, says: "This same way of salvation by faith in Christ He declared unto us before by the holy prophets, saying: 'Yet a little, little while, and He that cometh shall come, and shall not tarry. And whosoever shall draw back, in him My soul shall not have pleasure'" (*op. cit.*, Homily 86). Further, in the *First Epistle of Clement* (chap. xxiii), we read:

> Far from us be that which is written, "Wretched are they who are of a double mind, and of a doubting heart; who say, These things we have heard even in the times of our fathers; but, behold, we have grown old, and none of them has happened unto us."... Of a truth, soon and suddenly shall His will be accomplished, as the Scripture also bears witness saying, "Speedily will He come, and will not tarry."

Some of those who had professed faith in Christ had been filled with fear because of the persecution of their former brothers in the Hebrew religion and because of their own impatience. They are reminded that God "will have no pleasure in those who for fear draw back," and that the just (the true believer or the righteous) will have eternal life through faith.

v. 39. But we are not of them who draw back unto perdition; but of them that believe to the saving of the soul.

The meaning of the expression "my soul shall have no pleasure in him" becomes clear. "Pleasure" is *evdokia*, as in "good will toward men;" in verse 38, the related verb *evdokei* is used. The consequence of shrinking back or going back on one's commitment is perdition or condemnation. The verb *hypostellō* is used in both v. 38 and v. 39; it has not only the primary meaning of "shrink back," but also the secondary meaning of "conceal" or "suppress through fear." St. Gregory of Nazianzus declares that although he has never been silent on the subject of the Son of God, he is now "even more bold to declare the truth, that I may not (to use the words of Scripture) by drawing back fall into the condemnation of being displeasing to God" (*Third Theological Oration*, "On the Son," no. 1). Thus, one must not only hold this truth, but he must also proclaim it.

The Apostle's use of "we" in connection with not drawing back and having faith or believing indicates his hope that his readers may share that faith with him. This is the faithfulness that will bring them their salvation.

Chapter 11

v. 1. Now faith is the substance of things hoped for, the evidence of things not seen.

Having referred to faith in the last two verses of Chapter 10 as essential to the true follower of Christ, to his life and finally to his salvation, the Apostle now goes on to define faith. While it may seem that the whole of this present chapter is a kind of digression and constitutes a complete tractate in itself, its link with what precedes can be found in the call for patience of 10:36. The relation between faith and patience is well established in other Epistles (Romans 4:18, Titus 2:2, and James 1:3, for example).

The Christian has complete confidence in what God has promised him (II Peter 1:4). These promises, the object of his hope, have reality (II Corinthians 1:20), and they become reality or acquire substance (*hypostasis* in Greek) through faith. In his chapter "on Faith," St. John of Damascus defines faith as "undoubting and unambiguous hope alike of what God hath promised and of the good issue of our prayers. The first [faith], therefore, belongs to our will, while the second [evidence or proof] is of the gifts of the Spirit [Galatians 5:5]" (*Exposition of the Orthodox Faith*, Book IV, chap. x).

For the Christian, faith is superior to knowledge, for it is the means by which he knows the invisible ("things not seen"), and response to their real existence follows. On the other hand, things seen force their acceptance on the observer: "For we are saved by hope: but hope that is seen is not hope . . ." (Romans 8:24). So, faith offers the evidence of the existence of the things which the believer has not seen, but hope for through the testimony and promises of God, and through those to whom God has spoken. Faith overcomes any uncertainty that there might be in the things hoped for (see Clement of Alexandria, *Stromata*, Book II, chap. ii).

v. 2. For by it the elders obtained a good report.

As in other cases earlier in this Epistle, an appeal is made to the pre-New Testament history of the Hebrews, a normal procedure, since the New Testament is the continuation of that history. The term "elders" (*presbyteroi* in Greek) is used in the same sense as "father" in other places, notably in 1:1. "They obtained a good report," that is, record of them has been left to us because they had faith; they are the heroes of salvation history because of their faith. The expression *emartyrēthēsan* in Greek literally means "they were witnessed to," or "testified to," implying that God in His word, the Holy Scriptures, testified to them. Their faith in the promises of God receives its reward in the birth of the Savior, and for this reason, a large portion of this chapter forms the Epistle reading for the Sunday before the Nativity of our Lord.

v. 3. Through faith we understand that the worlds were framed by the word of God, so that things which are seen were not made of things which do appear.

The rest of this chapter will be devoted to a review of some of the outstanding examples of faith in the Old Testament. This verse, however, puts forward beforehand an application of faith that is common to all mankind. It is the kind of faith by which all men perceive ("understand" as a result of contemplation, *nooumen* in Greek) that the world and the ages (*aiōnas* from *aiōn,* meaning "eternity," "age," or "period of time," or "the world," sometimes equivalent to *kosmos*) did not come into being by themselves nor were they formed from pre-existing materials. We men should understand by the use of our intelligence that God, by a word, brought the visible into being from nothing. "Because that which may be known of God is manifest in [among] them [men], for God hath showed it unto them. For the invisible things of Him, from the creation of the world are clearly seen, being understood by the things which are made . . ." (Romans 1:19-20, "understood" in v. 20 is *nooumena* there also).

St. Gregory of Nyssa, commenting on our present verse, stresses the fact that "any efforts of the powers of reasoning," cannot settle the question of God's existence: the faith resulting from contemplation, thus, has nothing to do with reasoning (*On the Soul and the Resurrection* [NPNF 2*nd* series, vol. 5, p. 457]).

The choice of "framed" (*katērtisthai* from *katartizō*) instead of "created" may be due to the Apostle's intention to show that it is the orderliness of creation and the compatibility of its parts that lead men to seek to know the Creator who is the Sustainer of this order:

> The prophet said, "The heavens declare the glory of God" [Psalm 18/19:1]. For what will the Greeks [heathens or pagans] say in that day? That "we were ignorant of thee?" Did ye then not hear the heaven sending forth a voice by the sight, while the well-ordered harmony of all things spake out more clearly than a trumpet? . . . All things abiding in order and by their beauty and grandeur, preaching aloud the Creator? (St. John Chrysostom, *On Romans,* Homily 3, on v. 20)

The "word of God" here refers to a spoken utterance, since the Greek word *hrēma* is in the text rather than *logos.* On the other hand, the Son or Logos of God was, as we have already seen, the active Agent of creation, and thus, we may conclude that here the Apostle means "the utterance of the Word of God Himself."

v. 4. By faith Abel offered unto God a more excellent sacrifice than Cain, by which he obtained witness that he was righteous, God testifying of his gifts: and by it he being dead yet speaketh.

Now having stated the general principles of faith, the Apostle goes on to call his readers' attention to the accomplishments by faith of their forefathers. The first in his list is Abel, who "by faith offered" a sacrifice, a blood-offering, that was more acceptable to God than the offering of his brother Cain. The latter as we know, committed the first murder, out of jealousy. The difference, according to the

Apostle, between the two offerings lay in Abel's faith, although the Genesis account (chap. 4) does not mention this specifically, and God's words to Cain seem to accuse him of ill will or some improper attitude in making his sacrifice.

Cain's offering's being unacceptable has caused puzzlement among interpreters of Genesis, both ancient and modern. The wording of the crucial verse in Genesis (4:7) which contains God's words to Cain, in versions translated from the Hebrew is quite different from that of the translations from the Septuagint (Greek version). The first has it that the Lord said: "If thou doest well, shalt thou not be accepted? and, if thou doest not well, sin lieth at the door." In the latter, it reads: "Hast thou not sinned if thou hast brought it rightly but not rightly divided it?" The holy Fathers, depending upon the Greek version, since it was the one is use by the Church, have been consistent in their understanding of the reason for God's rejection of Cain's offering (see the *First Epistle of Clement,* chap. iv; St. Irenaeus, *Against Heresies,* Book III, chap. xxiii, no. 4; St. John Chrysostom, *On Hebrews,* Homily 22, no. 3). For St. Irenaeus, the key word is "divided," missing in the Hebrew texts. He says: "He had not made an equitable division of that share to which his brother was entitled." Further, rather than accept the Lord God's conciliatory counsel to "be still," or repent, so that he might exercise his privilege as the first-born son, in anger and envy he murdered his brother.

God's acceptance of Abel's gift testifies to his righteousness, and there is evidence that he was regarded as righteous and faithful in the Hebrew tradition, as we see in two New Testament references (Matthew 23:35 and I John 3:12). His example of faithfulness has always been a witness, and the Apostle indicates that although he is dead, by his faith he still speaks to the Hebrews of his generation. God had said to Cain, "the voice of thy brother's blood crieth unto me from the ground" (Genesis 4:10).

> *v. 5. By faith Enoch was translated that he should not see death;*
> *and was not found, because God had translated him: for before*
> *his translation he had this testimony, that he pleased God.*

Enoch, a seventh-generation descendant of Adam through Seth's line, is the second example of one who had faith. Again, the story in Genesis makes no mention of his faith, but it does say that he "walked with God," and, as the Apostle will explain in the next verse, it is through faith that one comes or draws near to God. He was translated or removed from the earth so that he might not see death (Genesis 5:21-24). It is understood that his translation placed him in the immediate presence of God, in heaven.

St. John Chrysostom (*ibid.*, no. 5) has an instructive commentary on the first two examples of faith offered by the writer. It consists primarily in pointing out that if Abel's faith resulted in his death, mankind would not be much encouraged by his example. But God, who is a "rewarder" (see v. 6), overturns the law of death, and shows by the translation of Enoch that death is not the destiny of those who are pleasing to God. For St. John, it is very significant that Enoch's example immediately follows that of Abel: the fear that might be excited in men by the first one's fate is replaced by the zeal engendered by the second's reward.

Further, it may be noted that these first two examples of faith seem to point to the work of redemption to be carried out by the Son of God, "in the fullness of time." Here, even before the Law, Abel has perceived that it is by blood-offering that man will be justified. Enoch's deathless removal from the earth may be regarded as a pledge, however shadowy, that the righteous shall live and that death is not their end. On the contrary, by this translation, "immediately at the beginning, the human soul thereby receiving a hope of the destruction of death, and of the overthrow of the devil's tyranny . . ." (*ibid.;* see also Wisdom of Solomon 4:10 and Ecclesiasticus 44:16).

There is a fairly rich tradition concerning Enoch in Hebrew literature, including a Book of Enoch which is not considered canonical. In the Epistle of Jude, curiously, there is a quote from that book, one which attests to Enoch's being considered a prophet (v. 14).

> *v. 6. But without faith it is impossible to please him: for he that cometh to God must believe that he is, and that he is a rewarder of them that diligently seek him.*

This assertion is a kind of parenthesis or pause to allow the Apostle the opportunity to elaborate on something suggested to him by the mention of Enoch's faith. It matters little that the word "faith" does not occur in the Genesis record of Him; the goal of his faith was already attained in that "he walked with God," which state the Apostle describes in terms of his pleasing God.

The essential components of faith are given: first of all, one must believe that "He is," as it is stated in *The Shepherd of Hermas* (Book II, Commandment I): "First of all, believe that there is one God who created and finished all things, and made all things out of nothing." To say that one must also believe that God is a rewarder is to say that there is a response on His part to those who believe in His existence, but this is qualified: to believe that He is and to stop there is not acceptable, for if one truly believes that God is, he must actively seek Him, to know Him and to have a relation with Him. The Psalmist says, "Blessed are they that keep His testimonies, and that seek Him with the whole heart" (118/119:2). The Prophet Amos says, "For thus saith the Lord unto the house of Israel, Seek ye me, and ye shall live" (5:4). And our Lord Jesus Christ Himself says, "Seek and ye shall find" (Matthew 7:7).

Concerning this last instruction from the Lord, St. John Chrysostom has a message to people of all times, especially our own:

> For things sought after need much care, especially in regard to God. For many are the hindrances, many the things that darken, many that impede our perception. For as the sun is manifest, and set forth publicly before all, and we have no need to seek it; but if on the other

hand we bury ourselves and turn everything upside down, we need much labor to look at the sun; so truly here also, if we bury ourselves in the depth of evil desires, in the darkness of passions and of the affairs of this life, with difficulty do we look up, with difficulty do we raise our heads, with difficulty do we see clearly. (*ibid.*, no. 7)

v. 7. By faith Noah, being warned of God of things not seen as yet, moved with fear, prepared an ark to the saving of his house; by the which he condemned the world, and became heir of the righteousness which is by faith.

Returning now to his presentation of examples of faith among the Hebrews' forefathers, the Apostle brings forward that of Noah, who was warned by God of the impending judgment of the world and its destruction. There were no physical signs of the disaster; all was well, as Jesus pointed out on speaking to His disciples of His second coming: ". . . in the days of Noah . . . they did eat, they drank, they married wives, they were given in marriage . . . and the flood came, and destroyed them all" (Luke 17:26-27). Although he may have been laughed at for what he was doing, he placed his faith in God, "moved with fear" ("godly fear" or "piety," *evlabētheis* in Greek), built the ark and saved his family (see Genesis 6-9 LXX).

The lesson the Apostle expects his readers to derive from Noah's story is of enormous importance for today's Christian, for he too must condemn the faithless world (see Galatians 5:24 and 6:14). In this last, St. Paul declares that it is because of his faith in Jesus Christ that the world is crucified to him and he to the world, with its seeming well-being and self-satisfaction. By his faith, Noah became an heir of righteousness, that is, he inherited that relationship to God which is right according to God's plan for man, and which can be obtained only by faith.

St. Cyril of Jerusalem (*Catechetical Lecture XVII*, no. 10) calls our attention to the symbolism of the story of Noah. He calls the Lord Jesus Christ "the true Noah, the Author of the second birth," making Noah a type of Christ. The dove that went forth from the ark, being the bearer of the news of salvation, is thus a figure of the dove in whose form the Holy Spirit descended upon Christ at the beginning of His work of redemption and rescue. The Church is represented by the ark, in safety from the condemnation, the judgment of this world, and in it the irreconcilable are reconciled; thus, the animals that are normally enemies lived in harmony there. Salvation came to those in the ark through the faith of Noah, by a water-death of wickedness, and this is a figure of baptism, as St. Peter says (I Peter 3:20-21), and by the wood of the ark, a symbol of the wood of the cross. (See also St. Justin Martyr, *Dialogue with Trypho,* chap. cxxxviii.)

v. 8. By faith Abraham, when he was called to go out into a place which he should after receive for an inheritance, obeyed; and he went out, not knowing whither he went.

Abraham, the father of the Hebrew people, was the one to whom the Promise was originally given, the promise that was ultimately fulfilled in Christ. He is the greatest of all the examples of those who had faith in the history of God's people, "the father of faith" (St. Gregory of Nyssa, *Answer to Eunomius' Second Book;* see also Romans 4). His first act of faith was his obedience. When the Lord commanded him to get out of his country and go to the land that He would show him, he left not knowing where he was going (see Genesis 12:1-4).

v. 9. By faith he sojourned in the land of promise, as in a strange country, dwelling in tabernacles with Isaac and Jacob, the heirs with him of the same promise:

The second evidence of Abraham's faith is his endurance and patience. Although the Lord Himself had promised him the land, he lived there "as in a strange country." His was a nomadic life, living in tents ("tabernacles"), as if his stay were intended to be temporary, having no city of his own. His immediate descendants, Isaac and

Jacob, were also heirs of the same promise, for the Lord gave it to them (Genesis 26:3, 28:13), and they also continued to live as aliens in the land.

v. 10. For he looked for a city which hath foundations, whose builder and maker is God.

The Apostle now gives us the key to Abraham's understanding of the deeper nature of the Promise. There was something much greater in God's plan for the Hebrew people than a whimsical preference for them to occupy some new, perhaps more favorable, land, because He liked them more than those who already inhabited it. His was a

> journey worthy of a prophet eager for the knowledge of God. For no local migration seems to me to satisfy the idea of the blessings which it is signified that he found. For going out from himself and from his country, by which I understand his earthly and carnal mind, and raising his thoughts as far as possible above the common boundaries of nature, and forsaking his soul's kinship with the senses,—so that untroubled by any of the objects of sense his eyes might be open to the things which are invisible, there being neither sight nor sound to distract the mind in its work,—"walking," as saith the Apostle, "by faith, not by sight," he was raised so high by the sublimity of his knowledge that he came to be regarded as the acme of human perfection, knowing as much of God as it was possible for finite human capacity at its full stretch to attain. (St. Gregory of Nyssa, *ibid.* [NPNF 2nd series, vol. 5, p. 259])

The fact that God identifies Himself to Moses as "the God of Abraham, and the God of Isaac, and the God of Jacob" (Exodus 3:6) testifies to His acceptance of their vision of Him.

Neither Abraham, nor his son Isaac, nor his grandson Jacob, seem to have been much concerned about the earthly or material benefits which the land of promise might have brought them. The city which they sought was one which had particular foundations (in Greek *tous themelious,* "the foundations"), which is explained as the city of which God is both the designer and maker. No Canaanite city had these foundations. That city, as subsequent passages of the Epistle will make clear, is the heavenly city, the heavenly Jerusalem.

The Christian, then, must understand that he too is a sojourner in a strange country, that there is no permanent ("continuing," *menousan* in Greek) city for him here on earth, and that his citizenship, because of his faith in Christ's promises, is the eternal city, which is the kingdom of God (see 13:14).

v. 11. Through faith also Sara herself received strength to conceive seed, and was delivered of a child when she was past age, because she judged him faithful who had promised.

In Genesis (18:10-15), when God promised Abraham that his wife, Sara, in spite of her age and her barrenness, would have a son, it is recorded that she laughed (v. 12). So, many commentators have had some problem in reconciling our author's attributing faith to her, in view of her first reaction to the promise. St. John Chrysostom, on the other hand, does not find any difficulty with Sara's being another example of faith. For him, her mood changed from disbelief to faith, when it was recalled that nothing is "too hard" for the Lord (vv. 14-15). Her denial, "I laughed not," is rather a retraction than a lie. "Nay, while her laughter indeed was from unbelief, her fear was from Faith, for to say, 'I laughed not,' (Genesis 18:15) arose from Faith. From this, then, it appears that when unbelief had been cleared out, Faith came in its place" (*op. cit.*, Homily 23, no. 5).

She received strength "for the conception of seed," to retain it so as to have a child. The expression, "and she was delivered of a child," is omitted in some Greek texts, but since such was the case, it does not alter the sense of the whole passage.

Her faith in God's promise, even though it was the result of later reflection, was more consistent with her spiritual state and earns her a place in the list of Old Testament faithful. She is cited among those barren women, whose miraculous birth-giving was due to God's intervention, and whose offspring played a prominent role in the history of salvation; among them are Elizabeth and Anne (St. Cyril of Jerusalem, *Catechetical Lecture XII,* nos. 27-31; see also St. Nicholas Velimirovic, *The Prologue from Ochrid,* Part III, Sept. 9).

> *v. 12. Therefore sprang there even of one, and him as good as dead, so many as the stars of the sky in multitude, and as the sand which is by the sea shore innumerable.*

It was both Abraham and Sara who were old and, except for God's intervention, incapable of having a child: what is said of one of them can be applied to both. Now it is the husband that is called "as good as dead," (*nenekrōmenou* in Greek, "having become dead or impotent") insofar as his ability to beget is concerned. And from them as from one person came descendants as numerous "as the stars of the sky" (Genesis 15:5) or as countless as "the grains of sand by the sea shore" (Genesis 22:17). Those descendants are not only the whole Hebrew race, but all those who become Israelites through faith in Christ. The Lord's admonition, "And think not to say within yourselves, We have Abraham to our father: for I say unto you, that God is able of these stones to raise up children unto Abraham" (Matthew 3:9), tells the Hebrews that their unfaithfulness and unrighteousness will result in their being replaced as children of Abraham. Then we have St. Paul's declaration: "Know ye therefore that they which are of faith, the same are the children of Abraham" (Galatians 3:7).

> *v. 13. These all died in faith, not having received the promises, but having seen them afar off, and were persuaded of them, and embraced them, and confessed that they were strangers and pilgrims on the earth.*

The heirs of the promises (the patriarchs) did not see their fulfillment, yet they died with their faith unshaken. These men of faith were convinced that these promises would be fulfilled, even if not in their own lifetime. They were persuaded (in Greek, *peisthentes*) of them and they embraced them (*aspasamenoi,* as in a greeting). The Apostle obviously means here to contrast the attitude of those who had seen the fulfillment of the promises in Christ and yet were tempted to go back to a state of expectation with that of the Old Testament men of faith. St. Gregory of Nyssa chides Christians of his own generation in similar terms:

> If they, then, bear the delay who by faith only and by hope saw the good things "afar off" and "embraced them," as the apostle bears witness, placing their certainty of the enjoyment of the things for which they hoped in the fact that they "judged Him faithful Who has promised," what ought most of us to do, who have not, it may be, a hold upon that better hope from the character of our lives? (*On the Making of Man,* chap. xxii, no. 7)

Their confession (a word used for declarations of basic beliefs, *homologēsantes*) that they were strangers (*xenoi,* or foreigners) and pilgrims (*parepidēmoi,* or sojourners) shows that they held as an article of faith that their homeland was not anywhere on the earth. Speaking of Christians, it was said, "They dwell in their own countries, but simply as sojourners. As citizens, they share in all things with others, and yet endure all things as if foreigners. Every foreign land is to them as their native country, and every land of their birth as a land of strangers" (*Epistle to Diognetus,* chap. v). Among those who confessed that they were strangers and sojourners in the land was David (Psalm 38/39:12).

v. 14. For they that say such things declare plainly that they seek a country.

Those who call themselves foreigners and pilgrims make it clear that they are in search of their true fatherland. This stance, attributed by the Apostle to the patriarchs, would have also been proper to the Christians to whom he addresses the Epistle. It is also true that in our times, Christians sometimes lose this perspective of their continued existence on the earth, as it was obviously so in St. Basil's day:

"Thus, we all look to the East at our prayers, but few of us know that we are seeking our own old country, Paradise, which God planted in Eden in the East" (*On the Holy Spirit*, chap. xxvii, no. 66).

> *v. 15. And truly, if they had been mindful of that country from whence they came out, they might have had opportunity to have returned.*

The Apostle immediately adds this explanation, so as to dispel any notion that they might have been homesick, filled with nostalgia for the country from which Abraham came originally. In spite of all uncertainties, their faith remained firm. Could the Apostle have had in mind those Hebrews who were tempted to stay in the lands of their captivity, Egypt and Babylonia—or once having left, to return—where they could be more certain of food and shelter, even if it was at the cost of their freedom? The faithful of old could have found a way to return too, if they had not had the vision of that better thing which God had prepared for them.

> *v. 16. But now, they desire a better country, that is, an heavenly: wherefore God is not ashamed to be called their God: for he hath prepared for them a city.*

The fatherland (rather than "country," as used in v. 14, and implied in both 15 and 16, *patris* in Greek) they seek, then, is better than any thing this world can offer, because it is the dwelling place of God Himself. "Now" is not used to introduce a contrast to some former state of mind; here it is something like "therefore" or "this being the case." From this fact, that heaven as their true fatherland is their destination, God is not ashamed to be called their God, to be identified with their names, because their whole life revolved around the destiny He had prepared for them. He would be known as the God of Abraham, of Isaac and of Jacob (see v. 10; Exodus 3:6,15). This assertion of God is quoted by our Lord Himself, and to this He adds, "God is not the God of the dead, but of the living" (Matthew 22:32), from which we understand that these three are alive.

St. John Chrysostom exhorts his hearers: "Let us even now become strangers; that God may 'not be ashamed of us to be called our God.' For it is a shame to Him, when He is called the God of the wicked, and He is also ashamed of them; as He is glorified when He is called the God of the good and the kind . . ." (*op. cit.*, Homily 24, no. 7).

Heaven is called "a city" because it will be life in perfect community, of which all earthly cities are poor imitations. The word "city" for heaven, the dwelling place of God and of the saints, occurs several times in this Epistle (11:10; 12:22; 13:14) and in the Revelation (20:9; 21:14,18,23). Jerusalem was, so to speak, the icon of the heavenly city, and St. John testifies to this in his vision: "And I John saw the holy city, new Jerusalem, coming down from God out of heaven, prepared as a bride adorned for her husband" (21:2).

vv. 17-18. By faith Abraham, when he was tried, offered up Isaac: and he that had received the promises offered up his only-begotten son, of whom it was said, That in Isaac shall thy seed be called.

Although the Apostle has digressed briefly, he now returns to his main theme, Abraham's faith, and demonstrates that there is no example of a faith greater than his. He had been put to the test before, and now we are told of his greatest test. God had already told Abraham that it would be through his son Isaac that "his seed would be called," (Genesis 21:12) that is, descendants as numerous as the stars of heaven (Genesis 15:5). Now He tells him to offer that same son in sacrifice (Genesis 22:2). In spite of the evident contradiction, Abraham's faith remained unshaken (see St. Cyril of Alexandria, *Commentary on the Gospel of St. Luke,* Homily 58).

In the very act of sacrificing, Abraham's raised hand was stayed by divine intervention (Genesis 22:11-12), yet, he had already determined to do what he had been commanded to do. In a sense, then, he had already made the sacrifice, as the first verb translated "offered up" (Greek *prosenēnochen,* perfect of *prospherō*) indicates: "in the exercise of obedience, he offered him as a sacrifice to God" (*First Epistle of Clement,* chap. x).

Isaac here is called the "only-begotten" son of the one "that had received the promises." Actually, he had another son, Ishmael, born of Sara's maid Hagar (Genesis 16:15), but it was to be the son of Sara, Abraham's wife, that would be counted as the only-begotten, or "beloved son" (*ton huion sou ton agapēton* Genesis 22:2 LXX). God Himself confirmed Sara's insistence that Ishmael would not be the one through whom Abraham's seed would be called (Genesis 21:10-12). See also St. Paul's treatment of this matter of the two sons of Abraham in Galatians (4:22-31).

The classic Orthodox interpretation of this whole episode is given by St. Athanasius:

> And, in offering his son, he worshipped the Son of God. And, being restrained from sacrificing Isaac, he saw the Messiah in the ram [lamb], which was offered up instead as a sacrifice to God. The patriarch was tried, through Isaac, not however that he was sacrificed, but He who was pointed out in Isaiah; "He shall be led as a lamb to the slaughter, and as a sheep before his shearer he shall be speechless" [Isaiah 53:7 LXX].... Thus God accepted the will of the offerer, but prevented that which was offered from being sacrificed. For the death of Isaac did not procure freedom to the world, but that of our Savior alone, by whose stripes we all are healed. (*Paschal Letter VI,* no. 8)

v. 19. Accounting that God was able to raise him up, even from the dead; from whence also he received him in a figure.

Abraham's faith is such that even in face of a seeming change in God's plan for him he reasons (*logisamenos* in Greek) that God will raise his son from the dead so that the promise will be faithfully carried out. So, when the Lord stopped the sacrifice and provided a lamb to be slain in Isaac's place, in a figure (in Greek, *en parabolē*), he received him, as it were, back from the dead. Thus, we have a symbol of the resurrection from the dead.

St. Cyril of Alexandria (*ibid.*) concludes that Abraham was taught many things by the event. In particular, he learned

> that God is able to raise again, even from the dead. And, moreover, he learned what is more important, and more worthy of account, I mean the mystery of Christ; that for the salvation and life of the world God the Father was about to yield His own Son to the sacrifice: even Him, Who by nature was beloved, that is, Christ. And the blessed Paul confirms this, saying of Him: "He that spared not His own Son, but delivered Him up for us all" [Romans 8:32].

v. 20. By faith Isaac blessed Jacob and Esau concerning things to come.

In verse 9 of this chapter, we find that Isaac and Jacob were "heirs with Abraham" of the same promise. They too dwelt in the promised land as strangers and pilgrims. The blessing that Isaac gave his twin sons, Jacob and Esau, according to the Apostle, concerned things to come, that is, things neither he nor they would live to see. He, like his father Abraham never lost his faith in God's fulfilling His promise, and in blessing his sons as he neared death, he gives evidence that his faith was very much alive.

The rather complex story of the conflict between the two brothers, which began in their mother's womb (Genesis 25:22), and which culminated in the reversal of the law of primogeniture (Genesis 25:33), is finally revealed to be the working of God's providence for the preservation of the hope for the fulfillment of the promise. In spite of the "subtilty" (*dolos* in Genesis 27:35 LXX, "deceit" or "treachery") whereby Jacob acquired Esau's birthright, Jacob is obviously God's own choice to take his place in the line of patriarchs who held to the promise. Esau turned out to be a wicked man: his willingness to sell his birthright for "a mess of potage," his alliance through marriage with the enemies of God, and his hatred of Jacob. Jacob, on the other hand, married according to his father's charge (Genesis 28:1), and received a second blessing from Isaac, which included "the blessing of Abraham" (28:4). God's will for Jacob was manifested in his dream of the ladder (vv. 11-22), and confirmed by appearances of God's angels to him (31:11, 32:1).

We find a meditation on the character of the two brothers in the troparia of the Fourth Ode of the Canon for Compline on Tuesday of the First Week of the Great Fast.

v. 21. By faith Jacob, when he was a dying, blessed both the sons of Joseph; and worshipped, leaning upon the top of his staff.

The Apostle continues to show that the righteous men of the Old Testament had faith in "the things to come," the very things that in his time had come to pass. The Lord Jesus Christ told his disciples that many prophets and righteous men "have desired to see those things which ye see, and have not seen them . . . " (Matthew 13:7), and He refers to the fulfillment of God's promises in Himself. Jacob, who had received the blessing of faith from his father, passes it on., and although eventually he blesses all his sons, the Apostle has chosen this earlier blessing of Joseph's sons, his grandsons Manasseh and Ephraim, because of the significant act of "leaning upon the top of his staff" (Genesis 48:14-16 and 49). The unusual thing in this blessing is that Jacob insisted on blessing the younger Ephraim first, even "guiding his hands crosswise" (Genesis 48:14). Jacob "saw in spirit the type of people to arise afterwards" (*Epistle of Barnabas,* chap. xiii). The whole incident suggests that Jacob foresaw by faith the means of the fulfillment of God's promise, the cross, many generations later.

After having extracted from Joseph the promise to take him out of Egypt and to bury him with his fathers, Jacob, the Scripture says, "worshipped, leaning upon his staff" (Genesis 47:31). Both the crosswise blessing and the top of his staff are taken to symbolize the cross, upon which redemption was accomplished. "Jacob prefigured thy cross in days of old, O Christ, when he venerated the top of Joseph's staff, in which he foreshadowed the dread sceptre of thy kingdom; and now we venerate thy cross in faith for ever" (Matins for the Sunday of the Cross, Canon, Ode 8; see also Matins for Monday of the Fourth Week of the Great Fast, Canon, Ode 9).

v. 22. By faith Joseph, when he died, made mention of the departing of the children of Israel; and gave commandment concerning his bones.

In St. Stephen's statement before the council, he cites Joseph: "And the patriarchs, moved with envy, sold Joseph into Egypt: but God was with him, and delivered him out of all his afflictions" (Acts 7:9-10). Commenting on this verse, St. John Chrysostom declares him to be a "type of Christ. Though they had no fault to find with him, and though he came on purpose to bring them their food, they thus ill-treated him. Still here again the promise, though it is a long while first, receives its fulfillment" (*On the Acts of the Apostles,* Homily 16).

Joseph also had faith in God's promise, and here specifically that which concerned the return of the children of Israel to the promised land and their inheriting it (Genesis 12:7, etc.), after 400 years of servitude in a strange land (Genesis 15:13-14). On his death bed, he mentioned the "exodus" and gave instructions concerning his own remains (Genesis 50:25). Moses, in fact, did take Joseph's bones with him in his wanderings (Exodus 13:19). St. John Chrysostom (*On Hebrews,* Homily 26, no. 2) explains the significance of these instructions: "He then not only believed himself, but led on the rest also to Faith: that having the Exodus always in mind . . . they might look for their [own] return to Canaan."

v. 23. By faith Moses, when he was born, was hid three months of his parents, because they saw he was a proper child; and they were not afraid of the king's commandment.

Moses is the next model of faith in the list, standing next to Abraham in greatness, but the Apostle devotes more lines to his praises than to Abraham, in the same spirit of the defence of St.

Stephen before the council (Acts 7). The next few verses will describe the things accomplished in him by faith; the first instance has rather to do with the faith of his parents, however. He really owed his earthly existence to their faith, or better, to God who inspired them to do so, since they, in defiance of Pharaoh's order (Exodus 1:22-2:3), hid the child to keep him from being killed. They were not afraid of the tyrant's command, because they obeyed a higher law. They saw in their son one who would be "exceeding fair" (in Stephen's words) in the sight of God. Moses prefigured Christ in many signs and symbolic acts: here he escapes a tyrant's order of mass murder of children, just as the Lord was spared being a victim of the command of another tyrant, Herod. (For a completely symbolic interpretation of all the events of Moses' life, see St. Gregory of Nyssa's *Life of Moses,* especially Book II, "Contemplation of the Life of Moses"; see also the Great Canon, Tuesday of First Week of the Great Fast, first troparion.)

> *v. 24. By faith Moses, when he was come to years, refused to be called the son of Pharaoh's daughter;*

Moses had been rescued from the water by Pharaoh's daughter, and after having been nursed by his own mother, he was brought back to the princess and became her son: "she called his name Moses, saying, I took him out of the water" (Exodus 2:1-10; the Egyptian word for water was *mou*). When he was grown he consciously rejected what lay within his power: to forget his own people and to be an Egyptian (Exodus 2:11-15; Acts 7:22-23). The Exodus account of Moses' action is stated simply: "Moses having grown, went out to his brethren the sons of Israel, and having noticed their distress..." But St. Stephen, having more information of the Hebrew tradition concerning Moses, reminds the council that he "was learned in all the wisdom of the Egyptians, and was mighty in words and deeds. And when he was full forty years old, it came into his heart to visit his brethren the children of Israel." It can be said that he realized or had faith that God had chosen the Hebrew people for a special calling, even though their lot at that time did not make it too apparent. His refusal of the princess as his mother represents something much broader: the rejection of the Egyptians, all their wealth and wisdom, everything they stood for. (See St. Gregory of Nyssa, *ibid.;* St. Ambrose of Milan, *Duties of the Clergy,* Book I, chap. xxvi, no. 123.)

> *v. 25. Choosing rather to suffer affliction with the people of God, than to enjoy the pleasures of sin for a season;*

He saw the Hebrews' great suffering at the hands of their cruel overlords, but he still preferred to throw in his lot with them, because he had faith that God would fulfill His promise to them.

> He "chose" to suffer for others, and voluntarily threw himself into so many dangers, when it was in his power both to live religiously, and to enjoy good things.... If then he accounted it "sin" not to be ready to "suffer affliction with" the rest, it follows that the suffering affliction must be a great good, since he threw himself into it from the royal palace. (St. John Chrysostom, *ibid.*, no. 4)

To have remained with the Egyptians would have meant participation in their idolatry, an apostasy of which the Hebrews too would be guilty later. Moses teaches by his example, when he killed the Egyptian who was beating a Hebrew, to take "our stand with virtue as with a kinsman and kill virtue's adversary. The victory of true religion is the death and destruction of idolatry" (St. Gregory of Nyssa, *ibid*, Book II, no. 14). His example is brought to present-day Christians in this sense: "O miserable soul, thou hast not struck and killed the Egyptian mind, as did Moses the great. Tell me, then, how wilt thou go to dwell through repentance in the wilderness empty of passions?" (Great Canon, Tuesday, First Week of the Great Fast, third troparion). Thus, this first act on leaving the Egyptians is seen as a figure of his calling.

Whatever advantages there may have been in remaining with the Egyptians, Moses had understood that their enjoyment was temporal ("for a season," *proskairon* in Greek) and not eternal. By faith, then, he had begun to identify himself with those who would be redeemed by the Redeemer, and whose relation to the world St. Paul describes in these terms: "We look not at the things which are seen, but at the things which are not seen: for the things which are seen are temporal [the word used in our present verse]; but the things which are not seen are eternal" (II Corinthians 4:18).

v. 26. Esteeming the reproach of Christ greater riches than the treasures of Egypt: for he had respect unto the recompense of the reward.

The spiritual riches of God's Christ—in a sense, the whole chosen people was the "anointed" or the Christ—were preferred by Moses, even if the wealth of Egypt was great and to reject it took an enormous courage of conviction. Furthermore, the reproach or hard lot of Israel was a figure of the sufferings of Jesus Christ: Israel, the anointed race, was a type of the Savior. Because of his God-given vision, it can be said that Moses, the God-appointed leader of the race, beheld Christ Himself (see St. Cyril of Jerusalem, *Catechetical Lecture X,* no. 7).

Moses looked eagerly (*apeblepen,* in Greek) toward the kind of recompense that results from faith in God, but this reward was in the future for both him and his people, but his faith in it determined his choice ("recompense of the reward" translates a single Greek word *misthapodosian,* "payment of wages").

v. 27. By faith he forsook Egypt, not fearing the wrath of the king: for he endured, as seeing him who is invisible.

Moses left Egypt twice, and the first time it was out of fear of the king's wrath (Exodus 2:14-15). Although he was fearless in his initial rejection of Egypt (v. 24), he did fear for his life when he fled and hid himself at Midian; this was perhaps because he already perceived that he had a special calling and needed to preserve his life for that.

What is more, he would not tempt God by throwing himself into dangers prematurely (see St. John Chrysostom, *ibid.*, no. 5).

Even in his long absence from Egypt after his first departure, some forty years, he kept the vision of his destiny before him and remained full of faith, resolved to return when God told him to do so. It was as if he had already seen God; yet this great miracle, which was to earn him the title of God-seer, was to take place later.

This example of Moses' faith is a lesson to us Christians today: "If then we too always see God with our mind, if we always think in remembrance of Him, all things will appear endurable to us, all things tolerable; we shall bear them all easily, we shall be above them all" (St. John Chrysostom, *ibid.*, no. 6).

v. 28. Through faith he kept the passover, and the sprinkling of blood, lest he that destroyed the firstborn should touch them.

The last of the ten plagues which God brought upon Egypt for Pharaoh's refusal to let His people go was to be the death of all male first born (Exodus 12:2). In accordance with the Lord's directions, only in those houses (that is, of the Israelites) of which the door posts were sprinkled with the blood of the sacrificed lamb, were the children to be spared the destruction of the angel of death. Moses, in faith, followed God's command, and thus, the passover as a type of the saving sacrifice of Christ was observed for the first time.

> "If then the blood of a lamb preserved the Jews unhurt in the midst of the Egyptians, and under so great a destruction, much more will the blood of Christ save us, who have had it sprinkled not on door-posts but in our souls. For even now also the Destroyer is going about in the depth of the night: but let us be armed with that Sacrifice. (He calls the "sprinkling" anointing [*proschysin*].) For God has brought us out from Egypt, from darkness, from idolatry. (St. John Chrysostom, *op. cit.,* Homily 27, no. 1)

Similarly, "Salvation was assured to them [the Hebrews] by 'the shedding of the blood' " (St. Gregory of Nyssa, *op. cit.,* Book I, no. 28).

v. 29. By faith they passed through the Red Sea as by dry land: which the Egyptians assaying to do were drowned.

It was by faith that Moses stretched forth his hand causing the waters of the Red Sea to part so that the Israelites might pass through the sea as on dry land and escape the pursuing Egyptians. It was his closing the sea again by faith that caused the enemies' destruction when, as they tried to do the same, they were drowned in the waters. The Israelites who followed Moses also had faith in God's working through His servant (see Exodus 14:21-31).

For St. John Chrysostom (*ibid.*, no. 2), what happened at the Red Sea was another example of the change in the actions of nature and other things, such as animals, to participate in effecting God's redeeming purpose. "That which was spread under the one as land, overwhelmed the others as sea. In the former case it forgot its nature: in the latter it even armed itself against them [the Egyptians]." Not only did this happen in the case of Israel's crossing the Red Sea, but also with Daniel in the lions' den and the three holy Children in the furnace of fire (see Daniel 6 and 3; Wisdom 19:18-21).

v. 30. By faith the walls of Jericho fell down, after they were compassed about seven days.

It was Joshua, the son of Nun, who in faith led the siege of Jericho: the Israelites, bearing the ark of the covenant, marched around the city once a day for six days, their priests going ahead blowing their trumpets; and, as the Lord promised, at the great blast of the ram's horn on the seventh day, the walls collapsed (Joshua 6).

Joshua, whose name in Hebrew and Greek is "Jesus" (*Iēsous;* see Acts 7:45 and Hebrews 4:8), meaning "God saves," was Moses' servant and minister, being with him when God spoke with him (Exodus 3:11). Finally, he became Moses' successor; at God's command Moses ordained him, laying his hand upon him (Numbers 27:18; Deuteronomy 34:9). He was one of the twelve spies sent by Moses to "spy out" the land of Canaan, and for this special task, Moses renamed him Jehoshua or Jeshua, his original name having been Oshea (Numbers 13:8, 16). Because of God's special calling, his practically blameless life, and his name, he is one of the principal Old Testament types of Christ: "Joshua . . . who subdued five kings [Joshua 10] and brought the Gibeonites into subjection [*ibid.*], that he might be the figure of a Man of his own name Who was to come . . ." (St. Ambrose, *On the Christian Faith*, Book V, no. 12). God Himself confirmed his special vocation in a vision (Joshua 5:13), and this confirmed his faith: he recognized the Leader of the heavenly host, and "after he believed, he forthwith conquered, being found worthy to triumph in the battle of faith" (*ibid.*, no. 126).

> *v. 31. By faith the harlot Rahab perished not with them that believed not, when she had received the spies with peace.*

The only woman other than Abraham's wife (see v. 11) mentioned in this review of Old Testament faithful is the harlot Rahab (Joshua 2). Her faith consisted of her acceptance of the God of the Israelites as the true God of heaven and earth (2:11), and to Him she became obedient. Her work by which, according to St. James (2:25), she was justified rather than by faith, was her concealing of the Israelite spies. For this she and her household were spared when the city was overrun and its inhabitants killed. Her home was marked by a scarlet rope or cord (in Greek, *spartion*) in a window of her house. She did not die with them "that believed not" (*apeithēsasin* in Greek indicates willful disbelief or "not being persuaded"), the people of Jericho who resisted God's will.

St. Ambrose (*ibid.*, no. 127) finds a mystical significance in the scarlet cord because of the color:

> [she] uplifted a sign of her faith and the banner of the Lord's Passion; so that the likeness of the mystic blood, which should redeem the world, might be in memory. So, outside, the name of Joshua was a sign of victory to those who fought; and inside, the likeness of the Lord's passion was a sign of salvation to those in danger. Where-

fore, because Rahab understood the heavenly mystery, the Lord says in the Psalm [86/87:4]: "I will be mindful of Rahab and Babylon that know me" [that is, of her and those of the city who repented and came to faith].

This same interpretation is found in the *First Epistle of Clement*, chap. xii.

v. 32. And what shall I more say? for the time would fail me to tell of Gideon, and of Barak, and of Samson, and of Jephthah; of David also, and Samuel, and of the prophets:

Although the Apostle has already mentioned a number of the great men of faith from the time of Adam to Joshua, there obviously remain many more if his list is to be complete. Since time and space do not permit him to summarize the accomplishments through faith of all the righteous men of the past, he mentions six by name and makes a general reference to "the prophets." According to St. John Chrysostom (*ibid.*, no. 4), the change of pace is well timed and the choice judiciously made. St. Athanasius (*Encyclical to the Bishops of Egypt and Libya*, no. 21), exhorting the hierarchs to contend against the Arians, cites this verse and its list of saints as evidence that it is both by having faith and by being loyal to the faith that they were justified. The following order is not chronological, but the recounting of their exploits in the next verse is.

For Gideon's story we may consult Judges 7 and 8; for Barak's, Judges 4; for Samuel's, Judges 13-16; for Jephthah's, Judges 11, etc. St. John Chrysostom admits that "some find fault with Paul because he puts Barak, and Samson, and Jephthah in these places," but he insists on the appropriateness of their inclusion: "After having introduced the harlot, shall he not introduce these? For do not tell me of the rest of their life, but only whether they did not believe and shine in Faith" (*ibid.*). The list goes on to name David, the ideal king, and example of humility and repentance, the forefather of Christ in the flesh, and himself a type of Christ; and Samuel, the fifteenth and last of the judges of Israel, accepted as prophet, priest and judge by the people, especially chosen by God, is known as the head of the prophets (St. Nicholas Velimirovic, *The Prologue from Ochrid,* Vol. 3, Aug. 20; see also Acts 3:24).

v. 33. Who through faith subdued kingdoms, wrought righteousness, obtained promises, stopped the mouths of lions,

With the above listing of men of faith in mind, the Apostle specifies some of their achievements. David conquered the Philistines and others (II Kings/II Samuel 8:1-8); Gideon, the Midianites (Judges 7); and Jephthah, the Ammonites (Judqes 11:32-33). "And Samuel judged Israel all the days of his life" (I Kings/I Samuel 7:15), that is, he exhorted the people to repentance and governed the nation with equity and justice. They did obtain the promises, God's promise of the land of Canaan (Joshua 21:43). Thus, those who had faith in the fulfillment of the promise of the land, but who did not see it in their lifetime, are represented by those who were under Joshua's command. Both David (I Kings/I Samuel 17:37) and Daniel (6:22), by their faith, were delivered from "the mouth of lions."

St. Ambrose (*Duties of the Clergy,* Book I, chap. xxxv, nos. 175-178), in his exhortation to pastors to fortitude, justice and prudence, refers specifically to the accomplishments of the men of faith given in this verse.

v. 34. Quenched the violence of fire, escaped the edge of the sword, out of weakness were made strong, waxed valiant in fight, turned to flight the armies of the aliens.

As in the preceding verse, no names are mentioned in connection with the exploits to which it refers, but they are easily identified. Daniel and the three holy Children, Hananiah, Mishael and Azariah (Shadrach, Mesach and Abednego, as they were renamed by the prince of Nebuchadnezzar's eunuchs), immediately come to mind: Daniel, for the reason mentioned above, and the three youths, because, through their faith, they came out of fiery furnace unharmed (Daniel 1:3,6,7; 3:20,27). According to St. Ambrose (*Letter LXIII*, no. 67), along with their unwavering faith in the God of Israel, their ascetic life and purity, which they maintained even while living in the royal palace, prepared them for their trial. St. John Chrysostom (*ibid.*) thinks the "escaped the edge of the sword" also refers to the same youths. It would also have been appropriate to include Elijah (III/I Kings 19:3) and Elisha (IV/II Kings 6:16) among them.

There is no reason to suppose that the Apostle has in mind only those patriarchs, prophets and kings he has already named. The Scriptures furnish many examples of the last three manifestations of the working of faith given in this verse. Many received strength even at moments of great weakness: Judith (Judith 13:7), Samson (Judges 16:28-30), and Hezekiah (Isaiah 38:1-6), to mention only three. David is perhaps the greatest example of one who "waxed valiant" or became strong in war (I Kings/I Samuel 17). The last phrase no doubt refers to all who were able, because of their faith, to put the enemies of the people of God to flight. One might mention Jonathan (I Kings/I Samuel 14:13), and the Israelites who out of weakness in the Babylonian Captivity became strong and defended themselves.

v. 35. Women received their dead raised to life again: and others were tortured, not accepting deliverance; that they might obtain a better resurrection:

It was by faith that Elijah raised the son of the widow from Sarepta from the dead (III/I Kings 17:22) and that Elisha accomplished the same in the case of the Shunammite woman's son (IV/II Kings 4:34). Two examples of torture which may have been in the Apostle's mind are recorded in II Macabees, Eleazar's (6:19) and the seven brothers with their mother (7:1-23). In view of the next statement, "not accepting deliverance; that they might obtain a better resurrection," it seems rather certain that it was indeed the seven brothers that the Apostle was recalling. The second brother, having been offered his freedom if he would deny his religion, told his torturers: "Thou like a fury takest us out of this present life, but the King of the world shall raise us up, who have died for His laws, unto everlasting life" (II Macabees 7:9). For St. John Chrysostom (*ibid.*, no. 5), it is to such heroes of the New Covenant as John the Baptist and James that the Apostle alludes: "It was in their power to abstain from reproving sinners, and yet they chose to die; even they who had raised others chose to die themselves, 'that they might obtain a better resurrection.'"

vv. 36-37. And others had trial of cruel mockings and scourgings, yea, moreover of bonds and imprisonment: they were stoned, they were sawn asunder, were tempted, were slain with the sword: they wandered about in sheepskins and goatskins; being destitute, afflicted, tormented;

The persecution of the Hebrews described in First and Second Macabees includes the types of suffering mentioned here (I Macabees 7:34, 9:26; II Macabees 7:1, etc.); others are to be found elsewhere in the Old Testament (III/I Kings 22:24; Jeremiah 20:2; Genesis 39:20). Chains and imprisonment were the fate of others, such as Jeremiah (Jeremiah 37:15; 38:13).

Stoning was a common method of execution in Israel. Zechariah the Prophet (II Chronicles 24:21; see also Matthew 23:37) was thus put to death. Tradition has it that Isaiah suffered the fate of being sawn in two with a wooden saw (St. Cyril of Jerusalem, *Catechetical Lecture II*, no. 14). They were tempted, in that release or freedom was offered to some for denying their faith in God, as we found in verse 35.

Some were banished and had to seek refuge away from their people, being reduced to extreme poverty and privation. They were clothed in rags, in sheepskins and goatskins, having nothing to eat and being tormented by their enemies (see the *First Epistle of Clement,* chaps. xvii-xix; also St. John of Damascus, *Exposition of the Orthodox Faith,* Book IV, chap. xv).

> *v. 38. (Of whom the world was not worthy:) they wandered in deserts, and in mountains, and in dens and caves of the earth.*

The world, that is, the society that does not know God, rejects those who put their trust in Him and who live their lives in accordance with His will. It is not worthy of the very ones it rejects. The sign of the righteous' not being accepted by society is their having to inhabit places normally considered uninhabitable by human beings.

For Theodoret (*Letter LXXVII*) the sufferings of the blessed prophets provided the model for the divine apostles who "traveled preaching over all the world, without home, bed, bedding, board, of any of the necessities of life, but scourged, racked, imprisoned, and undergoing countless kinds of death," and which he adduces in his exhortation to Bishop Eulalius not to abandon his flock in the Persian persecution.

For St. Symeon the New Theologian (*Discourses VI, VII, and XXII*), those sufferings provide the encouragement and inspiration for those ascetics and monastics who voluntarily accept the same, so that they may witness to the need for living for Christ alone and that they may pray for the world and its salvation.

> *vv. 39-40. And these all, having obtained a good report through faith, received not the promise: God having provided some better thing for us, that they without us should not be made perfect.*

The Apostle now sums up the whole argument of this chapter. The faith of all those named above is testified to in the Scriptures. The promise that was the object of their faith was Christ, and they all died in the hope of its fulfillment. God's plan involved the salvation of the whole human race, and the Hebrew faithful had had to wait for God's coming to call all men to Himself. They were the fore-runners, the ones chosen to prepare the way. His "better thing" was the New Covenant, which those who were living at the Apostle's time had the privilege of seeing established. The Old Testament saints could not have had their hope completed ("should not be made perfect") without the participation of those who put their faith in the Incarnate Word, in Him who is the one promised, prophesied and prefigured in the Old Testament.

The New Covenant brings forth the perfecting of God's people: the full revelation of God in His Son (1:1), His perfect Covenant to replace the Old (8:7-13), and His perfect sacrifice. Referring to the righteous mentioned above, St. John Chrysostom asks,

> They have not yet received it [the reward of the promise], but are still waiting. . . . They gained their victory so many ages ago, and have not yet received their reward. And you who are yet in the conflict, are you vexed? Do you also consider what a thing it is, and how great, that Abraham should be sitting, and the Apostle Paul, waiting till thou hast been perfected, that then they may be able to receive their reward. For the Savior has told them before that unless we also are present, He will not give it them . . . And art thou vexed, that thou hast not yet received the reward? What then shall Abel do, who was victor before all, and is sitting uncrowned? And what Noah? And what, they who lived in those early times: seeing that they wait for them and those after thee? Dost thou see that we have the advantage of them? For "God" (he says) "has provided some better thing for us." In order that they might not seem to have the advantage of us from being crowned before us, He appointed one time of crowning for all; and he that gained the victory so many years before, receives his crown with thee. Seest thou His tender carefulness? (*op. cit.*, Homily 28, no. 2; see also St. Gregory of Nyssa, *On the Making of Man*, chap. xxii, no. 7)

Chapter 12

v. 1. Wherefore seeing we also are compassed about with so great a cloud of witnesses, let us lay aside every weight, and the sin which doth so easily beset us, and let us run with patience the race that is set before us.

The Epistle contains several exhortations (2:1-4; 3:1-4,13; 5:11-6:20; etc.). Usually they follow the exposition of some doctrinal truth and urge the reader on to increased patience, humility, submission to God's will, deeper faith, and a way of living consistent with that truth. The present chapter begins with such an exhortation, but it focuses on the need to follow the example of the Saints whose faith and obedience were pointed to in the preceding chapter, and to take courage and inspiration from their faithfulness so as to remain true to the Christian calling (see the *First Epistle of Clement,* chap. xix).

Since the Apostle is addressing the first generation of Christians, all his examples are taken from the Old Testament. Later, with the passing of time, this cloud of witnesses will include hundreds of New Covenant witnesses, particularly martyrs. The Greek word in this first verse, *martys,* means and is translated by both "witness" and "martyr," a martyr being one who witnesses unto death. The Old Testament figures recalled in Chapter 11 can be called martyrs in that "they witnessed to the greatness of God," in spite of the dangers to which their witness exposed them, and "the remembrance of those holy people re-establishes and recovers the soul which had been weighed down by woes, as a cloud does him who is burnt by the excessively hot rays of the sun" (St. John Chrysostom, *On Hebrews,* Homily 28, no. 3).

For his imagery, the Apostle make use of a certain athletic stadium vocabulary, such as we find in other Epistles (I Corinthians 9:24-26; Galatians 2:2; Philippians 2: 6 and 3:13-14; I Timothy 6:12; II Timothy 2:5). He advises the Christian to prepare himself as an athlete does for the games: "lay aside every weight," that is, anything that could be an encumbrance or a hindrance to participation, even seemingly small and insignificant distractions that could impede the singleness of vision of which the Lord spoke (Matthew 6:22) and of heart, which characterized the life of the first disciples (Acts 2:46). The "sin" on the part of the runner of the race, that is a fundamental problem, is two-fold—a lack of faith in the very purpose of the race and in his own capacity for finishing it. St. John Chrysostom (*ibid.*) thinks that the term translated "doth easily beset us," *evperistaton* in Greek, really means in this context, "which can easily be circumvented," for, as he says, "It is easy, if we will, to overcome sin."

The word for race (*agōn* in Greek) refers specifically to an athletic contest, and indicates that the Christian's race is a real contest and that his opponent is the devil himself; it is a life-long struggle and the contestant can never take his attention away from his goal. The race is not without pain either (*agōn* is the root for our English word "agony), and it must be run with patience and endurance. (See 6:12, where you find *makrothymias,* and 12:10 for *hypomonēs,* which is used in the present verse.) The race is "set before" the Christian; it is not optional, for the struggle is an essential feature of the life in Christ. St. Ignatius pleads with those who would save him from his martyrdom, saying, "If you do, I shall again have to run my race" (*Epistle to the Romans,* chap. ii; see also Clement of Alexandria, *Stromata,* Book IV, chap. xvi).

Finally, it is evident that the "cloud of witnesses," in view of all that has been said, can in no way be likened to the spectators at an athletic event. Herein, the Apostle parts with his "stadium" frame of reference. The witnesses (the Saints) not only provide the needed examples of steadfastness, firmness of conviction and faithfulness, but they actively participate in the contest through their intercessions. They are those "constant luminaries who illuminate us, and as favored ones, plead for our souls." (All Saints Sunday, Vespers, sticheron on "Lord, I have cried"—the same concept of the role of the Saints is found in many of the hymns and verses for this feast.)

v. 2. Looking unto Jesus the author and finisher of our faith;
who for the joy that was set before him endured the cross,
despising the shame, and is set down at the right hand of the
throne of God.

"Looking unto" (*aphorōntes* with *eis* in the Greek text) means "keeping the sight fixed on something or somebody" or "looking away from everything else." Thus, the Christian must see Jesus only, for He is both the Author (*archēgos*) and the Finisher (*teleiōtēs*) of the faith, that is, the faith of the witnesses the Apostle has reviewed in Chapter 11, as well as the faith of those who now propose to follow Him. He has already called Jesus the *archēgos* of the salvation (2:10) of those whom He will bring to glory, and His work is finished, perfected, through suffering. Jesus Himself had spoken of His completing, finishing or perfecting His work through His resurrection (Luke 13:32), following His voluntary suffering. St. Peter twice calls Jesus *archēgos,* in speaking to the Jews and to the Sanhedrin (Acts 3:15 and 5:31—in both cases the word is translated "prince" in most English versions.)

Since the term *archēgos* is composed of two roots, one meaning "beginning" and the other meaning "lead or bring to," Christ is in every sense the *archēgos.* In this verse, it means both the originator of life and of faith (as God) and the leader who is the perfect example of faith which is fulfilled in His death (as the perfect Man). "He has put the faith within us . . . He put the Beginning into us, He will also put on the End" (St. John Chrysostom, *ibid.*). St. Gregory of Nyssa (*The Great Catechism,* chap. xxxv) speaks of the affinity established between Christ, the Author of life, and those who follow Him, specifically in His baptism. Baptism is the mystery in which we follow Christ in His death, burial and resurrection (Romans 6:4; Colossians 2:12). Thus, in His taking on human nature and becoming one of us, He first runs the race of faith, and only if we keep Him in our sight shall we also be able to finish the race.

The joy that the Apostle speaks of is the joy that was His as the Son of God, who always participates in the complete blessedness of the life of the All-Holy Trinity. This "for the joy that was set before Him" possibly alludes to the Son's self-emptying, the *kenoō* of Philippians 2:7, since the "for" of the above phrase translates *anti* of the Greek text and can mean either "because of" or "instead of." In order to rescue the human race, He chose to endure the cross and the shame that went with it, rather than "abide in His own dignity and honor" (St. Gregory of Nazianzus, *Oration XII*, "To His Father," no. 4). It was to this joy that He returned after His work was completed. This return is expressed by the phrase "and is set down at the right hand of God"—the place He always had occupied. On the other hand, there is a new dimension to the Son's joy: in assuming our nature, redeeming it and deifying it, He has taken it with Him into the heavenly realm in His ascension (Ephesians 1:3).

v. 3. For consider him that endured such contradiction of sinners against himself, lest ye be wearied and faint in your minds.

Having reminded the Hebrew Christians that Jesus has been the highest possible example of faithfulness, the Apostle now urges them to consider, by way of comparison, the rebelliousness and opposition He suffered. This "contradiction" (in Greek, *antilogia*) was foretold by the prophets: to Ezekiel, for example, the Lord said, "I send thee to the children of Israel, to a rebellious nation that hath rebelled against me . . . " (Ezekiel 2:3), although the terms used are not *antilogia* or some form of it, yet the meaning is quite the same. The word we find in this verse is found in the Old Testament and is variously translated as "provocation," "rebellion" or "strife," for example, "the water of strife" (Numbers 20:13). There is also a figure of this rebelliousness, such as that against Moses and Aaron, "the gainsaying *[antilogia]* of Korah," which led to the destruction of the rebels (Jude 11).

The Lord had prepared His disciples for persecution and rejection: "the servant is not greater than his lord. If they have persecuted me, they will also persecute you . . . " (John 15:20). Perhaps some of the Lord's persecutors were among those who were persecuting those who had become Christians. They are rightly described as sinners (Matthew 26:45; Mark 14:41).

They must overcome the opposition, keeping Jesus always in their mental view, if they are to finish the race set before them: otherwise, they may collapse in the midst of the race, like runners, being wearied and faint in their "souls" (see also Galatians 6:9).

v. 4. Ye have not yet resisted unto blood, striving against sin.

Although the Christians to whom the Apostle is speaking have suffered persecution as a result of their adherence to Christ and their acknowledging Him to be the Messiah (see 10:32, "after ye were illuminated, ye endured a great fight of afflictions"), they have lost no more than their standing in the community, even property, and have not yet been threatened with death. The sin they are striving against or "fighting" against (*antagōnizomenoi,* another term often used in athletic contests, as in IV Macabees 17:11-16) is no doubt the temptation to return to their old ways and to renounce the Christian faith. The One they are urged to look to (v. 2) and consider (v. 3) did indeed contend against sin, all the sins of mankind, even "unto blood."

> *vv. 5-6. And ye have forgotten the exhortation which speaketh unto you as unto children, My son, despise not thou the chastening of the Lord, nor faint when thou art rebuked of him: for whom the Lord loveth he chasteneth, and scourgeth every son whom he receiveth.*

The exhortation which the Apostle brings to the readers' attention is from Proverbs (3:11-12). In this connection St. Clement of Rome quotes Job 5:17-26: "Blessed is the man whom the Lord reproveth, and reject not thou the warning of the Almighty . . ." (*First Epistle of Clement,* chap. lvi). This calls to mind Psalm 93/94:12-13, "Blessed is the man whomsoever thou shalt chasten, O Lord, and shalt teach him out of thy law; to give him rest from evil days, until a pit be digged for the evil one," and finally James 1:12: "Blessed is the man that endureth temptation: for when he is tried, he shall receive the crown of life, which the Lord hath promised to them that love Him." This rather gentle reminder demonstrates that the tradition to which they are heirs both as Christians and as Hebrews speaks of a training or discipline inherent in being of the elect (not "punishment"—the Greek is *paideia*). God might even allow persecution or any number of adversities, and for those who have faith this is proof of His love (see St. John Cassian, *Conference of Abbot Theodore,* chap. xi).

Even if the Lord's chastisement is the consequence of one's failure to keep His commandments, it is always given for correction. With this verse in mind, St. Ambrose reminds us (*Concerning Repentance,* Book I, chap. xii) of what the Psalmist says about the chastisement of God: "If they profane my statutes and keep not my commandments, I will visit their offenses with the rod and their sins with scourges, but my mercy will I not take from them" (Psalm 88/89:31-32), and: "The Lord hath chastened me sore, but He hath not given me over unto death" (Psalm 117/118:18). St. Paul also testifies to the reason the Lord chastens those whom He loves: " . . . we are chastened of the Lord, that we should not be condemned with the world" (I Corinthians 11:32). St. Gregory the Great, citing the Lord's own words, gives perhaps the most important reason of all: "The fruitful branch is said to be purged, because it is cut down by discipline that it may be brought to more abundant grace." (*Epistles,* Book IX, chap. xxxiii; see John 15:1-2).

v. 7. If ye endure chastening, God dealeth with you as with sons; for what son is he whom the father chasteneth not?

The Apostle continues to make the point that God's correction is to be expected since He has received them as His children in their rebirth in baptism (6:4; 10:32). It is normal for a father, even in an earthly family, to concern himself with the discipline, the moral and spiritual growth of his children. (The noun *paideia* and the verb *paidevō,* having to do with "upbringing, education and discipline," and the application of the same to children, are used here.) So much more does God's care for His children whom "He receiveth" manifest itself in the trials He allows them to undergo. As Hebrews, whom the Apostle addresses, they should have remembered that God had consented for their forefathers to endure trials and tribulations for their own correction (see Isaiah 53:5 and Jeremiah 30: 14).

> *v. 8. But if ye be without chastisement, whereof all are partakers, then are ye bastards, and not sons.*

The absence of discipline would be a sign that they were not really His children, for when they became Christians, they became partakers of (*metochoi,* "sharers in") God's family, and, as true children, expressed their willingness to accept His divine guidance, which would necessarily include correction and reproof. With reference to this idea, St. John Chrysostom (*op. cit.,* Homily 29, no. 3) concludes: "If then not to be chastened is a mark of bastards, we ought to rejoice at chastisement, if this be a sign of legitimacy. 'God dealeth with you as sons' for this very cause."

> *vv. 9-10. Furthermore we have had fathers of our flesh which corrected us, and we gave them reverence: shall we not much rather be in subjection unto the Father of spirits, and live? For they verily for a few days chastened us after their own pleasure; but he for our profit, that we might be partakers of His holiness.*

The Hebrews are reminded that they have always respected their fathers in the flesh, that is, their earthly fathers, even when they were corrected or disciplined by them. In view of the fact that their present trials are evidence of the heavenly Fathers's loving care for them (vv. 5-6), the Apostle insists that the only proper way to respond is to accept this discipline and submit to it. The reward for their obedience is life, both life in the world to come and the godly life in accordance with God's plan in the present. The Book of Proverbs has much to say about the salutary consequences of a father's correction (again, *paideia*) of his child. "Foolishness is bound in the heart of a child, but the rod of correction shall drive it far from him" (22:15). "Withhold not correction from the child: for if thou beatest him with the rod, he shall not die. Thou shalt beat him with the rod, and shalt deliver his soul from death" (23:13-14 LXX). Obviously the heavenly Father's correction has one purpose: to save His children (see St. Paul's testimony to the Corinthians, cited above, vv. 5-6).

God's fatherhood is contrasted with men's: He is the Father of spirits (or souls), while our earthly fathers have a limited relationship with their children. St. John Cassian, having quoted our verse 9, asks: "What could show more clearly than this distinction, that he laid down that men were the fathers of our flesh, but always taught that God alone was the Father of souls?" (*The Second Conference of Abbot Serenus*, chap. xxv).

Human fathers are limited in two ways: their discipline lasts only till we come of ages ("for a few days"), and their ability to train their children is fallible. Being subject to human ignorance and victims of emotion, they sometimes discipline wrongly or even for their own benefit. ("After their own pleasure" translates *kata to dokoun avtois*, that is, "in their judgment," or "as it seems to them.")

The heavenly Father's correction and training are, by contrast, infallible. He knows what we need and what is for our own good, and, furthermore, He has a design or will for those who follow Him (Ephesians 5:17): to become partakers of His divine life or of the divine nature (II Peter 1:4). Holiness is God's, and therefore the real goal of the life in Christ is to become holy, that is, to share in His holiness.

The writer of II Maccabees encourages the Jews under persecution, by reminding them that God permits this for their own purification. " . . . that they be not discouraged for these calamities, but that they judge those persecutions not to be for destruction, but for a chastening of our nation" (6:12). The Jews of the Apostle's time could take heart from their own past if they remembered these admonitions.

v. 11. Now no chastening for the present seemeth to be joyous, but grievous: nevertheless afterward it yieldeth the peaceable fruit of righteousness unto them which are exercised thereby.

God applies His discipline to His children because He wills their ultimate good. He knows that their present trials cannot be pleasant for them, since no discipline or even medicine is at the time it is administered. For this reason, the Apostle exhorts them to keep their faith in God's plan for them, and not consider their difficulties a sign of His abandoning them. If they are aware of how the Lord dealt with their ancestors, they should remember how He chastened them in the past. For their idolatry, the Lord had said, "I will bring evil upon them" (Jeremiah 11:11), a saying which St. John Cassian paraphrases, "Evil, that is, sorrows and losses, with which they shall for the present be chastened for their soul's health, and so shall at length be driven to return and hasten back to Me, whom in their prosperity they scorned" (*Conference of Abbot Theodore*, chap. vi).

Their present training ("those who are exercised by it," *gegymnasmenois* in Greek), like the athlete's, will yield the desired results or bear fruit: the latter will be rewarded with a temporal victory, but they will be rewarded with salvation, described as a "peaceable" state "of righteousness."

vv. 12-13. Wherefore lift up the hands which hang down, and the feeble knees; and make straight paths for your feet, lest that which is lame be turned out of the way; but let it rather be healed.

The Apostle now turns from his gentle reminders to a rather sharp command to come alive and, so to speak, put their heart into their struggle. For this, he again makes use of a figurative language appropriate to the athletic field, language almost identical to that used by the Prophet Isaiah (35:3) to encourage the people of Israel. It is likewise reminiscent of the language of Eliphaz, who reproved Job (Job 4:3-4) in the latter's desolate state, reminding him of how he had come to the rescue of others. Now that the Messiah has come and some of them have believed in Him, they need the same kind of encouragement, because the many who have not believed are trying to discourage them. The signs of weakening are hands that grow weary or "hang down" (*pareimenas* in Greek) and knees that are feeble or "paralyzed" (*paralelymena*). Perhaps some are even feigning weakness because of their fear (see St. Symeon the New Theologian, *Discourse V,* no. 21).

In both of these verses, the whole church is exhorted and encouraged. Using the language of Proverbs 4:26, which the Apostle makes plural, he urges them to set out on the race that they have chosen, and for that it is necessary to make the racetrack (*trochias*) straight and smooth. In this manner, even the weaker members, the lame or limping (*chōlon*), may take courage from the whole band and not fall away, but rather regain their strength (see St. John Chrysostom, *op. cit.,* Homily 30, no. 1).

> *v. 14. Follow peace with all men, and holiness, without which no man shall see the Lord.*

In order to finish the race set before them, the Hebrew Christians are reminded that they must follow (or rather, "pursue" and "strive for" as the Greek *diōkete* indicates) the two things that, perhaps more than anything else, characterize the life in Christ: peace and holiness (St. John Chrysostom, *ibid.;* see also St. Paul's almost identical expression in Romans 14:19 and II Timothy 2:22). The Lord had given peacemaking as one of the primary virtues of His followers: "Blessed are the peacemakers, for they shall be called the children of God" (Matthew 5:9). Further, He said, "My peace I give unto you" (John 14: 27), not as the world gives, but that which is the product of love, first among Christians themselves but also with all men, even one's enemies (St. Cyril of Jerusalem, *Catechetical Lecture XIII,* no. 14). Holiness is that state of purity which brings the believer into communion with God: "Blessed are the pure in heart, for they shall see God" (Matthew 5:8). "Take away the tears, and you remove with them purification; but apart from being purified there is no one who is saved, no one whom the Lord calls blessed, no one who sees God" (St. Symeon the New Theologian, *Discourse XXIX,* no. 7). St. Basil, in his *Letter LIV* (to the Chorepiscopi) insists that holiness is a primary requisite for those who would minister at the altar. St. Gregory the Great, in his *Letter XLVI* (Book XI, to Isacius, the Bishop of Jerusalem), urges him to "let his holiness mitigate some evils by repressing them, and others by bearing them, so as in all respects to conserve the peace of them that dwell together in the holy Church of Jerusalem." All of these Fathers cited had particular reference to this present verse from Hebrews.

> *v. 15. Looking diligently lest any man fail of the grace of God; lest any root of bitterness springing up trouble you, and thereby many be defiled;*

The mutual responsibility and interdependence of Christians is stressed here. They must have concern for their brethren in the Faith. The verb translated "looking diligently" is *episcopountes* in Greek, from which *episcopos,* bishop, is derived. It means "watch over," or even "examine," but implies that this must be done in the spirit of love. The particular concern is that any one of their number might fall short of the grace of God, that is, lose faith "in the good things to come, the Gospel, the best course of life" (St. John Chrysostom, *op. cit.,* Homily 31, no. 1). As St. Paul puts it in another place, "for all have sinned, and come short of the glory of God" (Romans 3:23), and the sin of particular concern to the Apostle here is that of falling back into the Law with all its sacrifices, in other words, apostasy and idolatry. Thus, the term translated "fail," *hysterōn* in Greek, describes those who have come short or failed to see that all things in the Old Covenant have been replaced in the New by God's grace.

The expression "lest any root of bitterness springing up trouble you" repeats essentially the warning to the Hebrew people found in Deuteronomy 29:18: it specifically concerns those who were in danger of falling into apostasy and idolatry, of serving the gods of other nations. The obvious danger is that the falling away of one could corrupt many others. This same word "root" (*rhiza* in Greek) is used in I Macabees 1:10 and in St. Matthew's Gospel 13:21, in the first case, to describe the wicked Antiochus, and in the second, in the Parable of the Sower, the one who received the word in a stony place and in whom the word did not take root. Here the word is used to describe the way in which sins and the temptation to commit them invade the community unnoticed and suddenly spring up and take hold. Bitterness is often used in Scripture as an equivalent of sin and evil (see Acts 8:21; Romans 3:14; Ephesians 4:31).

St. Cyril of Alexandria applies the warning expressed in the present verse to an incident recounted in Luke 9:46, where we read that "there entered a thought among them [the disciples], which of them is the greatest." He shows how the Lord responded to this ambition: "He saw in the disciples' mind this thought, springing up, in the words of Scripture, like some bitter plant; He saw the tare, the work of the wicked sower; and before it grew high; before it struck its root down deep . . . and took possession of the heart; He tears up the evil by the very root" (*Commentary on the Gospel of St. Luke,* Homily 54). For both St. Gregory of Nyssa (*Against Eunomius,* Book VIII, no. 1) and St. Gregory of Nazianzus (*Oration XXXVI,* no. xxii), our Apostle's "root of bitterness" is heretical doctrine, especially that of Arius and Sabellius, which must be uprooted, lest it defile so many. The first says, for example, "that this deceit obtains much support, as men of feebler mind are pressed by this superficial bit of plausibility, and led to acquiesce in the blasphemy."

> *vv. 16-17. Lest there be any fornicator, or profane person, as Esau, who for one morsel of meat sold his birthright. For ye know how that afterward, when he would have inherited the blessing, he was rejected: for he found no place of repentance, though he sought it carefully with tears.*

Christians have a birthright, the heritage that is given them in being born again in baptism. In the Old Law, the birthright normally belonged to the first-born son: he became heir to his father. Now Esau sold his birthright to his brother Jacob "for a mess of potage" (Genesis 25:29-34). No mention is made of his being a fornicator in the literal sense of the word, but he was considered to be guilty of every immoral act. He was a profane person, the opposite of a holy, pious person, because he thought more of material advantage, however brief its duration, than of spiritual things. Anyone who sells his spiritual heritage for material profit is a "fornicator." Israel's abandoning their God and turning to other gods is labeled "going a whoring" (Judges 2:17; 8:33; Psalm 105/106:39—*exepornevsan* or *epornevsan* in LXX).

From St. Cyril's use of this verse (*Catechetical Lecture IV,* no. 24), we see that he understood that not only was apostasy a problem in that early Christian community, but, on the part of some, there was also a loss of commitment, a failure to keep vows, all of which led to immoral behavior. With respect to vv. 14-16, he warns his catechumens: "Enrolled henceforth in the angelic books for thy profession of chastity, see that thou be not blotted out again for thy practice of fornication."

Verse 17 stresses the irreversibility of Esau's loss. An analogy with the loss that will be suffered by those who fall away is no doubt intended. After having despised his birthright (Genesis 25:34), he still begged his father to bless him, as was the custom when a father was approaching death, but he was rejected. The reason is that he "found no place of repentance," repentance that included a change of his father's decision and the opportunity for him to be truly sorry for what he had done. He sought the first kind of change with tears (Genesis 27:38), but his own repentance in the second sense was not sincere, in view of his hatred for and his vow to kill Jacob (Genesis 27:41; see also St. John Chrysostom, *ibid.,* no. 3).

vv. 18-19. For ye are not come unto the mount that might be touched, and that burned with fire, nor unto blackness, and darkness, and tempest, and the sound of a trumpet, and the

voice of words; which voice they that heard intreated that the
word should not be spoken to them any more:

The use of the conjunction "for" (*gar* in Greek) indicates that what follows is the reason for what has just been said. The Apostle has exhorted the Hebrew Christians to remain faithful; he has even implied that God's judgment on those who fall away is irreversible, like Isaac's upon Esau. He has contrasted the Covenants, the Old and the New, and now he emphasizes the difference in the very way they were given to the people: the first, in a terrifying revelation that instilled fear in them. "Take heed . . . whosoever toucheth the mount shall surely be put to death . . . whether it be beast or man" (Exodus 19:12-13). "And mount Sinai was altogether on a smoke, because the Lord descended upon it in fire: and the smoke thereof ascended as the smoke of a furnace, and the whole mount quaked greatly. And when the voice of the trumpet sounded long . . . Moses spake, and God answered him by a voice" (Exodus 19:18-19). "And all the people saw the thunderings, and the lightnings, and the noise of the trumpet, and the mountain smoking: and when the people saw it, they removed, and stood afar off. And they said unto Moses, Speak thou with us, and we will hear: but let not God speak with us, lest we die" (Exodus 20:11). "And ye drew near and stood under the mountain; and the mountain burned with fire up to heaven: there was darkness, blackness and tempest . . ." (Deuteronomy 4:11 LXX).

The second, however, was given by the quiet, humble entrance of the Son of God into the world, and now, as Christians, they do not have to be filled with fear and come to the mountain, as did Moses and his people, to a tangible (that "might be touched"), earthly place with its blazing fire, blackness, darkness and tempest. These physical phenomena are often used in Scripture as signs of God's presence, and of His wrath provoked by the sinfulness of His people (see Deuteronomy 4:1-13; Judges 13:20; III/I Kings 8:12; Nahum 1:3; Exodus 20:18). St. Gregory of Nazianzus, by way of explanation of the fear that provoked his taking refuge in Pontus, calls up the whole episode summarized in the above paragraph, insisting that he was not worthy of the privilege of approaching God at His altar (*In Defense of His Flight to Pontus,* no. 92). Later, of course, he realized that it was necessary for him to attend precisely to the way that the coming of the Son of God into the world had made it possible for man to draw near to God (Hebrews 7:19).

> *v. 20. (For they could not endure that which was commanded, And if so much as a beast touch the mountain, it shall be stoned, or thrust through with a dart:*

The people were so filled with fear, because they believed that man heard the voice of God only at the peril of death (see Deuteronomy 5). They recognized that Moses was exempt from this condemnation, and they wanted him to be the mediator who would convey to them God's commandments. They had heard that the Lord would descend to Mount Sinai and that the mountain would thus become holy, and, although it could be touched, neither man nor beast could touch it without being put to death (Exodus 19:12-13). On the other hand, according to God's word to Moses (Deuteronomy 5), if they kept His commandments and feared Him in purity of heart, they too could hear Him and live.

Some "critical editions" of the New Testament omit the second part of the consequence of a beast's touching the mountain, "thrust through with a dart," since it is not found in some manuscripts of this Epistle, although it is certainly found in the verse from Exodus (19:13 LXX) that is quoted.

> *v. 21. And so terrible was the sight, that Moses said, I exceedingly fear and quake:)*

So awesome and terrifying was the sight that even Moses, the chosen friend of God, as he himself said, was filled with fear and trembling. This is recorded in Deuteronomy 9:19, and describes his reaction to his discovering Israel's rebellion and their making the golden calf for an idol, after the fearful sight on Mount Sinai. Yet, there must have been a tradition independent of the Scriptures themselves that attributed the same fear and trembling to Moses at that moment as well. St. Stephen, in his discourse before the council, says essentially the same (Acts 7:32; see also Exodus 3:6). In any event, the sight he had witnessed at the time of God's descent upon the mountain could have had as much to do with his fear at the sinfulness of Israel. He feared that what they had done would provoke God's wrath, especially because of what he had just seen.

> *v. 22. But ye are come unto Mount Sion, and unto the city of the living God, the heavenly Jerusalem, and to an innumerable company of angels,*

Having pointed out that the Hebrew Christians to whom this Epistle is written have not drawn near, as their forefathers had, to the earthly burning mountain from which the Law was given, the Apostle now instructs them that what they have approached is the spiritual mountain, "Mount Sion, the city of the living God, the heavenly Jerusalem." (Note that the verbs of both v. 18 and this one are the same, *proselēlythate* in Greek.) These three titles mean heaven, the dwelling place of God, and the Kingdom of God in the world to come. Sion, the site of Abraham's sacrifice, the temples, the places where God was worshipped (Psalm 64/65:1) and the place from which the Messiah was to come (Psalm 2:6) should have had a special meaning for all Hebrews. But all that took place there was a figure and pointed to the spiritual Sion which has now been made accessible. The angels, who are the choirs that praise God and the ministers of His will, attest to the otherworldly nature of this Sion. Jerusalem, the holy city, prefigures the city of God's kingdom where His reign will be complete.

For St. Gregory of Nazianzus, those who, like his sister Gorgonia, live their lives in faith and love, in the hope of the resurrection and of life with Christ in His kingdom, have as their "native land the Jerusalem above, the object, not of sight but of contemplation, wherein is our commonwealth, and whereto we are pressing on . . ." (*Funeral Oration on His Sister Gorgonia,* no. 6) In his *Second Oration on Pascha,* he urges his people who are partaking of the festival, "Let us make our Head, not the earthly Jerusalem, but the heavenly City, not that which is now trodden under foot by armies [Luke 21:20-24], but that which is glorified by Angels" (chap. xxiii).

v. 23. To the general assembly and church of the firstborn, which are written in heaven, and to God the Judge of all, and to the spirits of just men made perfect,

The "mount" to which the Christian Hebrews have drawn near is further described as the "general assembly" (Greek *panēgyrei,* a solemn or festal assembly, usually of a whole nation) and "the church of the firstborn, which are written in heaven." This Church no doubt includes the patriarchs, the just of the Old Covenant and the saints of the New, as well as those faithful still on earth whose "true country is the heavenly Jerusalem;" and their "fellow-citizens and their compatriots are 'the first-born which are written in heaven'" (St. Basil the Great, *Hexameron,* Homily IX, no. 2; see also Luke 10:20).

The picture painted by the Apostle is one of great rejoicing, in which angels and men, both in heaven and on earth, join together in the praise of God (St. Athanasius, *Paschal Letter VI,* no. 9, in which he speaks specifically of the Paschal celebrations). The "spirits of just men made perfect" are in St. John Chrysostom's words, "the souls of those who are approved." (*op. cit.,* Homily 32, no. 4) The use of "spirits" recalls verse 63 of the "Song of the Three Children": "O ye spirits and souls of the just, bless ye the Lord" (see also Matins for Palm Sunday, Canon, the heirmos of Ode 6). St. Peter speaks of Christ's going to the "spirits in prison" (I Peter 3:19). "Made perfect" translates the Greek *teteleiōmenōn,* and has the meaning of "having completed, finished, fulfilled" what was set before, that is, the race, and in this sense is equivalent to "approved," as noted above; they are those who have carried out God's will for them, and those on earth who do God's will; according to St. Cyril of Alexandria (*op. cit.,* Homily 74) they contemplate the "spiritual beauty of the spirits above in heaven." That the Apostle had in mind the festal assembly of the Church, the Eucharist at Pascha, is taken for granted by St. Athanasius (see the quote above). This same understanding of v. 23 is the theme of the Seventh Ode of the Matins Canon, First Sunday of the Great Fast: "The triumphant assembly and the Church of the firstborn rejoices as it now beholds the people of God cry aloud with one accord: 'Blessed art thou, O Lord, in the temple of thy glory.'"

The Apostle's insertion of "to God the Judge of all" serves to remind his readers that those who are approved and live in the heavenly realm have come before the Judge, who is God, and that all men must come before Him for judgment.

v. 24. And to Jesus the mediator of the new covenant, and to the blood of sprinkling, that speaketh better things than that of Abel.

Finally the Apostle mentions that it is Jesus to whom we draw near, to Him who in His two natures, as God and Man, ascended into heaven, and "sat down on the right hand of the Majesty on high" (1:3). His place is Mt. Sion, the heavenly mountain, while Moses stood trembling at the foot of Mt. Sinai. Moses could only convey what was given to him, but Jesus spoke directly to the people as the divine Law-giver. Jesus is the Mediator of the New Covenant, that is, He established the new pact between God and man, since He partakes of both natures. Just as the Old Covenant was confirmed by the "blood of sprinkling," so too the New, but by the blood of the God-Man. "The spirits of the righteous [just men] cried aloud in joy: 'Now is a new covenant granted to the world: let the people be renewed through sprinkling with the Blood of God.'" (Palm Sunday, Matins Canon, see above).

Although Abel's blood was that of the innocent victim who was unjustly murdered by his brother, it could only cry out for vengeance. The blood of Christ proclaims forgiveness, reconciliation, and invites all men to partake.

Did then the blood "of Abel" speak? "Yea," he saith, "and by it he being dead yet speaketh" [11:4]. And again God saith, "The voice of thy brother's blood crieth unto Me" [Genesis 4:10]. . . . But not in such a way as that of Christ. For this has cleansed all men, and sends forth a voice more clear and more distinct, in proportion as it has greater testimony. (St. John Chrysostom, *ibid.,* no. 2)

"And if the blood speaks, much more does He who, having been slain, lives" (*ibid.,* no. 4). The superiority of Christ's sacrifice over all those of the Old Testament, and here it seems that Abel's was the greatest, has already been emphasized (see chaps. 8-10; also St. John Chrysostom, *On the Acts of the Apostles,* Homily 54; St. Athanasius, *Paschal Letter I,* no. 9).

v. 25. See that ye refuse not him that speaketh. For if they escaped not who refused him that spake on earth, much more shall not we escape, if we turn away from him that speaketh from heaven:

The apostle's exhortation now becomes stronger, as the opening "see that" indicates. Its connection with the foregoing verse is effected by the repetition of "speak" (Greek *lalounta,* from *laleō*). Jesus the Mediator speaks through His shed blood; thus the hypothesis proposed, "If they escaped not who refused Him that spake on earth," leads us to conclude that "He that spake on earth" refers to Jesus. A different Greek verb, however, is employed in this second sentence: *chrēmatizonta,* one which normally has to do with God's speaking, either through the Holy Spirit, as in Luke 2:26, or through another medium, such as an angel or angels (Acts 10:22), or by means of a dream (Matthew 2:12-23). Now Moses was the one who conveyed God's speaking, principally His giving the Law, but we find that even in this, the medium was an angel or angels (Acts 7:38,53), and he was the mediator of the Old Covenant. The Divine Law-giver had thus spoken "on earth." Moses was the one who heard His voice, because the people could not bear hearing it. Jesus, then, being the only one who came down from heaven, spoke "from heaven" in His saving work among men, and continues to speak after having ascended into heaven (see John 3:12-13).

The point here is that the consequences of turning away from the One who has spoken to them "from heaven," albeit directly or face-to-face, are far greater than what happened to their forefathers who refused Him. The latter perished in the wilderness not reaching the land of promise, but the former will lose the reality of which the land was but a figure. Even the verbs chosen emphasize the difference: "refuse" (Greek *paraitēsamenoi*) can indicate rejection even of something or someone unknown, while "turn away from" (Greek *apostrephomenoi*) is applied to those who have known the truth, Christ Himself, and have turned their backs on Him or deserted Him (see II Timothy 4:4 and Titus 1:14).

vv. 26-27. Whose voice then shook the earth: but now he hath promised, saying, Yet once more I shake not the earth only, but also heaven. And this word, Yet once more, signifieth the removing of those things that are shaken, as of things that are made, that those things which cannot be shaken may remain.

"Thou art praised above all, O Christ our God, who shakest the earth, that the dwellers upon it may turn and be saved: and thou makest it firm once more in thy love and ineffable compassion" (Troparion of the Prophecy, Sixth Hour, Friday in the Fifth Week of the Great Fast): thus the Church sings of the motivation and the purpose of the Lord's shaking the earth, His love and compassion, and that the dwellers on earth may be saved.

We have seen that the voice of God shook the earth when the Law was given: "And Mt. Sinai was altogether on a smoke . . . and the whole mount quaked greatly" (Exodus 19:18). And He promised that He would once again "shake the heavens and the earth" (Haggai 2:6; also Isaiah 2:19).

The holy Fathers (for example, St. John Chrysostom, *On Hebrews*, Homily 32, no. 5, and St. Gregory of Nazianzus, *Fifth*

Theological Oration, "On the Holy Spirit," no. xxv) teach that this prophesied shaking signifies the final destruction of the earth and the consummation of all things. The latter says:

> There have been in the whole period of the duration of the world two conspicuous changes of men's lives, which are also called two Testaments, or, on account of the wide fame of the matter, two earthquakes; the one from idols to the Law, the other, from the Law to the Gospel. And we are taught in the Gospel of a third earthquake, namely, from this Earth to that which cannot be shaken or moved.

Elsewhere (*Oration on the Great Athanasius,* no. 25) he says:

> "Yet once more," I hear the Scripture say that the heaven and the earth shall be shaken, inasmuch as this has befallen them before, signifying, as I suppose, a manifest renovation of all things. And we must believe St. Paul when he says, that this last shaking is none other than the second coming of Christ, and the transformation and changing of the universe to a condition of stability which cannot be shaken [see Isaiah 65:17; II Peter 3:13; Revelation 21:1].

The Apostle wants the Hebrews to understand that they must not fall into the apostasy of reverting to the Old Law, even though because of having become followers of Christ, they may find the persecution almost unbearable. God's judgment is more to be feared than that of men, especially in view of the promised end of all things. St. John Chrysostom's moral application of these verses makes an appeal to their (and our) confidence in the Lord's promises: "All things therefore will be taken away, and will be compacted anew for the better. Why then do you grieve when you suffer in a world that will not endure; when you are afflicted in a world which will very shortly have passed away?" (*ibid.*).

The "things which cannot be shaken" are the things to come, the things of eternal life with Christ in His kingdom. The created "things" will be taken away—only that which is eternal cannot be shaken and removed.

v. 28. Wherefore we receiving a kingdom which cannot be moved, let us have grace, whereby we may serve God acceptably with reverence and godly fear:

The eternal kingdom of heaven, which has been the theme of Christ's preaching and the content of His followers' hope, is the unshakable, indestructible thing that will remain when everything else passes away. The kingdom is present because of God's sojourn among men, but its full realization belongs to the age to come. In the Church, the kingdom is participated in by the faithful in this life, and the Church is the ship of salvation, the destination of which is the kingdom to come.

So that the Christian may persevere and overcome all obstacles and not fall away from the Church, which is the worshipping assembly of the faithful, he must have or hold fast to the grace that has been given to him (see 4:16 and 12:12-15 in this Epistle).

In the fidelity and steadfastness which the Apostle has not ceased to recommend to his readers, they must fulfill their primary duty toward God, to worship Him. The English word "serve" may contain the sense of worship, but the Greek verb *latrevōmen* is in this case specifically worship. To worship Him acceptably is no doubt to do so in accordance with His own commandments, and with reverence (*aidous* in Greek may be translated "humbly" or "with dignity") and godly fear (*evlabeias,* with "piety" or "sobriety"). The worship which the Lord specifically commanded is the Eucharist (Luke 22:19; I Corinthians 11:23-24; see also St. Irenaeus, *Against Heresies,* Book IV, chap. xviii, no. 1).

It is noteworthy that, as the Epistle reaches its climax and is about to be concluded, the primary function of the Church should be emphasized. The activity of the Church in the first days of her existence after the descent of the Holy Spirit is described as revolving around its daily worship.

> And they continued steadfastly in the apostles' doctrine and communion, and in breaking of bread, and in prayers . . . and they

continuing daily with one accord in the temple, and breaking bread
from house to house, did eat their meat with gladness and singleness of heart, praising God, and having favor with all the people.
And the Lord added to the Church daily such as were being saved.
(Acts 2:42,46-47)

v. 29. For our God is a consuming fire.

The Apostle concludes his warnings and his exhortations with a
quotation from the Old Testament: "For our God is a consuming
fire" (Deuteronomy 4:24). Although the emphasis in the New
Covenant has been on God's love and compassion for man as the
motivation for all His redeeming and saving work, the Old Testament truth about God as a jealous God who will punish is not to be
forgotten.

That "our God is a consuming fire" must be understood as a
means of describing His ineffable holiness and righteousness, before
which all that is unholy and unrighteous is consumed. There are
many places in Scripture in which fire is the sign of God's presence
(Genesis 15:17; Deuteronomy 4:24; Ezekiel 1:4). Not only is God's
presence signaled by fire, but the Savior Himself, in prophecy, is
compared to fire (Malachi 3:2), as is the Holy Spirit (Matthew 3:11).

The Lord's second coming, according to St. Paul, will be accompanied by "a flaming fire" (II Thessalonians 1:8). The Lord tells His
disciples, "I am come to send fire upon the earth, and what will I, if
it be already kindled?" (Luke 12:49). According to the Blessed Theophylact, *Explanation of the Gospel according to St. Luke,* this means,
"How greatly do I desire that it be already kindled," that is, a "fiery
zeal for the good." His very presence, further, is a fire that purges the
earth of its evil. The descent of the Holy Spirit at Pentecost is related
thus: "And there appeared cloven tongues like as of fire, and it sat
upon each of them. And they were all filled with the Holy Spirit . . .
" (Acts 2:3-4). The Apostles were inflamed by His indwelling so that
they could carry out their mission, as the whole Book of the Acts of
the Apostles testifies.

While the reminder of God's being a consuming fire at the end of the apostle's exhortation is designed to teach the Hebrews tempted to apostasize that they must face God's judgment and that He will deal severely with those who turn their backs on Him, we also discover by a careful examination of the Scriptures that this fire of God's presence comes for mankind's benefit, purification, restoration and salvation.

St. Athanasius characterizes the diligent and careful servant of the Lord as "burning like a flame, so that when, by an ardent spirit, he has destroyed all carnal sin, he may be able to draw near to God, who according to the expression of the saints, is called 'a consuming fire'" (*Paschal Letter III,* no. 3).

St. Ambrose (*Treatise on the Gospel of St. Luke,* Book VII, no. 132) interprets the Savior's saying quoted above in a very positive way:

> It is not a fire that destroys the good, but one that makes good will sprout and grow, enriches the vessels of gold in the house of God, burning up the hay and stubble [see I Corinthians 3:11-15]; that divine fire which parches earthly desires which are generated by carnal pleasures, which must perish as works of the flesh; that fire was certainly the one which burned brightly in the bones of the prophets, as that great saint Jeremiah says: "But His word was in mine heart as a burning fire shut up in my bones . . ." [Jeremiah 20:9]; in fact, the fire concerning which it is written: "A fire goeth before Him" [Psalm 96/97:3], is the Lord's fire. And the Lord Himself is that fire, as He says Himself, "I am a burning, and not a consuming fire" [Exodus 3:2; see also 24:17; Deuteronomy 4:24]. The Lord's fire is an eternal light, and it is with this fire that those lamps are lighted: "Let your loins be girded about, and your lights burning" [Luke 12:35]. And since the day of this life is like night, a light is necessary. . . . The Lord will come at the end with the sign of fire [Isaiah 66:15-16], with the object of destroying, at the time of the resurrection, all vice, to fill the desires of each one with His presence and cast light upon the deserving and [clarify] the mysteries.

Chapter 13

Coming now to the last chapter of the Epistle, we feel obliged to call attention to another controversy concerning authorship. Some scholars have held that this chapter, in view of its subject matter, was the work of a different author and that it was added later. Again, we prefer not to enter into a discussion of this question, although we shall treat it as the concluding part of the original work, as did the holy Fathers of the Church, confining ourselves still to an explanation of its contents. The whole chapter is a final exhortation, in which the Hebrew Christians are urged to live in accordance with the teachings of the Gospel, and in so doing, to witness to their faith.

vv. 1-2. Let brotherly love continue. Be not forgetful to entertain strangers: for thereby some have entertained angels unawares.

The first virtue to which the Apostle calls attention, the very foundation of the Christian community's unity, is brotherly love (*philadelphia* in Greek). St. Paul also exhorts the Romans (12:10) to "be kindly affectionate one to another with brotherly love," and commends the Thessalonians in his first Epistle to that Church (4:9) for their brotherly love for those who are in Macedonia (compare I Peter 1:22 and II Peter 1:7).

St. John Chrysostom (*On Hebrews*, Homily 33, no. 1) explains the use of the verb, "let continue" (in Greek, *menetō*): "See how he enjoins them to preserve what they had. . . . He did not say, 'Be loving as brethren,' but 'Let brotherly love continue.'" Apparently they had already shown their love for one another, and it is necessary, in view of the difficulty of the times, for them to continue doing so both as an aid to and a product of their faithfulness to their profession. For St. Augustine, commenting on I John 4:12-16, and citing this verse from Hebrews, the one virtue that is not ever to cease or become less fervent is brotherly love. "Let love within have no intermission; let the offices of love be exhibited according to the time" (Homily 8, no. 3).

The Apostle's second mark of Christian behavior, "be not forgetful to entertain strangers," is also echoed in the chapter from Romans cited above (v. 13), "given to hospitality." St. John Chrysostom (*ibid.*) says of this, "He did not say, 'Be hospitable,' as if they were not, but 'Be not forgetful of hospitality,' for this was likely to happen owing to their afflictions."

Attention should be called to the Greek word *philoxenia,* translated here as "entertain strangers" and in Romans as "hospitality." The first element of the word is *philo,* which is love or friendship. Thus, it means more than simple hospitality—not a sentimental or subjective response, but really "love for strangers." We should remember that the Lord extended the Hebrew idea of "love of one's neighbor" (Parable of the Good Samaritan) to include love of all who are in need, and not simply love of others of the same religion or nation.

Saying "for thereby some have entertained [received] angels unawares," the Apostle probably has in mind Abraham's hospitality (Genesis 18:1-22) or Lot's meeting with two angels (Genesis 19:1 ff.). (See also Judges 13 and Tobias 5:2.) Even more importantly, remember that the Lord Himself may come to us in other people in their hours of need. He did say, "inasmuch as ye have done it unto one of the least of these my brethren, ye have done it unto me." One of the works of love He had enumerated was, "I was a stranger, and ye took me in" (see Matthew 25:36-40).

v. 3. Remember them that are in bonds, as bound with them; and them which suffer adversity, as being yourselves also in the body.

The sympathy of Christians for other Christians, whether they be "in bonds" ("prisoners," Greek *desmiōn*) or "afflicted" ("being evil-treated," Greek *kakouchoumenōn*) is that of brothers, "For baptism renders a man a brother, and the partaking of the divine mysteries" (St. John Chrysostom, *On Matthew,* Homily 79, no. 1). So, when a brother is imprisoned or ill-treated, his brothers are in spirit imprisoned and ill-treated. St. Paul tells the Romans (12:15) that they must "rejoice with them that do rejoice, and weep with them that weep."

The reason the Apostle gives for those Christians' co-suffering with those who are evil-treated is that they themselves are "in the body." It is not very likely that he means that as long as they are still in this life the same thing could happen to them at any time. In view of what has been said concerning those who are imprisoned, it is more probable that he has reference to the body to which they all belong, the Church that is the Body of Christ. St. Paul (I Corinthians 12:25-27) gives us the key to understanding this phrase, "in the body"—"the members should have the same care one for another. And whether one member suffer, all the members suffer with it; or one member be honored, all the members rejoice with it. Now ye are the body of Christ, and members in particular."

v. 4. Marriage is honorable in all, and the bed undefiled: but whoremongers and adulterers God will judge.

The absence of the verb "is" in the Greek text could lead us to conclude that the Apostle has intended us to read the verse as part of the exhortation; thus, "Let marriage be honorable," etc. The holy Fathers, among them St. John Chrysostom, St. Gregory of Nazianzus, St. Athanasius and St. John of Damascus, take it instead to be a declaration or definition. The latter, for example, states unequivocally: "For we know that the Lord blessed marriage by His presence, and we know him who said, 'Marriage is honorable, and the bed undefiled' " (*Exposition of the Orthodox Faith,* Book IV, chap. xxiv). Although generally the Fathers declare virginity or chastity to be a higher state (see St. Athanasius, *Letter XLVIII,* "To Amun"), others, like St. Cyril of Jerusalem, praise "the ascetics and virgins who maintain the angelic life in this world," but warn against despising marriage and take pride in their virginity: "Nor again, on the other hand, in maintaining thy chastity, be thou puffed up against those who walk in the humbler path of matrimony." He quotes our present verse in a hortatory form: "Let marriage be had in honor among all, and let the bed be undefiled" (*Catechetical Lecture IV,* no. 25).

The "bed" (normal sexual relations in marriage) is undefiled if both husband and wife are faithful: "He is blessed who, being freely yoked in his youth, naturally begets children. But if he uses nature licentiously, the punishment of which the Apostles writes shall await whoremongers and adulterers" (St. Athanasius, *ibid.*). The Saint's words echo the sentiments of Proverbs (5:18-20), along with the implied warning, "Why wilt thou, my son, be ravished with a strange woman, and embrace the bosom of a stranger?" The whole present verse is a warning against sexual promiscuity and a reminder that in God's judgment "Marriage is honorable, and the marriage-bed undefiled. For on both Christ has given His blessing, eating in the flesh at the wedding in Cana, turning water into wine and revealing His first miracle, to bring thee, my soul, to a change of life" (Great Canon of St. Andrew, Thursday, First Week of the Fast, Second Canon, Ninth Ode).

v. 5. Let your conversation be without covetousness; and be content with such things as ye have: for he hath said, I will never leave thee, nor forsake thee.

The first clause in the original text has no verb, as in verse 4. Translators generally have supplied an introductory "let your"— properly so in this case, we would say, because of the hortatory nature of the whole verse. "Conversation" translates the Greek *tropos,* which means manner or way of living or conduct, even style of life, and the characteristic of the Christian way is "without love of money" (such is the meaning of the Greek *aphilargyros*). St. Paul teaches us that "the love of money is the root of all evil: which while some coveted after, they have erred from the faith" (I Timothy 6:10). Further, what he tells Timothy fits the spirit of this verse in Hebrews; especially so, since earlier in the Epistle to Timothy he had stressed the need for Christians to be content with what they had (vv. 6-9). This precept is also taught in the Gospels (Matthew 6:34; Luke 3:14) and by St. Paul elsewhere (such as II Corinthians 9:8). The Christian's being able to do so is due to the Lord's promise never to abandon him, nor forsake him, although the reference is from the Old Testament (Deuteronomy 31:6,8 and Joshua 1:5). If it was so under the Law, how much more is it applicable to those who have chosen to follow Christ?

For those who would be missionaries and preachers of the Word, St. Cyril of Alexandria says: "It was absolutely necessary for those whose business it would be to proclaim the saving message of the Gospel to have a mind careless about wealth, and occupied only with the desire for better things" (*Commentary on the Gospel of St. Luke,* Homily 27). St. Symeon the New Theologian applies God's promise never to forsake His own especially to those who repent and confess their sins (*Discourse V,* no. 9).

> *v. 6. So that we may boldly say, The Lord is my helper, and I will not fear what man shall do unto me.*

If they lead the life outlined tersely in the first five verses, Christians are given to understand that they may "boldly say," because they will be assured that the Lord has promised never to leave them. The word translated "boldly" here is not the same word similarly translated elsewhere in the Epistle. This one is *tharrountas,* a form of *tharreō,* meaning "to have courage" or confidence. In other verses, "with boldness" or "boldly" was used to translate *parrēsia* (4:16; 10:19).

What the devout Christian may say with all confidence is, "The Lord is my Helper, and I will not fear what man shall do unto me," the exact words of Psalm 117/118:6 LXX, (which calls to mind Psalm 26/27:1 and Psalm 29/30:10). Both Psalms 117 and 26 are reflected in the Great Canon of St. Andrew, Ode 1, Heirmos: "He is my Helper and Protector, and is become my Salvation . . . ," so that the Christian, on beginning the Great Fast, may have confidence in the Lord's promise.

> *v. 7. Remember them which have the rule over you, who have spoken unto you the word of God: whose faith follow, considering the end of their conversation.*

In order for us properly to understand this verse, we must analyze several of its key words. We do this in light of the way in which

St. John of Damascus makes use of the verse in his chapter "Concerning the Honor Due to the Saints and Their Remains," (*ibid.*, chap. xv).

The Greek *mnēmonevete*, translated "remember," implies much more than a simple recollection or recalling. The corresponding noun *mnēmosynon*, as can be seen in other places in the New Testament (Mark 14:9; Acts 10:4), means a "memorial" or "a remembrance in honor of." St. John (*ibid.*) bears this out, in that he includes the Mother of God, St. John the Baptist, the martyrs, the ascetics and the patriarchs before the Law, as those who must be remembered and honored as "those who have the rule," better translated as "leaders" (*hēgoumenōn* in Greek, from *hēgeomai*), that is, those who have led or shown the way. They have spoken the word of God unto the then present generation of Christians by their example and their teaching.

"Have the rule" is misleading, except when applied to those who presently lead by the proclamation of the word and the ministration of the holy mysteries. This sense is also included, as we see in the word's use in verses 17 and 24 of this chapter.

The word translated "conversation" is *anastrophēs* and not the *tropos* of verse 5. (See also Galatians 1:13; Ephesians 4:22; James 3:13; 1 Peter 2:12; and II Peter 2:7.) The distinction between *tropos* and *anastrophē* is a fine one: we might say of the first that it refers to that which characterizes, a life style, while the second means "those things which have been done," or "behavior." We must carefully review and adopt as our own their behavior and conduct, and strive to have the same "end" (*ekbasis* in Greek), which means outcome or result.

St. John concludes the chapter we have referred to as follows: "Let us carefully review the life of these men, and let us emulate their faith and love and hope and zeal and way of life, and endurance of sufferings and patience even to blood, in order that we may be sharers with them in their crowns of glory."

v. 8. Jesus Christ the same yesterday, and today, and for ever.

The object of that faith is Jesus Christ, the God-Man and Incarnate Word, whether it be of those who faithfully held to the promise and died without seeing it, or of those who have now seen fulfilled all the expectations of the Old Covenant faithful. What can the Apostle do at this point but call forth Him specifically in His eternal being? St. Athanasius, in his *First Discourse against the Arians,* (chap. x, no. 36), explains:

> The Image of the unalterable God must be unchangeable; for "Jesus Christ is the same yesterday, today and forever." And David in the Psalm says of Him, "Thou, Lord, in the beginning hast laid the foundation of the earth, and the heavens are the work of Thine hands. They shall perish, but Thou remainest . . . and they shall be changed, but thou art the same, and thy years shall not fail" [Psalm 101/102:25-26].

And in his *Letter LIX* ("To Epictetus," no. 5) he says, "The very Essence of the Word . . . is incapable of alteration or change. For the Saviour Himself [through the Prophet] says: 'Behold, behold, it is I, and I change not' [Malachi 3:6]."

Many other holy Fathers make use of this verse, which is apparently a line from an early hymn or creedal statement, in their struggle against heresies, especially those errors concerning our Lord's person. (See St. Ambrose, *On the Christian Faith,* Book V, chap i, no. 25; St. Gregory of Nazianzus, *Oration XXXVIII,* "On the Theophany," chap. ii, among others.)

The "word of God" spoken by those who guide the Christian community, according to St. John Chrysostom (*On Hebrews,* Homily 33, no. 6), has to do with Christ's unchangeableness and His continued presence and working in the Church: "Do not think that then indeed He wrought wonders, but now works no wonders. He is the same. This is [what is meant by], 'remember them that have the rule over you.'"

v. 9. Be not carried about with divers and strange doctrines. For it is a good thing that the heart be established with grace; not with meats, which have not profited them that have been occupied therein.

Although there may have been many ("various" or "many colored," *poikilais* in Greek) doctrines and teachings that were strange ("foreign," in Greek *xenai*), that is, were departures from the "apostles' doctrine" (Acts 2:42), by which men might have been carried away (see Ephesians 4:14), here the Apostle has in mind specifically an apparent continued preoccupation with the food laws of the Old Covenant. These he summarizes under the title of "meats," ("foods," *brōmasin* in Greek). He contrasts these things of the Old with the grace of the New Law. "The Law was given by Moses, but grace and truth came by Jesus Christ" (John 1:17). He is no doubt recalling what the Lord Himself had said, quoting from Isaiah (29:13): "This people draweth nigh unto me with their mouth ... but their heart is far from me. But in vain they do worship me, teaching for doctrines the commandments of men ... Not that which goeth into the mouth defileth a man; but that which cometh out of the mouth, this defileth a man" (Matthew 15:8-11).

The response to grace must be faith; those whose life revolves around (*peripatēsantes*, here translated "occupied") the observance of external rites were not profited by them. Faith, on the other hand, is effective in that it brings purification; thus, grace establishes (*bebaiousthai* in Greek) or confirms the heart.

"There is one observance, abstaining from sin. For what profit is it, when some are so polluted, as not to be able to partake of the sacrifices? So that it did not save them at all; although they were zealous about the observances. But because they had not faith, even thus they profited nothing" (St. John Chrysostom, *ibid.*). This same Father was of the opinion that there may have been some among the Hebrew Christians who had tried to introduce "the observance of 'meats,'" (*ibid.*, no. 3) that is, make this a part of their Christian way of life.

Whether the Apostle also has in mind the temptation of some among them to eat the sacrificial foods of the pagans, we cannot be sure, but elsewhere we find warnings against this, as in I Corinthians 10:20 (see also Clement of Alexandria, *The Instructor*, Book II, chap. i).

v. 10. We have an altar, whereof they have no right to eat which serve the tabernacle.

The altar that we Christians have is Christ; He was both the priest and the victim in the supreme sacrifice that He offered for the sins of the world. He was the reality pointed to by all the Old Testament figures or types, including the tabernacle (and temple) and its altar. The Apostle would surely ask why those who have the "real thing" might be tempted to continue to participate in the "shadow of things to come" (Colossians 2:16-17). Those who serve (here the Greek is *latrevontes*, "worship") the tabernacle have no right to eat at the Christian altar. By this the Apostle must mean not only the spiritual eating or communion with Christ that one has by believing in Him, but also, and rather directly, by participation in the divine Eucharist, wherein one receives the body and blood of Christ. The warning of St. Paul (referred to in v. 9) concerning the eating of pagan sacrificial offerings is no doubt applicable here. "Ye cannot drink of the cup of the Lord, and the cup of devils: ye cannot be partakers of the Lord's table, and of the table of devils" (I Corinthians 10:21).

In the Ninth Ode of the Compline Canon for Wednesday of Holy Week, we find this troparion: "The upper room wherein Christ kept the Passover was revealed as a heavenly tabernacle; the supper without shedding of blood is our reasonable worship; the table on which the Mysteries were celebrated there is our spiritual altar."

v. 11. For the bodies of those beasts, whose blood is brought into the sanctuary by the high priest for sin, are burned without the camp.

The Old Testament ritual prescription which the Apostle recalls here is found in Leviticus (16:27): the blood of the bullocks and goats that was offered for the sins of the people on the day of Atonement was brought into the sanctuary, but the bodies were then burned without (outside) the camp. Although here it is stressed that it was the blood of the animals that were burned outside the camp that constituted the sacrifice for the sins of the people, it is true that the phrase "without the camp" will also be applied to the place of the supreme and final sacrifice of Jesus Christ (see v. 12). The Old Testament ritual was then a figure of the reality of the New; the blood of the perfect victim also was shed outside the city, but His blood was not taken into the tabernacle (temple) which was only a type of the heavenly tabernacle.

> Thus Christ, suffering "without," fulfilled all. Here he [the Apostle] makes it plain too that He suffered voluntarily, showing that those things were not accidental, but even the [Divine] arrangement itself was of a suffering "without." [He suffered] without, but His blood was borne up into heaven. Thou seest then that we partake of Blood which has been carried into the Holy Place, the True Holy Place; of the Sacrifice of which the Priest [Jesus] alone had the privilege. We therefore partake of the Truth [the Reality]. (St. John Chrysostom, *ibid.*, no. 7)

v. 12. Wherefore Jesus also, that he might sanctify the people with his own blood, suffered without the gate.

Of this Theodoret says,

> All the Old Testament, so to say, is a type of the New. It is for this reason that the divine Apostle plainly says—"the Law having a shadow of good things to come" [Hebrews 10:1] and again "now all these things happened unto them for ensamples" [I Corinthians 10:11]. The image of the archetype is very distinctly exhibited by the lamb slain in Egypt, and by the red heifer burned without the camp, and moreover referred to by the Apostle in the Epistle to the Hebrews, where he writes "Wherefore Jesus also . . . suffered without the gate." (*Dialogue III,* "The Impassible" [NPNF 2*nd* Series, vol. 3, p. 226])

St. Cyril of Alexandria, after considering various symbolic interpretations of the Parable of the Prodigal Son, concludes that Jesus Christ's sacrifice "outside the gate" of the city was effective for the sanctification and redemption of all people, both the Jews within and the Gentiles without:

> He was sacrificed, not for the Gentiles only, but that He might also redeem Israel, who by reason of his frequent transgression of the law had brought upon himself great blame. And the wise Paul bears witness to this, saying, "Jesus also, that He might sanctify the people by His blood, suffered outside the gate." (*op. cit.*, Homily 107)

It is also important to note that criminals were executed outside the city, and it was God's design that His Son, who bore man's sin and shame to the fullest, should suffer the same condemnation. Thus it was Jesus, who came to save Israel, was an outcast from His own people. But His blood offered for the sins of the whole world was brought into that Holy Place not made with hands, the heavenly sanctuary. (See Chapter 9 and the commentary on the foregoing verse.)

In the Aposticha for Matins, Wednesday in the Sixth Week of the Great Fast, we find:

> Israel was clothed in purple and fine linen, arrayed in the glory of priestly and royal garments; rich in the Law and the Prophets, it rejoiced in the worship of the old Covenant. But it crucified Thee outside the gates, O Benefactor who hast made thyself poor, and it rejected thee when thou hast returned alive after the crucifixion.

v. 13. Let us go forth therefore unto him without the camp, bearing his reproach.

All those who believe in Jesus Christ and follow Him faithfully must also realize that they must willingly become outcasts as far as the world is concerned. Just as He was cast out of the city, Christians too must be ready to bear the rejection and shame of their Lord. The Hebrew Christians, particularly, had to face the consequences of putting their faith in Christ, that is, to go out to be with Him, to remain "outside the gates," to be cut off from Judaism. St. Paul says: "I am crucified with Christ" (Galatians 2:20), "they that are Christ's have crucified the flesh" (5:24), and "But God forbid that I should glory save in the cross of our Lord Jesus Christ, by whom the world is crucified unto me, and I unto the world" (6:14).

St. John Chrysostom says (*ibid.,* no. 7), "But what is, 'Let us go forth unto Him?' Let us have fellowship with Him in His sufferings; let us bear His reproach. For He did not simply bid us to dwell 'outside the gate,' but as He was reproached as a condemned person, so also we."

v. 14. For here we have no continuing city, but we seek one to come.

"Those in whom Christ dwells by faith have a mind raised aloft . . . and while walking upon earth, their thoughts are set upon those things which are above, and 'their dwelling is in heaven'" (St. Cyril of Alexandria, *op. cit.,* Homily 141). The city out of which He and those who unite themselves to Him have been cast out has become a symbol of this world or "this worldism," and its impermanence, because of its rejection of Him. Both the religious and political worlds combined to reject Him, the Jews and the Romans. The city that is to come and that is sought by Christians is the same that was the destination of Abraham (see 11:10), the destination that has been revealed and realized by the Mediator of the New Covenant, Christ (see 12:22). St. Paul reminds Christians of their true home or fatherland, when he says, "our community [*politevma,* "state" or "commonwealth"] is in heaven" (Philippians 3:20). In spite of the vast distance (spiritual and moral) between heaven and earth, "for us the Lord has consecrated a way through His blood, and has made it easy" (St. Athanasius, *Paschal Letter XLIII*). He also indicates in the same letter that the moment when we manifest most clearly that "we are seeking the city that is to come," is during the Paschal Liturgy, the celebration of the Feast that elevates us up to heaven.

v. 15. By him therefore let us offer the sacrifice of praise to God continually, that is, the fruit of our lips giving thanks to his name.

Two words in this verse deserve special consideration: "sacrifice" (in Greek *thysian,* which is singular and without an article, thus "a sacrifice"); and "giving thanks," from *homologountōn,* which has as its primary meaning "confess" and by extension "give thanks." Thus, the last clause might be rendered, "the fruit of our lips which confess to His name."

Since the great sacrifice of our Lord Jesus Christ was offered once and for all, as has been emphasized earlier in the Epistle (see 7:27; 9:12; 10:10), there is no necessity for any new sacrifice. The Christian community's response, then, is to offer up (*anapherō* in Greek) through Him a continual sacrifice of praise (*thysian aineseōs* in Greek, a phrase which forms part of the people's initial response in the Divine Liturgy to the exhortation, "Let us stand aright . . . that we may offer the holy oblation in peace"). Or, as St. Gregory of Nazianzus says, "every day and every moment, offering ourselves" (*Second Oration on Pascha*, no. xxii).

It is in hymns of praise and confession, the fruit of our lips which confess to His name—as the expression of our faith—that we participate in the Lord's sacrifice. That this verse refers to the Eucharist we have the very early witness of St. Irenaeus (*Fragment of a Lost Writing*, no. xxxvii), quoting this verse:

> Now these oblations are not according to the law, the handwriting of which the Lord took away from the midst by canceling it, but they are according to the Spirit, for we must worship God "in spirit and in truth" [John 4:24]. And therefore the oblation of the Eucharist is not a carnal one, but a spiritual; and in this respect it is pure. For we make an oblation to God of the bread and the cup of blessing, giving thanks in that He has commanded the earth to bring forth these fruits for our nourishment. And then, when we have perfected the oblation, we invoke the Holy Spirit, that He may exhibit this sacrifice, both the bread the body of Christ, and the cup the blood of Christ, in order that the receivers of these antitypes may obtain remission of sins and life eternal.

v. 16. But to do good and to communicate forget not: for with such sacrifices God is well pleased.

The repetition of "forget not" (see v. 2) seems to put "doing good" and "communicating" in the same category of "entertaining strangers," that is, as such essential characteristics of Christian behavior that to neglect them would be a serious matter. Again, these two virtues are not something new to the community. In any event, all of the positive exhortations intervening between v. 2 and the present verse emphasize those things that brotherly love and the experience of the unity of participation in the holy Eucharist must naturally produce. Such participation is the means for the transformation of each member of the community.

Both words in the first part of the verse are nouns, *eupoiia* and *koinōnia,* the second deserving some further consideration. It is used by St. Paul in several of his Epistles: I Corinthians 10:16, where it clearly denotes communion of the body and blood of Christ in the holy Eucharist; II Corinthians 13:14, in which it means unity in the grace of the Son, in the love of the Father, and in the communion of the Holy Spirit (see St. John Chrysostom, *On II Corinthians,* Homily 30, no. 3); and Romans 15-16, where he uses it in the sense of sharing and contributions to the poor. St. John uses the same word in his First Epistle to mean unity in doctrine (1:3), in way of life (1:6), and in the Church (1:7). Its being coupled with "doing good" leads us to conclude that sharing with others may be what is intended here; however, the other meanings could well be in the mind of the Apostle also: the unity and love of the community in Christ, manifest in the holy Eucharist, find expression in their making sacrifices for others. This is indeed acceptable to God.

Of this St. Cyril of Alexandria says,

"But alms and communication forget not; for which such sacrifices God is content." For He loveth not the incense of the worship according to the law, but requireth rather the pleasantness of the sweet spiritual savor. But the sweet spiritual savor unto God is to show pity unto men, and to maintain love towards them . . . the daughter of love is pity for poverty. (*op. cit.,* Homily 112)

v. 17. Obey them that have the rule over you, and submit yourselves: for they watch for your souls, as they that must give

account, that they may do it with joy, and not with grief: for
that is unprofitable for you.

Earlier in this chapter (v. 7), the Hebrew Christians are urged to
follow the faith of their superiors, because it was they who preached
the word of God to them. Now they are told to obey them and submit themselves to them. It is understood that those leaders have an
appointment according to the will of God (see the *First Epistle to
Clement,* chap. xxi) and are entrusted with the care of the flock. All
the ranks of the priesthood are responsible before God ("as the ones
who must give account," *os logon apodōsontes* in Greek) for their
subjects, must be blameless and above accusation, and are to be reverenced and obeyed. According to St. Ignatius,

> For since ye are subject to the bishop as to Jesus Christ, ye appear
> to me to live not after the manner of men, but according to Jesus
> Christ, who died for us, in order, by believing in His death, ye may
> escape from death. It is therefore necessary that, as ye indeed do, so
> without the bishop ye should do nothing . . . to the presbytery, as
> the apostle[s] of Jesus Christ . . . [and] the deacons as being [the
> ministers] of the mysteries of Jesus Christ." (*Epistle to the Trallians,*
> chap. ii [shorter version])

The ruler may, in some cases, be unworthy in his own life, but if
he does not depart from the Faith, he is to be followed in matters of
Faith. The Lord Himself has said: "The scribes and Pharisees sit in
Moses' seat: all therefore whatsoever they tell you observe, do; but
do ye not after their works" (Matthew 23:2). "Let those who rule
[you] also hear, and not only those who are under their rule; that as
the subjects ought to be obedient, so also the rulers ought to be
watchful and sober" (St. John Chrysostom, *On Hebrews,* Homily 34,
no. 2).

It is the obedience of the subjects that causes the leaders to do
their work with joy. It is not profitable to the disobedient subject
to cause them grief, for they too are held accountable for their
actions.

vv. 18-19. Pray for us: for we trust we have a good conscience,
in all things willing to live honestly. But I beseech you the rather
to do this, that I may be restored to you the sooner.

In the rest of the verses of this chapter, the Apostle closes his letter in a customary way. A request for the readers' or hearers' prayers
is found also in St. Paul's Epistles to the Thessalonians (I, 5:25; II,
3:1) and to the Ephesians (6:18-19). In the second and third of these
referenced cases, it is specifically that he, and those with him, may be
enabled to proclaim the word of the Gospel effectively. Here, it is the
Jews whom he asks to pray for him, and, if indeed St. Paul is the
author, we can understand why he adds, "for we trust we have a good
conscience, in all things willing to live honestly," as a defense of his
preaching among the Jews generally. We recall that he had infuriated
them and that they had sought to have him killed, because, according to their accusation, he had forsaken Moses and the Law. (See Acts
21-26; also St. John Chrysostom, *ibid.,* no. 4.)

The Apostle declares his conviction (*pepoithamen* in Greek, "we
are persuaded" or "convinced") that in all that he had taught and in
his way of living he had had a "good conscience" (in Greek, *kalen
syneidisin*). St. Paul had testified before both the Jews and the Romans
that he had done his work among them with the same "good" or
"clean" conscience (Acts 23:1; 24:16; see also I Timothy 1:5,19; 3:9 and
II Timothy 1:3). His desire has been to live "honestly," "following that
which is good," and his conscience bears witness to this desire. The
word translated "live" is *anastrephesthai,* to "conduct oneself" or "to
behave" (see also I Timothy 3:15 and II Corinthians 1:12), and that
which is translated "honestly" is simply "well," *kalōs* in Greek.

According to St. John Chrysostom (*ibid.*), he is writing to "persons grieved with him," and he asks prayers for himself of "those
who hate him," just as he might ask "those who love him." His conviction of having a good conscience in what he teaches means that
"our conscience in nothing hurts us" nor "have we done anything
with deceitfulness or hypocrisy." "Not as an enemy but as a friend,"
he addresses them.

His reason for asking their prayers and further evidence of his love for them is that he wishes to be with them. Their prayers can hasten his being restored to them. *Tachion* in Greek means "more quickly," a comparative of *tachys,* and the verb is *apokatasthathō,* a passive of *apokathistēnō,* to restore, or reestablish. What the restriction or obstacle to his returning as quickly as he desires is not made clear, and it would be useless to suppose some reason.

> *vv. 20-21. Now the God of peace, that brought again from the dead our Lord Jesus, that great shepherd of the sheep, through the blood of the everlasting covenant, make you perfect in every good work to do his will, working in you that which is wellpleasing in his sight, through Jesus Christ; to whom be glory for ever and ever. Amen.*

The second part of the Epistle's close consists of a beautiful blessing and prayer for the author's readers. Its form and language suggest a liturgical formula in use at the time of writing.

Whatever its origin, among the names of God that denote His works, "the God of peace" has been chosen perhaps because it can be said to capture the essence of the Lord's mission. It serves here as a reminder that God has established peace between Jew and Gentile (see Ephesians 2:14) and made them one in Christ, and as a prayer that there be no divisions among the Christians he addresses. St. Paul uses the name several times: II Corinthians 13:11; Romans 15:33; 16:20; Philippians 4:9; 1 Thessalonians 5:23. (See also St. Gregory of Nazianzus, *In Defense of His Flight to Pontus,* no. 117.)

The clause "that brought again from the dead our Lord Jesus," using *anagagōn* (literally "brought up" or "brought back"), is reminiscent of the language of Isaiah 63:11. St. Cyril of Jerusalem (*Catechetical Lecture XIV,* no. 20) quotes this passage using one of the Septuagint variants, "from the earth," and thus, for this Saint, the passage is a prophecy of the Resurrection. (See also I Corinthians 15:15 and I Peter 1:21.)

The appositive, "that great Shepherd of the sheep," recalls our Lord's own words calling Himself "the good Shepherd," who gives His life for His sheep and who knows them (John 10:11,14; and I Peter 2:25; 5:4). In this latter reference, He is called the "chief Shepherd" (in Greek, *archipoimenos*). St. Cyril (*ibid.*) says that our author has added "great" to distinguish Him from the shepherds that had gone before Him.

Our Lord's work of making His followers "perfect" (or "complete" according to the Greek word *katartisai*, from *katartizō*, meaning "refit," "repair," or "restore"), completing the work of their restoration, is accomplished through the "blood of the everlasting covenant" (see Ezekiel 37:26; Matthew 26:28; Mark 14:24; Hebrews 9:13-15). "For that is made 'perfect' which having a beginning is afterwards completed" (St. John Chrysostom, *ibid.*). Even the peace that has been made between the Jews and the Greeks is a consequence of the blood of the cross (Colossians 1:29). St. Paul uses the same verb *katartizō* with the sense of restoration (I Thessalonians 3:10), as does St. Peter (I Peter 5:10).

It is by conformity with God's will, expressed in His word and made effective in the Son's work, that the restoration or completion of the believer is accomplished (his ascetic struggle), so that what he does may be well-pleasing in God's sight. (See I Thessalonians 2:13; also St. Symeon the New Theologian, *Discourse I*, no. 2.)

The ending of the second verse is apparently an expression used in the liturgy of the Church at this early period of its history.

v. 22. And I beseech you, brethren, suffer the word of exhortation: for I have written a letter unto you in few words.

The sense of this addition to the Epistle is clear enough: the Apostle exhorts those to whom it is addressed to bear or allow his message, which he now characterizes as an exhortation. Both the verb translated "beseech" and the word for "exhortation" come from the same basic word *parakaleō: parakalō* and *paraklēseōs*—thus, he exhorts them to accept the exhortation. St. John Chrysostom advises us: "Observe his wisdom. He says not, 'I beseech you, suffer the word of' admonition, but 'the word of exhortation,' that is, of consolation, of encouragement" (*ibid.*, no. 6).

When he says, "a letter to you in few words," he undoubtedly means that, dealing with a subject as rich and as complex as the doctrine of Christ and His priesthood, he could have written much more, but he has kept it relatively short so as not to lose their attention.

> *v. 23. Know ye that our brother Timothy is set at liberty; with whom, if he come shortly, I will see you.*

The only Timothy (Timotheus) mentioned in the New Testament is the one who was a fellow-worker of St. Paul (Romans 16:21), and to whom the latter addressed two epistles, and whom he calls his son in the faith (I Timothy 1:2) and "our brother" (II Corinthians 1:1). He has apparently been released from prison, no doubt in Rome, where he was imprisoned with his father in the Faith (Philippians 2:19-24; Philemon 1). Here the Apostle expresses the hope that Timothy will be able to accompany him when he returns to the Hebrews. We may assume that the Apostle is confident that they will receive him well.

St. John Chrysostom, in the "Argument" at the beginning of his *Homilies on the First Epistle to Timothy,* says of him:

> The affection of Paul for him is a sufficient evidence of his character. For he elsewhere says of him, "Ye know the proof of him, that as a son with a father, he hath served with me in the Gospel" [Philippians 2:22]. And to the Corinthians again he writes: "I have sent unto you Timothy, who is my beloved son, and faithful in the Lord" [I Corinthians 4:17]. And again: "Let no man despise him, for he worketh the work of the Lord, as I also do" [I Corinthians 16:10-11]. And to the Hebrews he writes: "Know ye that our brother Timothy is set at liberty." Indeed his love for him is everywhere apparent, and the miracles that are now wrought still attest his claims.

(For the account of the miracles wrought by the bones and relics of St. Timothy, see St. John Chrysostom's *First Homily on the Statues,* no. 4.)

v. 24. Salute all them that have the rule over you, and all the saints. They of Italy salute you.

This last part of the closing contains this greeting to be conveyed by the people to whom the letter is addressed, to the leaders and then to all "the saints," that is, the holy people of God. Exactly who "they of Italy" are is not known, perhaps Aquila and Prisca (or Priscilla), the only people described in the New Testament as such (see Acts 18:2; II Timothy 4:19). It could be that this statement gives the key as to where the Epistle was written; but since the two had to leave Rome and were found in Corinth by St. Paul, again, if he indeed is the author, he calls them "they of Italy" writing from the latter city (see Acts 18:2).

v. 25. Grace be with you all. Amen.

Since this final blessing was a formula no doubt already in wide use in the liturgy, it is certainly a fitting conclusion for the Epistle. Also it seems appropriate to us to quote St. John Chrysostom's words on this short close as our final note to this study:

> But how does "Grace" come to be "with" us? If we do not do despite to the benefit, if we do not become indolent in regard to the Gift. And what is "the grace?" Remission of sins, Cleansing: this is "with" us. For who (he means) can keep the Grace despitefully, and not destroy it? For instance; He freely forgave thee thy sins. How then shall the "Grace be with" thee, whether it be the good favor, or the effectual working of the Spirit? If thou draw it to thee by good deeds. For the cause of all good things is this, the continual abiding with us of the "grace" of the Spirit. For this guides us to all [good things], just as when it flies away from us, it ruins us, and leaves us desolate. (*On Hebrews,* Homily 34, no. 6)

Index of Scripture References in the Epistle to the Hebrews

The number(s) in parentheses refer to the verse(s) in Hebrews were the scripture is cited.

OLD TESTAMENT

Genesis

1:26-30 (2:7)
2: 2 (4:4)
4 (11:4)
4:7 (11:4)
4:10 (11:4; 12:24)
5:21-24 (11:5)
6-9 (11:7)
12:1-4 (6:13; 11:8)
12:2 (6:14)
12:7 (11:22)
14:18-20 (7:1)
15:5 (11:12; 11:17-18)
15:13-14 (11:22)
15:17 (12:29)
16:15 (11:17-18)
17:4 (6:13)
17:5 (6:13)
17:16 (6:13)
18:1-22 (13:1-2)
18:10-15 (11:11)
18:14 (6:14)
18:18: (11:11)
19:1 (13:1-2)
21:10-12 (11:17-18)
21:12 (11:17-18)
22:2 (11:17-18)
22:11-12 (11:17-18)
22:16-17 (6:13; 6:15)

22:17 (11:12)
22:18 (6:17)
25:22 (11:20)
25:29-34 (12:16-17)
25:33 (11:20)
25:34 (12:16-17)
26:3 (11:9)
27:35 (11:20)
27:38 (12:16-17)
27:41 (12:16-17)
28:1 (11:20)
28:4 (11:20)
28:11-22 (11:20)
28:13 (11:9)
31:11 (11:20)
32:1 (11:20)
47:31 (11:21)
48:14-16 (11:21)
49 (11:2)
49:10 (7:15)
50:25 (11:22)

Exodus

1:22-2:3 (11:23)
2:1-10 (11:24)
2:11-15 (11:24)
2:14-15 (11:27)
2:24 (11:27)
3:6 (11:10; 11:16; 12:21)

3:8 (4:5)
3:11 (11:30)
3:15 (11:16)
10:10 (5:1)
12:2 (11:28)
13:19 (11:22)
14:21-31 (11:29)
17:1-7 (3:7-11)
19:6 (7:19)
19:12-13 (12:18-19)
19:13 LXX (12:20)
19:18 (12:26-27)
19:18-19 (12:18-19)
20:18 (12:18-19)
20:19 (12:18-19)
24 (9:18-20)
24:1 (9:18-20)
24:3-8 (9:21-22)
24:4 (9:18-20)
24:7 (9:18-20)
24:7-8 (9:18-20)
24:8 (9:18-20; 10:22)
25-26 (9:2)
25:4 (9:18-20)
25:16 (9:4)
25:21 (9:4)
25:31-37 (9:2)
26 (9:3)
28 (5:4)
30:6 (9:4)

30:22-29 (9:21-22)
35 (3:2)
39:1 (9:18-20)
40:20 (9:4)
40:34-38 (7:13-14)

Leviticus

1:4 (6:2)
4:3-21 (5:3)
4:13 (5:2)
8:33 LXX (5:9)
9:7 (5:3)
11 (9:10)
11:25 (9:10)
14:4-7 (9:21-22)
15:5 (9:10)
16:2 (9:7)
16 (7:27)
16:6,11 (5:3)
16:12 (9:4)
16:13 (9:7)
16:17 (9:7)
16:27 (13:11)
16:30 (9:7)
16:32-34 (9:4)
21 (7:26)
22 (7:26)
22:18 (3:1)
24:5-6 (9:2)
27:30 (7:5)

Numbers

4:11 LXX (12:18-19)
4:1-13 (12:18-19)
5 (12:20)
6:3,15 (9:10)
7:5 (8:2)
8 (9:10)
12:7-8 (3:5)
13:8 (4:8; 11:30)

13:16 (4:8; 11:30)
14 (4:7)
14:6-9 (4:8)
14:22-23 (3:11-17; 3:18)
14:29 (3:17)
14:30 (3:18; 4:2)
14:30-31 (4:5)
15:27-31 (9:7)
16 (5:4)
16:10 (5:4)
17:1-11 (9:4)
17:10 (9:4)
18:21 (7:5)
19 (9:10)
20:13 (12:3)
27:18 (11:30)
27:18-23 (4:8)
32:13 (3:17)

Deuteronomy

1:31,33 (8:9)
4:11 (1:7)
4:24 (12:29)
10:5 (9:4)
12:6-17 (3:1)
12:9ff (10:28)
13:6ff (10:28)
14 (9:10)
18:1-2 (7:5)
18:15 (3:5)
18-19 (3:5)
29:18 (12:15)
31:6 8 (13:5)
32:8 (7:1)
32:35-36 (10:30)
32:43 (1:6)
34:9 (11:30)

Joshua

1:4 (4:8)

1:5 (13:5)
2 (11:31)
2:11 (11:31)
5:3 (11:30)
6 (11: 30)
10 (11:30)
21:43 (11:33)

Judges

2:17 (12:16-17)
4 (11:32)
6:34 (1:1)
7 (11:33)
7-8 (11:32)
8:33 (12:16-17)
11 (11:32)
11:32-33 (11:33)
13 (13:1-2)
13-16 (11:32)
13:20 (12:18-19)
16:28-30 (11:34)

I Kings/I Samuel

7:15 (11:33)
14:13 (11:34)
16:13 (1:1)
17 (11:34)
17:37 (11:33)

II Kings/II Samuel

7:14 (1:5)
8:1-8 (11:33)
22:3 (2:3)
22:14 (7:1)
24:14 (10:31)

III Kings/I Kings

8:9 (9:4)
8:12 (12:18-19)

17:22 (11:35)
19:3 (11:34)
22:24 (11:36-37)

IV Kings/II Kings

4:34 (11:35)
4:43 (8:2)
6:16 (11:34)

II Chronicles

24:21 (11:36-37)

Tobit

5:2 (13:1-2)

Judith

13:7 (11:34)

Job

4:3-4 (12:12-13)
5:17-26 (12:5-6)

Psalms

2:6 (12: 22)
2:7 (1:5; 5:5)
2:7-8 (1: 5)
4:34 (10:5-7)
5:30 (10:5-7)
8:4-6 (2:6)
15/16:8-11 (5:7)
18/19:1 (11:3)
21/22:22 (2:12)
26/27:1 (13:6)
29/30:10 (13:6)
32/33:6 (1:2)
32/33:11 (6:17)
38/39:12 (11:13)
39/40 (10:5-7)

44/45:6 (1:8)
44/45:7 (1:8)
49/50 (10:30)
56/57:2 (7:1)
56/57:4 (4:12)
63/64:3 (4:12)
64/65:1 (12:22)
68/69 (7:15)
77/78:10 (8:8)
77/78:68 (7:15)
77/78:37 (8:8)
86/87:4 (11:31)
88/89:27 (1:6; 12:5-6)
90/91:11-12 12:5)
93/94:12-13 (12:5-6)
94/95 (3:7-12)
94/95:11 (4:3)
95/96:7 (1:6)
96/97:3 (12:29)
98/99:1 (6:12)
101/102:25,26
     (1:10;13:8)
102/103:9 (8:11)
102/103:20 (1:14)
103/104:4 (1:7)
105/106:6,7,24,26 (3:17)
105/106:39 (12:16-17)
109/110:1-4 LXX (7:1;
     7:8; 7:17; 7:20-21)
109/110:1 (1:13;5:10;
     6:13; 10:13)
109/110:4 (5:6; 6:18)
117/118:6 LXX (13:6)
117/118:18 (12:5-6)
118/119:2 (11: 6)

Proverbs

3:11-12 (12:5-6)
3:21 (2:1)
4:26 (12:12-13)

5:18-20 (13:4)
22:15 (12:9-10)
23:13-14 (12:9-10)

Ecclesiasticus (Sirach)

44:16 (11:5)

Wisdom (of Solomon)

4:10 (11:5)
19:18-21 (11:29)

Isaiah

2:19 (12:26-27)
5:1-7 (6:7)
8:18 (2:13)
9:6ff (7:15)
11:1 (7:15)
26:20 (10:37-38)
29:13 (13:9)
34:4 (1:11-12)
35:3 (12:12-13)
38:1-6 (11:34)
44:4 (2:1)
45:17 (2:2-3)
51:6 (1:11-12)
51:7-8 (1:11-12)
53:5 (12:7)
53:7 LXX (11:17-18)
54:13 (8:11)
63:9 (2:5)
63:11 (13:20-21)
63:13-14 (3:7-12)
65:17 (12:26-27)
66:15-16 (12:29)

Jeremiah

9:8 (4:12)
11:11 (12:11)
20:2 (11:36-37)

20:9 (12:29)
30:14 (12:7)
31:31-38/38:31-34 LXX
    (8:9; 9:15; 11:36-37)
37:15 (11:36-37)
38:13 (11:36-37)

Ezekiel

1:4 (12:29)
2:3 (12:3)
11:5 (1:1)
20:20 (7:18)
20:21,24 (7:18)
20:25 (7:18)
37:26 (13:20-21)

Song of the Three Children

v. 63 (12:23)

Baruch

3:35-37 (1:9)

Daniel

1:3,6,7 (11:34)
2:47 (4:12)

3:20,27 (11:34)
3 (11:29)
6 (11:29)
6:22 (11:33)

Hosea

8:1 (8:8)

Joel

3:10-11 (10:36)

Amos

5:4 (11:6)

Nahum

1:2 (10:27)
1:3 (12:18-19)

Habakkuk

2:3-4 LXX (10:37-38)

Haggai

2:6 (12:26-27)

Zechariah

1:14 (10:27)
12:8 (10:36)

Malachi

2:11 (8:8)
3:6 (1:11-12; 3:8)
3:2 (12:29)
4:2 (7:13-14)
4:2 (7:15)

I Maccabees

1:10 (12:15)
7:34 (11:36-37)
9:26 (11:36-37)

II Maccabees

6:12 (12:9-10)
6:19 (11:35)
7:1 (11:36-37)
7:1-23 (11:35)
7:9 (11:35)

IV Maccabees

17:11-16 (12:4)

NEW TESTAMENT

Matthew

2:12 (12:25)
2:23 (12:25)
3:9 (8:12; 11:12)
3:11 (12:29)
3:15 (7:2)
5:8 (12:14)
5:9 (12:14)

5:12 (10:34)
5:33-37 (6:16)
6:22 (12:1)
6:34 (13:5)
7:2 (5:2)
7:7 (11:6)
7:15 (2:1)
8:11 (8:12)

9:10-13 (10:5-7)
10:20-21 (6:11)
10:22 (3:6)
13:7 (11:21)
13:21 (12:15)
15:8-11 (13:9)
22:1-14 (8:12)
22:23 (6:2)

22:32 (11:16)
22:44-45 (1:13)
23:2 (13:17)
23:35 (11:4)
23:37 (11:36-37)
25 (4:16)
25:31 (1:6)
25:34 (4:3)
25:36-40 (13:1-2)
26:28 (13:20-21)
26:39 (5:7)
26:42 (5:7)
26:45 (12:3)
26:64 (10:11-12)
27:28 (9:18-20)
27:51 (10:20)
28:18 (7:16)

Mark

7:4 (6:2)
14:9 (13:7)
14:24 (13:20-21)
14:41 (12:3)
16:19 (10:11-12)

Luke

2:26 (12:25)
2:52 (5:8)
3:8 (8:12)
3:14 (13:5)
8:5-15 (6:7)
9:46 (12:15)
10:20 (12:23)
10:30-37 (12:1-2)
12:35 (12:29)
12:49 (12:29)
13:32 (10:14)
17:26-27 (11:7)
18:7 (6:15)
19:41 (5:7)

20:46 (2:1)
21:20-24 (12:22)
22:19 (12:28)
22:29-30 (8:5)
24:27 (2:1)

John

1:9 (1:3)
1:10 (1:6)
1:14 (2:14; 7:16; 9:2)
1:17 (10:1; 13:9)
1:18 (1:1)
2:18-21 (9:11)
3:12-13 (12:25)
4:24 (13:15)
4:34 (3:1)
5:17 (4:9)
5:19 (6:13)
5:22-23 (1:6)
5:26 (7:16; 10:20)
5:46 (3:3)
6:33-58 (6:4)
6:57 (9:13-14)
8:12 (1:3)
8:56 (6:13; 6:15)
10:11 (13:20-21)
10:14 (13:20-21)
10:17-18 (5:7)
11:35 (5:7)
11:40 (10:10)
12:27 (5:7)
12:32-33 (5:7; 5:10)
13:14 (11:10)
14:6 (2:10; 7:25; 9:8;
    10:20)
14:9 (1:14)
14:26 (8:10)
14:27 (7:2)
15:1-2 (12:5-6)
15:20 (12:3)

15:26 (3:7-12)
16:8-10 (7:2)
16:15 (5:7)
17:1 (5:5)
17:4 (4:10)
17:5 (5:5; 1:3; 1:4)
17:9 (5:7)
19:29 (9:18-20)
19:34 (9:18-20)

Acts

2:3-4 (12:29)
2:25-36 (1:5)
2:31 (5:7)
2:42 (13:9; 12:28)
2:46-47 (12:28)
2:46 (12:1)
3:15 (12:2)
3:24 (11:32)
4:31 (2:4)
5:31 (12:2)
6:6 (6:2)
7 (11:23)
7:9-10 (11:22)
7:22-23 (11:24)
7:32 (12:21)
7:45 (4:8; 11:30)
7:53 (2:2-3; 12:25)
8:23 (12:15)
10:4 (13:7)
10:22 (12:25)
14:3 (2:4)
15:12 (2:4)
18:2 (13:24)
19:1-6 (6:2)
20:28 (2:17)
21-26 (13:18-19)
23:1 (13:18-19)
24:16 (13:18-19)

I Corinthians

3:1-3 (5:13)
3:13 (10:25)
3:11-15 (12:29)
4:9 (10:33)
4:17 (13:23)
6:9 (13:4)
8:6 (2:10)
8:24 (11:1)
9:24-26 (12:1)
10:1-4 (3:3)
10:5 (3:17)
10:11-12 (3:19)
10:16 (13:16)
10:20 (13:19)
10:21 (13:10)
11:23-24 (12:28)
11:23-26 (8:5)
11:32 (12:5-6)
12:25-27 (13:3)
13:4 (6:15)
15:15 (13:20-21)
15:25 (1:13)
15:25-26 (10:13)
15:27-28 (2:5)
15:28 (2:8)
16:10-11 (13:23)

II Corinthians

1:1 (13:23)
1:12 (13:18-19)
1:20 (11:1)
3:3 (10:15-17)
4:4 (1:3)
4:18 (11:25)
5:16 (7:25)
5:18 (2:17)
5:19 (2:17; 5:10)
5:21 (4:14)
7:9 (8:12)

7:13,15 (2:1)
9:8 (13:5)
11:2 (10:27)
11:27-30 (10:29)
12:12 (2:4)
13:11 (13:20-21)
13:14 (13:16)

Romans

1:3 (1:5)
1:7 (3:1)
1:19-20 (11:3)
2:16 (4:12)
3 (7:11)
3:14 (12:15)
3:24-25 (8:12)
3:25 (10:15)
4 (7:11; 11:8)
4:12 (6:17)
4:18 (11:1)
5:3-5 (6:11)
5:8-10 (2:14)
5:10 (2:17)
6:3-4 (3:14; 10:22)
6:4 (12:2)
6:3,6 (6:6)
8:3 (2:14; 4:14; 7:18)
8:9 (3:7-11)
8:16-17 (1:2)
8:17 (1:14; 3:1)
8:26 (7:25)
8:29 (1:6)
8:32 (11:19)
12:10 (13:1)
12:13 (13:1-2)
12:15 (13:3)
12:19 (10:30)
13:11 (3:13)
14:19 (12:14)
15:4 (3:19)

15:16 (13:16)
15:33 (13:20-21)
16.20 (13:20-21)
16:21 (13:23)

Galatians

1:13 (13:7)
2:2 (12:1)
2:20 (13:13)
3 (7:11)
3:7 (11:12)
3:15 (6:16)
3:19 (2:2-3)
3:19,24 (8:7)
3:21 (7:18; 9:9)
3:29 (4:1)
4:19 (6:6)
4:22-31 (11:17-18)
4:26 (4:10)
5:1 (3:6)
5:5 (11:1)
5:10 (6:9)
5:24 (11:7; 13:13)
6:9 (12:3)
6:14 (11:7; 13:13)

Ephesians

1:3 (12:2)
1:4 (4:3)
1:11 (1:14)
1:20 (6:20)
2:6 (6:20)
2:19 (3:1)
3:10 (1:1)
4:5 (6:6)
4:14 (6:19; 13:9)
4:22 (13;7)
4:31 (12:15)
5:17 (12:9-10)
6:17 (4:12)

6:18-19 (13:18-19)

Philippians

1:7 (10:33)
2:6 (12:1)
2:7 (5:8; 12:2)
2:8-9 (1:4)
2:9 (7:26; 9:24)
2:10-11 (1:4)
2:19-24 (13:23)
2:22 (13:23)
3:13-14 (12:1)
3:20 (3:1; 9:23; 13:14)
4:9 (13:20-21)

Colossians

1:15 (1:3)
1:15-18 (1:6)
1:16 (1:2; 2:8)
1:16-17 (1:2)
1:18 (8:13)
1:20 (7:2; 13:20-21)
2:5 (5:12)
2:12 (12:2)
2:14-15 (2:14)
2:16-17 (13:10)
2:17 (10:1)
3:1 (10:11-12)

I Thessalonians

2:13 (13:20-21)
3:10 (5:12; 13:20-21)
4:9 (13:1)
5:4 (10:25)
5:23 (13:20-21)
5:24 (10:23)
5:25 (13:18-19)

II Thessalonians

1:3-5 (10:36)
1:7-8 (10:31)
1:8 (12:29)
3:1 (13:18-19)

I Timothy

1:5 (13:18-19; 7:19)
1:8 (7:19)
1:10 (13:4)
1:19 (13:18-19)
2:4 (10:8-9)
2:5 (7:25)
3:15 (13:18-19)
4:1 (2:1)
4:4 (12:25)
4:14 (6:2)
6:6-9 (13:5)
6:10 (13:5)
6:11-14 (10:23)
6:12 (12:1)
6:18-19 (6:9)

Titus

1:4 (2:1)
1:14 (12:25)
2:2 (11:1)
3:7 (6:11)

Philemon

1 (13:23)

Hebrews

1:1 (11:2; 11:39-40)
1:1-2 (7, Introduction)
1:3 (4:15; 12:24)
1:4 (2:2-3)
1:5 (2:6)

1:6 (2:5)
1:14 (2:2-3; 2:16)
2:1-4 (3:1; 12:1)
2:2 (10:35)
2:3 (5:11)
2:5 (2:6)
2:10 (4:10; 12:2)
2:14 (3:14)
2:17 (3:1; 4:14)
3:1 (4:14; 6:18)
3:1-6 (4:14; 12:1)
3:6 (4:16)
3:7-8 (4:7)
3:7 (9:8)
3:12 (5:11)
3:13 (12:1)
3:15 (4:7)
3:16 (4:2)
4:8 (11:30)
4:11 (5:11)
4:14-15 (5:1)
4:15 (2:17, 18)
4:16 (10:14; 10:19; 12:28; 13:6)
5:1 (8:3)
5:3 (4:15)
5:10-11 (6:3)
5:11-6:20 (12:1)
6:1 (9:13-14)
6:4 (12:7)
6:10 (10:35)
6:12 (12:1)
6:13 (6:16)
6:20 (4:6,10; 5:10; 7:19; 8:2; 10:34)
7 (5:6; 6:20)
7:13 (2:1)
7:16 (9:9)
7:17-20 (9:12)
7:19 (9:8,9; 12:18-19)
7:22 (2:2-3; 9:15)

7:24-25 (4:14)
7:25 (8:3; 10:13; 10:21)
7:27 (13:15)
7:28 (10:14)
8-10 (12:24)
8:1-2 (8:4)
8:6 (2:2-3; 9:15)
8:7 (9:9)
8:7-13 (11:39-40)
9 (7:22, 27; 13:12)
9:7-12 (10:19)
9:9 (7:11; 10:2)
9:10 (6:2)
9:12 (13:15)
9:14 (10:2)
9:15 (10:3)
9:28 (10:14)
10 (7:27)
10:1 (7:11)
10:10 (13:15)
10:12,14 (7:3)
10:19-20 (2: 10 13: 6)
10:25 (3:13; 4:3)
10:32 (12:4; 12:7)
10:35 (10:19)
10:36 (11:1)
11 (6:12; 12:2)
11:4 (12:24)
11:10 (13:14; 11:16)
11:26 (10:35)
11:39 (6:15)
11:39-40 (9:15)

12:2 (4:10)
12:12-15 (12:28)
12:22 (11:16; 13:14)
13:7 (13:17) 13:8 (1:11-12)
13:14 (11:16)

James

1:3 (11:1)
1:12 (12:5-6)
2:25 (11:31)
3:13 (13:7)
4:4 (13:4)

I Peter

1:21 (13:20-21)
1:22 (13:1)
2:9 (7:19)
2:12 (13:7)
2:25 (13:20-21)
3:18-19 (9:15)
3:19 (12:23)
3:20-21 (11:7)
3:22 (10:11-12)
5:4 (13:20-21)
5:10 (13:20-21)

II Peter

1:4 (2:10; 11:1; 12:9-10)
1:7 (13:1)
2:7 (13:7)

3:10 (3:13)
3:13 (12:26-27)

I John

1:3 (13:16)
1:5 (1:3)
1:6 (13:16)
2:25 (4:1)
2:27 (8:11)
3:12 (11:4)
4:1-3 (2:11)
4:12-16 (13:1-2)

Jude

11 (5:4; 12:3)
14 (11:5)

Revelation

1:5 (1:6)
1:6 (1:4)
1:16 (4:12)
5:10 (1:4)
5:8-14 (1:6)
13:8 (5:5)
20:9 (11:16)
21:1 (12:26-27)
21:2 (11:16)
21:14 (11:16)
21:18 (11:16)
21:23 (11:16)
21:26 (2:7)